The Cambridge Companion to Flaubert

This volume brings together a series of essays by acknowledged experts on Flaubert. It offers a coherent overview of the writer's work and critical legacy, and provides insights into the very latest scholarly thinking. While a central place is given to Flaubert's most widely read texts, attention is also paid to key areas of the corpus that have tended to be overlooked. Close textual analyses are accompanied by discussion of broader theoretical issues, and by a consideration of Flaubert's place in the wider traditions that he both inherited and influenced. These essays provide not only a robust critical framework for readers of Flaubert, but also a fuller understanding of why he continues to exert such a powerful influence on literature and literary studies today. A concluding essay by the prize-winning author Mario Vargas Llosa examines Flaubert's legacy from the point of view of the modern novelist. The *Companion* includes an invaluable chronology and bibliography.

D0140144

THE CAMBRIDGE
COMPANION TO
FLAUBERT

EDITED BY
TIMOTHY UNWIN
University of Bristol

CAMBRIDGE
UNIVERSITY PRESS

PUBLISHED BY THE PRESS SYNDICATE OF THE UNIVERSITY OF CAMBRIDGE
The Pitt Building, Trumpington Street, Cambridge, United Kingdom

CAMBRIDGE UNIVERSITY PRESS
The Edinburgh Building, Cambridge, CB2 2RU, UK
40 West 20th Street, New York, NY 10011–4211, USA
477 Williamstown Road, Port Melbourne, VIC 3207, Australia
Ruiz de Alarcón 13, 28014 Madrid, Spain
Dock House, The Waterfront, Cape Town 8001, South Africa

http://www.cambridge.org

First published 2004

Printed in the United Kingdom at the University Press, Cambridge

Typeface Sabon 10/13 pt.   *System* LaTeX 2_ε [TB]

A catalogue record for this book is available from the British Library

Library of Congress Cataloguing in Publication data
The Cambridge companion to Flaubert / edited by Timothy Unwin.
p.   cm. – (Cambridge companions to literature)
Includes bibliographical references and index.
ISBN 0 521 81551 7 – ISBN 0 521 89459 X (pbk.)
1. Flaubert, Gustave, 1821–1880 – Criticism and interpretation – Handbooks, manuals, etc.
I. Unwin, Timothy A.   II. Series.
PQ2249.C28   2004
843'.8 – dc22   2004052833

ISBN 0 521 81551 7 hardback
ISBN 0 521 89459 X paperback

CONTENTS

NOTES ON CONTRIBUTORS

ALISON FINCH is a Senior Research Fellow in French at Churchill College, Cambridge, and co-editor of *French Studies*. She is the author of *Proust's Additions* (1977), *Stendhal: 'La Chartreuse de Parme'* (1984), *Concordance de Stendhal* (1991), and *Women's Writing in Nineteenth-Century France* (2000). She is currently writing *A Cultural History of French Literature* for Polity Press.

ANNE GREEN is a Senior Lecturer in French at King's College London. She has published two books on historical fiction: *Flaubert and the Historical Novel. 'Salammbô' Reassessed* (1982) and *Privileged Anonymity. The Writings of Madame de Lafayette* (1996), as well as numerous articles on Flaubert. She is currently working on a book on Second Empire literature and a study of Flaubert's *Sous Napoléon III*.

AIMÉE ISRAEL-PELLETIER is Associate Professor of French at the University of Texas at Arlington. She is the author of *Flaubert's Straight and Suspect Saints. The Unity of 'Trois Contes'* (1991). She has published articles on Rimbaud and Impressionism, the reader, and the relationship between poetry and money. She has also written on the Comtesse de Ségur and biculturalism.

ROSEMARY LLOYD is Rudy Professor of French and Professor of Gender Studies at Indiana University. She has published on Baudelaire, Flaubert, Mallarmé, childhood and jealousy. Her most recent books are *Mallarmé: the Poet and his Circle* (1999), *Baudelaire's World* (2002) and *Out of the Valley: Memoirs of an Australian Childhood* (2003). She is currently completing a study of written still life.

MARY ORR is Professor of Modern French Studies at the University of Exeter. Her recent publications include *Intertextuality: Debates and Contexts* (2003) and *Flaubert: Writing the Masculine* (2000). Her current research projects include essays on male costume in Flaubert, a co-edited volume of feminist reappraisals of male canonical writers, and a monograph project to remap the history of ideas of nineteenth-century France through the lens of Flaubert's *La Tentation de saint Antoine*.

LAURENCE M. PORTER is Professor of French at Michigan State University. His books include *Critical Essays on Gustave Flaubert* (1986), *A Gustave Flaubert Encyclopedia* (2001), *Gustave Flaubert's 'Madame Bovary': A Reference Guide* (with Eugene F. Gray, 2002), and *Approaches to Teaching Flaubert's 'Madame Bovary'* (with Eugene F. Gray, 1995). He serves on the Editorial or Advisory Boards of *Nineteenth-Century French Studies*, *Studies in Twentieth Century Literature*, and *Women in French Studies*.

ALAN RAITT is Emeritus Professor of French literature in the University of Oxford, and an Emeritus Fellow of Magdalen College, Oxford. His publications on Flaubert include a study of *Trois Contes* (1991), books entitled *Flaubert et le théâtre* (1998) and *The Originality of 'Madame Bovary'* (2002), and editions of *L'Education sentimentale* and the texts that Flaubert wrote about his friend Louis Bouilhet.

LAWRENCE R. SCHEHR is Professor of French, Comparative Literature, and Gender and Women's Studies at the University of Illinois. His books include *Flaubert and Sons* (1986), *The Shock of Men* and *Alcibiades at the Door* (1995), *Rendering French Realism* and *Parts of an Andrology* (1997), and *Figures of Alterity* (2003). He is the co-editor of *Articulations of Difference* (1997) and *French Food* (2001).

MICHAEL TILBY is Fellow in French at Selwyn College, Cambridge. He has published widely on a number of nineteenth-century French authors, especially Balzac, and is currently completing a study of the novels Balzac published under pseudonyms in his early years as a writer.

ADRIANNE TOOKE is Fellow and Tutor in French at Somerville College, Oxford, and Lecturer in the University of Oxford. She has worked extensively on Flaubert, in particular on his travel writing and art commentaries. In addition to numerous articles, her publications include a critical edition of *Par les champs et par les grèves* (1987), a book entitled *Flaubert and the Pictorial Arts* (2000), and a translation of and introduction to *L'Education sentimentale*. She is currently co-editing volumes three to five of Benjamin Constant's correspondence.

TIMOTHY UNWIN is Professor of French at the University of Bristol. His publications on Flaubert include *Art et infini: l'œuvre de jeunesse de Gustave Flaubert* (1991) an edition of three early stories (*Trois Contes de jeunesse*, 1981), and an edition and translation of *Mémoires d'un fou* (2001). He also edited *Le Cœur à droite* by Louis Bouilhet (1993). His other publications include *The Cambridge Companion to the French Novel: 1800 to the Present* (1997), and *Textes réfléchissants: réalisme et réflexivité au dix-neuvième siècle* (2000). He is currently completing a study of Jules Verne.

MARIO VARGAS LLOSA, the acclaimed Peruvian writer, is the author of many prize-winning novels and critical essays. He wrote extensively on Flaubert in *The Perpetual Orgy* (1975). Recently he published *The Way to Paradise* (2003), an account of the lives of Flora Tristan and her grandson Paul Gauguin. In 2004 he gave a series of lectures in Oxford on Victor Hugo, to be published as *The Temptation of the Impossible: Victor Hugo's 'Les Misérables'*.

TONY WILLIAMS is Professor of French at the University of Hull. His publications on Flaubert include *'The Hidden Life at its Source': A Study of Flaubert's 'L'Education sentimentale'* (1987) and a genetic edition of the scenarios of *L'Education sentimentale* (1992). He was co-editor (with Mary Orr) of *New Approaches in Flaubert Studies* (1999).

PREFACE

Flaubert represents many things to many readers. He has been approached in vastly differing ways, and the body of critical and scholarly material devoted to him can seem confusing or daunting. The present volume, bringing together a series of essays by acknowledged experts, seeks to provide a coherent overview of the novelist's work and to offer various possible pathways through it, while at the same time offering the reader insights into the latest scholarly thinking. Close textual analyses are accompanied by discussion of broader theoretical issues, and by consideration of Flaubert's place in the literary and artistic traditions that he both inherited and influenced.

Rather than follow the chronological development of Flaubert's writing, chapters here have been organised thematically and arranged in clusters. Following an introductory account of the man and writer, a discussion of Flaubert's place in literary history describes in broad terms how his work responds to nineteenth-century artistic preoccupations, and how this response is taken forward by subsequent writers. Essays on specific aspects of the corpus (the early work, the travel writings, the correspondence) are then followed by a series of chapters which, from different perspectives, home in on the best-known texts in the Flaubertian canon (*La Tentation de saint Antoine, Madame Bovary, Salammbô, L'Education sentimentale, Trois Contes, Bouvard et Pécuchet*). These are examined not only in terms of major themes and aspects (history, death) but also in terms of techniques and approaches (modes of characterisation, stylistic innovations, compositional practices, uses of the visual). In the final stages, an evaluation of the importance of the theatre in Flaubert's work is followed by a chapter on the question of failure which runs throughout his writing and constitutes such an important part of his originality. The volume concludes with an essay by the contemporary novelist Mario Vargas Llosa, who examines Flaubert's legacy from a practising writer's point of view and stresses his fundamental impact on the techniques of modern fiction.

The chosen arrangement here not only allows significant texts and themes to be revisited at successive stages in the light of different critical or theoretical concerns, it also enables attention to be brought to key areas of the Flaubertian corpus (juvenilia, drafts and scenarios, letters, travel notes, theatrical writings) that can sometimes be overlooked. The essays stand both individually as interpretations of Flaubert, and collectively in their contribution to the overall picture that emerges. Each author has addressed from their own perspective the issues that commonly arise in discussion of Flaubert. The reader of this volume will find a variety of responses – sometimes contrasting, sometimes similar – which will, it is hoped, provide a robust critical framework and yield insights into why Flaubert's writing continues to fascinate and to exert such a powerful influence. The range of recurring topics here includes questions of genre, tradition and legacy; the Balzacian model; realism and positivism; pessimism; love, marriage and adultery; history and the past; humour and the grotesque; bourgeois society and the fascination with *bêtise* (stupidity); language and *idées reçues* (i.e., received ideas or platitudes); art and artists; gender, sexuality and death; saintliness, sin and the history of religion; text and intertext; self-consciousness and experiment; free indirect discourse and point of view; irony and ambivalence; and, of course, the question of writing itself. While the approaches adopted are intentionally diverse, they have the common goal of offering companionable ways into Flaubert's writing and through it to the broader issues it raises. Of course these essays do not propose definitive answers, nor do they close off further investigation. Rather, they provide a means by which Flaubert's work can be opened up, seen in context, and appreciated in its richness and diversity. As is the case with other volumes in the *Companion* series, there is an accompanying Chronology, and a selective Bibliography at the end of the volume. This includes a list of available translations of Flaubert's work. While the list of critical material is slanted towards works produced in or translated into English, it includes significant and major work on Flaubert in French.

I should like to thank all my contributors for their enthusiastic collaboration in bringing this project to completion, and for their helpful and prompt responses to my own editorial suggestions and queries. This is a collective enterprise, and as volume editor I have benefited greatly from the wisdom and insights that have been offered throughout by friends and colleagues. Special thanks are due to Tony Williams, who made perceptive comments on my own chapters; to Kay Chadwick, who provided much-needed guidance on presentational matters; to Mario Vargas Llosa, who kept his commitment to me despite an overwhelming number of other obligations; to John King, who provided a translation of Mario Vargas Llosa's essay at very short notice; and to Linda Bree at Cambridge University Press whose encouragement and advice at all stages of the project have been invaluable.

TIMOTHY UNWIN

12 December 1821	Birth in Rouen of Gustave Flaubert, second surviving son of Achille-Cléophas and Anne-Justine Flaubert. The first son Achille was born on 9 Feburary 1813
15 July 1824	Birth of Flaubert's sister Caroline
February 1832	Flaubert enrols as a pupil at the Collège Royal
Summer 1836	First meeting with Elisa Schlésinger in Trouville
1838	*Mémoires d'un fou*. Begins writing *Smar* which is completed early the following year
August 1840	Flaubert passes his baccalaureate as a private pupil, after being sent down from the Collège Royal. He travels to the Pyrenees and Corsica in the company of Dr Jules Cloquet
1842	Completes *Novembre*
1842–3	Law studies in Paris
January 1844	First nervous attack. Flaubert abandons his law studies and returns to the family home in Rouen
June 1844	The Flaubert family move to Croisset
1845	Completes the first *Education sentimentale*. In March, Flaubert's sister Caroline marries Emile Hamard. The family travel to Italy
15 January 1846	Death of Flaubert's father, Achille-Cléophas
23 March 1846	Death of Flaubert's sister Caroline, two months after giving birth to a daughter
July 1846	Flaubert meets Louise Colet who, with a gap from 1849–51, will be his mistress until 1855
May–August 1847	Flaubert and Du Camp travel through Brittany, then write *Par les champs et par les grèves*
February 1848	Flaubert and Bouilhet arrive in Paris and witness the uprising in the city

1849	Flaubert completes the first version of *La Tentation de saint Antoine* in September, then sets out on an eighteen-month journey to the Middle East with Maxime Du Camp
1851–6	Writes *Madame Bovary*, which will be published in the *Revue de Paris* from October 1856
1856	Rewrites *La Tentation de saint Antoine*
1857	Flaubert is put on trial for publishing *Madame Bovary*, and is acquitted. Begins working on *Salammbô*
April–June 1858	Flaubert travels to the site of Carthage for his research on *Salammbô*
1862	Completes *Salammbô*, which is published in the autumn
23 February 1863	Attends Sainte-Beuve's Magny dinners for the first time, and meets Tourgueniev
6 April 1864	Flaubert's niece Caroline marries Ernest Commanville
September 1864	Begins work on *L'Education sentimentale*
15 August 1866	Flaubert is named Chevalier de la Légion d'honneur
November 1868	Tourgueniev pays a visit to Croisset
18 July 1869	Death of Louis Bouilhet
13 October 1869	Death of Sainte-Beuve
17 November 1869	Publication of *L'Education sentimentale*
1870–1	During the Franco-Prussian War, Croisset is home to a group of occupying soldiers. Flaubert stays in his niece's flat in Rouen, returning to Croisset in April the following year after the armistice
8 November 1871	Elisa Schlésinger visits Flaubert at Croisset
6 April 1872	Death of Flaubert's mother. He completes the final version of *La Tentation de saint Antoine* in June, and begins work on *Bouvard et Pécuchet* in the autumn
1873	In April, Flaubert and Tourgueniev stay with George Sand in Nohant. Completes his play *Le Candidat* in November
1874	In March, Flaubert withdraws *Le Candidat* after a run of only four nights. The final version of *La Tentation de saint Antoine* is published and sells well

1875	During the autumn, Flaubert spends six weeks in Concarneau where he begins *La Légende de saint Julien l'Hospitalier*
1876	Death of Louise Colet on 8 March. Death of George Sand on 7 June. Flaubert completes *Un cœur simple* on 16 August
1877	Completes *Hérodias* in February. *Trois Contes* published in April. Flaubert resumes work on *Bouvard et Pécuchet*
8 May 1880	Death of Gustave Flaubert, before *Bouvard et Pécuchet* is completed

The following abbreviations are used in this volume to refer to works by Flaubert:

OC   *Œuvres complètes*, 2 vols. (Paris: Seuil, 1964)
CHH   *Œuvres complètes*, 16 vols. (Club de l'Honnête Homme, 1971–6)
OJ   *Œuvres complètes*, vol. i: *Œuvres de jeunesse* (Paris: Gallimard, Bibliothèque de la Pléiade, 2001)
Cor. *Correspondance*, 4 vols. (Paris: Gallimard, Bibliothèque de la Pléiade, 1973–98)

References to these works will be given in the form (OC i 75), (OC ii 140), (Cor. i 122), (OJ 525), (CHH xv 352), etc. The basic reference text will be the two-volume Seuil *Œuvres complètes*. However, texts up to 1845 will be referenced to the recently published first volume of the Pléiade *Œuvres complètes*. References to the correspondence up to 1875 will be to the Pléiade edition, and to the Club de l'Honnête Homme edition for 1876 onwards. References to other bibliographical items will be provided in full in a footnote on first mention, and in abbreviated form thereafter.

All quotations are accompanied by a translation into English. The translation usually precedes the original, but the order is from time to time reversed for the sake of clarity or precision. In chapter 9 ('The stylistic achievements of Flaubert's fiction'), extracts from the French normally precede their translations. Translations are those of the individual contributors unless otherwise specified. The main Bibliography lists published translations of individual works by Flaubert.

I

TIMOTHY UNWIN

Gustave Flaubert, the hermit of Croisset

Famously dubbed the 'novelist's novelist' by Henry James,[1] Flaubert has pre-occupied almost every generation of writers since the mid-nineteenth century. From the seclusion of a large family home on the banks of the Seine near Rouen, the so-called hermit of Croisset raises the art of prose narrative to new levels and reveals its modernity. As he stomps up and down the avenue of lime trees in his garden, sometimes in the company of his friend and mentor Louis Bouilhet, Flaubert bellows out the sentences of *Madame Bovary*, to the amazement or amusement of the folk in passing river craft. This is the legendary *gueuloir*, or 'yelling place', where the novelist puts his writing through the test of sound, rhythm and vocal fluidity, subjecting it to the final quality control. For, as he writes to his mistress Louise Colet on 24 April 1852, 'prose was born yesterday, that is what we must tell ourselves. Verse is the quintessential form of ancient literatures. All the combinations of poetry have been tried out. But as for prose, far from it' ['la prose est née d'hier, voilà ce qu'il faut se dire. Le vers est la forme par excellence des littératures anciennes. Toutes les combinaisons prosodiques ont été faites, mais celles de la prose, tant s'en faut' (Cor. II 79)]. And so, as he opens up new pathways in technical and formal experiment, Flaubert also heightens awareness of the complexities and the possibilities of the novelist's craft.

His impact on Maupassant, Zola, Joyce, Proust, James, Gide, Beckett, Borges, Calvino, Kundera and a host of key figures in the history of the genre is well documented, and his interest for theorists of literature is beyond doubt. Famously analysed by Lukács, Sartre, Poulet, Richard, Genette, Bourdieu and many others, Flaubert is one of those writers on whom almost everyone has had their say. His massive legacy extends to such votaries as Woody Allen (whose character Isaac in the 1979 film *Manhattan* listed *L'Education sentimentale* among the things that made life worth living);[2] Claude Chabrol who adapted *Madame Bovary* to the screen in 1991 with an icily intense Isabelle Huppert in the lead role; and Julian Barnes, whose unwavering enthusiasm for Flaubert has been expressed from *Flaubert's*

Parrot through to the recent collection of essays entitled *Something to Declare*.[3] As Mario Vargas Llosa will argue in the concluding essay to this volume, Flaubert is the first modern novelist, and he revolutionises the art of narrative fiction. But importantly, Flaubert's work is also grounded in the past (a point that will be discussed and developed here by Alison Finch in her discussion of Flaubert's stylistic achievements). His debt to Homer, Shakespeare, Cervantes, Rabelais, Montaigne, Byron, Rousseau, Goethe and many others is attested continuously throughout his novelistic writings and his correspondence. He is a writer who remains throughout his life a voracious reader, always supremely concerned with literature and with the questions it raises. Such questions include a preoccupation with boundaries and where they may or may not lie: boundaries between different literary genres and traditions, of course, but also the boundaries between literature and philosophy, or between literature and history, or literature and the visual arts. With Flaubert, as Barthes observed in his 1953 essay *Le Degré zéro de l'écriture*, literature turns in on itself as never before, scrutinises its own status and function, and emerges into truly modern self-awareness.[4] For all that, and perhaps because of that, Flaubert stands firmly at the crossroads of different styles and approaches, different literary traditions, different epochs. Amenable to vastly differing approaches, he is an exemplary literary case.

Strangely, despite Flaubert's reputation as one of the foremost technicians and philosophers of the genre, his work is also shot through with self-doubt and with a very modern anxiety about the novelist's authority. Where Balzac proclaims triumphantly that his fictional world is real, that novelists 'invent truth by analogy' ['inventent le vrai, par analogie'],[5] for Flaubert the truth-value of fiction is precisely what is in question. With him, fiction becomes a hall of mirrors in which uniform representation ceases to be a possibility and absolutely everything is problematised. There are no unassailable truths, and there is no longer any stable vantage point from which the novelist is able to depict his world. Moreover, as Aimée Israel-Pelletier will argue in her essay here, this holds as much for the visual as for the textual in Flaubert's work, which often highlights the instability of the human gaze and dramatises its inability to find coherence in a world of proliferating objects. And while Flaubert holds 'art' as the supreme value, he at the same time muses that art itself might be no more than a joke, a metaphysical hoax, at best a harmless obsession without meaning. 'Art', he writes to Louise Colet in November 1851, 'may be of no greater consequence than the game of skittles. Perhaps it's all just some immense joke' ['L'Art n'est peut-être pas plus sérieux que le jeu de quilles. Tout n'est peut-être qu'une immense blague' (Cor. II 16)]. From his earliest writings (as my own chapter in this volume will emphasise) we find him turning round the very beliefs on which his work is constructed, putting into question the novelist's or the narrator's apparent judgments on the world, and destabilising the framework within which textual meaning is established. Flaubertian irony is notoriously double-edged, exposing not only the illusions of the characters but also the potential errors of the novelist himself, and almost always, Flaubert writes in such a way as to challenge the very novelistic authority upon which his narrative also depends. The unfinished *Bouvard et Pécuchet* asks deeply uncomfortable questions about the relationship between narrative and knowledge, indeed about the novelist's own attempt to be original. In it, Flaubert uses cliché and recycled knowledge as the very building blocks of his novel, confronting himself with the near impossible challenge of finding novelty through his very refusal of it. The projected ending of the novel has the two clerks returning, armed with new learning, to their former profession as copyists – an allegory, it seems, of the novelist himself copying out the platitudes of his own characters in an attempt to recover meaning that may have regressed into infinite emptiness. Similarly, in *Un cœur simple*, a parrot becomes the symbol of pointless repetition, language without content, words without origin or purpose. That the central character, Félicité, should find both emotional and spiritual fulfilment in her relationship with such a creature, even after it has died, is suggestive of the novelist's own worst nightmare in which empty sentences are rehearsed, then merely remembered in some endless void. From the writer's point of view this is, as Mary Orr will argue later in this volume, not only a struggle with the death of meaning, but a confrontation with death itself and the 'meanings' it confers on human life.

It is hardly surprising, then, that even at a relatively early stage in his career Flaubert discovers 'the torments of style' ['les affres du style'], for he sees writing as an almost impossibly difficult balancing act. As he writes up his sections of the journey that he and his friend Maxime Du Camp had made through Brittany in 1847, in a text entitled *Par les champs et par les grèves*, he complains that he sees nothing but problems in even the simplest of passages: 'The more I progress, the more difficulty I have in writing the simplest things, and the more emptiness I see in those I had judged the best' ['Plus je vais, et plus je découvre de difficultés à écrire les choses les plus simples et plus j'entrevois de vide à celles que j'avais jugées les meilleures' (Cor. 1 486)]. (The crucial place of *Par les champs et par les grèves* in Flaubert's development as a writer will later be discussed by Adrianne Tooke.) Yet, if the writer is faced with the constant possibility of the failure of his own activity, it is Flaubert's paradoxical and inherently 'postmodern' achievement as an artist to have problematised that very issue – a point that will be developed in more detail in Lawrence Schehr's chapter, which analyses Flaubert's creative obsession with failure. Emptiness lurks everywhere, yet Flaubert seeks throughout his career to confront it, to sound out its possibilities, and to write it into his approach. This is where we find the depressing undercurrent of absurdity that lurks within even the most beautifully crafted passages in the Flaubertian *œuvre*. So complex is the task, so evanescent are the thoughts the artist is trying to fix on paper, that he is left with the constant sense that meaning may have escaped between the lines and eluded his grasp: 'There is so much thought between one line and the next! and what you sense most clearly remains floating on the white of the paper' ['Il y a tant de pensée entre une ligne et l'autre! et ce que l'on sent le mieux reste flottant sur le blanc du papier' (Cor. II 456)]. Art may itself end up as an empty and meaningless charade, yet Flaubert will, like Beckett a century later, stare long and hard into the void and seek to make sense of it. And there is sometimes a rich seam of gold in the most unpromising of locations. In *Un cœur simple*, Félicité finds her own spiritual fulfilment in the face of all odds. In *Madame Bovary*, Emma is, for all her tawdry and sentimental platitudes, capable of poetic feelings and mystical impulses that raise her beyond the inherent dreariness of her surroundings. If, for Rodolphe, 'Emma was like every other mistress' ['Emma ressemblait à toutes les maîtresses'], the narrator is quick to remind us that 'this man so full of experience could not distinguish the variety of feelings beneath the similarity of expressions' ['il ne distinguait pas, cet homme si plein de pratique, la dissemblance des sentiments sous la parité des expressions'], and that for Emma, as for everyone else, the problem is that language itself is a faulty, inadequate instrument that cannot register the complexity of her emotions, 'as if the plenitude of the soul did not on occasions spill over in the emptiest of metaphors, since no one can ever give the exact measure of their feelings' ['comme si la plénitude de l'âme ne débordait pas quelquefois par les métaphores les plus vides, puisque personne, jamais, ne peut donner l'exacte mesure de ses sentiments' (OC I 639)]. (Further discussion of this crucial passage will be found later, in Alison Finch's chapter on Flaubert's stylistic achievements.) Thus *Madame Bovary* becomes, like so much of Flaubert's work, a wager to find the poetic in the trivial, an attempt to extract richness from the banal monotony of daily life. As Flaubert himself was to put it on one occasion, it is a novel 'suspended over the double abyss of the lyrical and the vulgar' ['suspendu entre le double abîme du lyrisme et du vulgaire' (Cor. II 57)], seeking beauty in combinations never before associated with art. In this respect, there are clear parallels between what Flaubert does with the novel in the mid-nineteenth century, and what Baudelaire does with poetry, for each works their art in new spaces and with new materials. Between them, they usher in a radically new concept of beauty, and pave the way towards a modernist aesthetic.

Although by Flaubert's own admission there is a side of him that is 'enchanted by *shouting*, lyricism, great flights of the eagle, all the sonorities of the sentence and the summits of the idea' ['épris de *gueulades*, de lyrisme, de grands vols d'aigle, de toutes les sonorités de la phrase et des sommets de l'idée'], there is another 'which searches and digs out truth as much as it can, and which likes to bring out the small fact as powerfully as the big one' ['qui fouille et creuse le vrai tant qu'il peut, qui aime à accuser le petit fait aussi puissamment que le grand' (Cor. II 30)]. From 1845 onwards, the year in which he completes the first *Education sentimentale* – this early novel has little but the title in common with the more famous work of 1869 – the process of tracking down the hidden details and the unlikely truths is one that is painstakingly built into Flaubert's method. Voracious reading and research is accompanied by extensive jottings and notes, progressively honed through many stages. No longer will writing be a question of putting the sentences spontaneously on paper as the mood dictates. It is an exacting task accompanied by constant self-criticism, and involving repeated redrafting and reworking, as well as being a journey through vast terrains of scholarship or along the highways and byways of literary history itself. It is in the 1840s, in particular as he is writing the first *Education sentimentale*, that Flaubert first develops this concept of literature. At the same time – and partly because, following an epileptic seizure in January 1844, he abandons his law studies in Paris and renounces the prospect of an active professional life – he establishes himself as the hermit of Croisset, withdrawing officially into the world of his writing and devoting himself wholeheartedly to it. After the deaths of his father and his sister in 1846, there is no longer any looking back. Croisset will be the shared home of Flaubert and his mother until the latter's death in 1872. To be a writer now is, in Flaubert's view, to live in and through literature, to think and feel in terms of his writing. He will declare to Louise Colet in 1852: 'I am a man of the quill. I feel through it, because of it, in relation to it, and much more with it' ['Je suis un homme-plume. Je sens par elle, à cause d'elle, par rapport à elle, et beaucoup plus avec elle' (Cor. II 42)]. One of the consequences of this approach to writing is that Flaubert left thousands and thousands of pages of jottings, drafts, plans and scenarios which, strictly speaking, have to be considered as much a part of the corpus as the completed texts. For the body of work that Flaubert left is a continuum which, in the eyes of many commentators, can be seen to extend seamlessly from rough notes through to the finished product. As Tony Williams will demonstrate in his essay here, it is in the nature of the questions that Flaubert raises about literature that we have on occasions to return to the *avant-texte* ['pre-text'] and set it alongside the completed version, by way of entering into the creative processes and the decisions involved in writing.

Another reason why we might find ourselves wishing to delve into earlier versions of the Flaubertian text is that the final draft, rich and multifaceted as it is, is almost invariably a pared down and reduced version of what came earlier. Flaubert proceeds by distilling and condensing his material, excluding what is deemed either factually or artistically superfluous. Many lines of research that are conducted for, say, *Salammbô*, may only appear fleetingly if at all in the final text, yet Flaubert's overall understanding of his subject is second to none, and following publication of his novel in 1862 he was able to take on the archaeologist Guillaume Froehner in a very public quarrel in the Parisian press. And as Anne Green will argue here, the presence of history is absolutely central throughout Flaubert's work, informing his approach both to his own era and to earlier ones and underpinning his meticulous and exacting method. Yet what is excluded and unspoken in the Flaubertian text is nonetheless sometimes as important as what is actually said, and this applies not only to the factual details or the research that goes into the making of narrative, but also to the complex web of ironies that is woven around so many apparently 'innocent' and deadpan sentences. One of the fascinations of reading Flaubert is that he often seems able to say so much with so little. A small phrase such as '. . . and the violin started again' ['. . . et le violon recommença' (OC 1 592)], when Emma sees the Viscount waltz back onto the dance-floor with a new partner at the Vaubyessard ball, is loaded with a terrible, tragic irony, and a sense of finality all the greater for its being so blandly understated. Of comparable status is the final line of *Salammbô* which offers an ironically simplified and falsified explanation of the death of the heroine: 'Thus died Hamilcar's daughter, for having touched the mantle of Tanit' ['Ainsi mourut la fille d'Hamilcar pour avoir touché au manteau de Tanit' (OC 1 797)]. And then there is the devastating line at the end of the penultimate chapter of the 1869 *Education sentimentale*, when Madame Arnoux leaves for the final time, making her exit both from Frédéric's life and from his heart: 'And that was all' ['Et ce fut tout' (OC 11 161)]. (The rich resonances of this final 'judgment' on Frédéric's love for Madame Arnoux will be more fully developed in Mary Orr's essay in this collection.) These small transitional or concluding moments, infinitesimal in terms of their relation to the overarching narrative, are where Flaubert steeps his text with layers of emotion and irony. At such points, he is capable of turning the telescope around, shrinking the macro-narrative to tiny proportions while placing the fleeting transitional statement absolutely in the foreground – a reversal of perspective which, as Alison Finch will remind us in her essay here, was very much at the heart of Proust's fascinating response to Flaubert. This is the sort of procedure that delights enthusiasts of Flaubert, confirming their conviction that meaning in the Flaubertian text is to be sought in places where it may not immediately be apparent. Of course, for such elements of the text to operate successfully, they have to be prepared well in advance through long sequences of narrative. The more alert we are to Flaubert's writing, the more we become aware of these complex operations embedded in the tiniest details of the text, often stretching over several chapters. It also means that Flaubert is quintessentially a writer who repays both close reading and frequent rereading. This, no doubt, is one of the consequences of his habit of progressive working and reworking of the text.

Flaubert's method of work and composition is thus radically different from that of, say, Balzac or Stendhal. Stendhal, with magical spontaneity, wrote *La Chartreuse de Parme* over a period of fifty-two days, much of it dictated. Balzac found himself working against the clock to complete *La Cousine Bette* after serial publication of the novel had already begun. Flaubert could never have contemplated writing in such a manner or in such circumstances. Of the author of the *Comédie humaine* he once wryly observed: 'What a great man Balzac would have been if he had known how to write!' ['Quel homme eût été Balzac, s'il eût su écrire!' (Cor. II 209)] Flaubert himself took several years over each of his main novels and reserved his spontaneity for correspondence when his day's work was done. There is no value-judgment in this; rather it is the mark of Flaubert's particular approach to writing, which is based on the minute assembly of detail in an overall framework. Of course, Balzac remained a crucial model for him, as much to work with as to work against, a vital point that Michael Tilby will develop and explain in the next chapter. But Flaubert's ascetic commitment to his own vocation as a writer involved the working through of each project from initial preparatory jottings and research through to plans, composition and redrafting, including the test of the *gueuloir*. Like most writers, he had notebooks full of plans and scenarios that were never used, but the projects that were followed through show an extraordinary degree of care. Meanwhile, 'normal' life was, it seems, put on hold. We know from the many letters to Louise Colet that the novelist's proposed meetings with his mistress, often planned to coincide with the end of a section or a chapter in the writing of *Madame Bovary*, were regularly put off. Whilst Flaubert manfully tried to persuade Louise that they were companions in art above all, and that this sacrifice was all in the name of the higher love that bound them together, she was having none of this excuse-making and saw right through it. (For more on the strategies Flaubert adopts with different correspondents, and the fascinating revelations that the correspondence vouchsafes about him, see the chapter by Rosemary Lloyd.) We shall briefly revisit the question of Flaubert's turbulent and surprisingly busy amorous life, though it is a basic truth that his commitment to writing overshadowed his commitment to human relationships.

Apocryphally, his mother confronted him with this when she uttered the withering and memorable phrase: 'Your obsession with sentences has dried up your heart' ['Ta rage des phrases t'a desséché le cœur']. It is true that, for Flaubert, the adventures of prose narrative were, despite its enormous difficulties and frustrations, often the most fulfilling and the most reward-ing form of engagement. As happens in his novels, life itself is sometimes viewed through the wrong end of the telescope, and a fleeting, passing sen-tence assumes overwhelming proportions in the daily drama of his existence. As the scandal of *Madame Bovary* is brewing and he is about to be put on trial, he writes to Elisa Schlésinger: 'And so I am going to resume my poor, dreary, tranquil existence in which sentences themselves are adventures and where the only flowers I gather are metaphors' ['Je vais donc reprendre ma pauvre vie si plate et tranquille, où les phrases sont des aventures et où je ne recueille d'autres fleurs que des métaphores' (Cor. II 665)]. After all, Flaubert had long maintained that life itself is such a hideous thing that the only way to put up with it is by immersing oneself in art.

It is perhaps inevitable that critics of Flaubert focus on his misanthropy, suggesting that this contaminates his art and restricts his vision of the human condition. It is true that a fascination with stupidity (*bêtise*) and a sense of the grotesque are everywhere in his work, as will become apparent from many of the essays in this volume, and that there is often cruelty in his dissection of human folly. To George Sand, he once offered a highly revealing insight into one of his motives as a writer when he claimed that dissection is an act of revenge (Cor. III 711). But while Flaubert is perhaps a long way from having the Olympian qualities he so admires in Homer and Shakespeare, it would be quite wrong to dismiss him as a writer devoid of compassion or psychological finesse. Generations of readers have identified with Emma Bovary and rightly found extraordinary richness and delicacy in Flaubert's portrayal of her tragic predicament.[6] That Flaubert's techniques and modes of character representation are astonishingly varied and complex is, more-over, brought out later in this volume by Laurence Porter. But it may well be precisely *because* Flaubert cultivates a stance of aesthetic detachment that he is the better able to enter into the complexities and nuances of human feeling. Condemning the emotive approach of Romantic writers like Alfred de Musset, for whom strong and passionate feeling is the basis on which the poet or artist must build, Flaubert decides early in his career as a writer that he must stand outside or above his own (and therefore his characters') emotions and hold them in check, in order the more fully to explore them. At the end of the first *Education sentimentale*, the artist-hero Jules understands that 'you have to be sober to sing of the joys of the bottle, and entirely with-out anger to portray the rages of Ajax' ['il faut être à jeun pour chanter la bouteille, et nullement en colère pour peindre les fureurs d'Ajax' (OJ 1041)]. Every emotion and every state of mind has unique resonances that the artist is better able to perceive if he contemplates it lengthily, without sentimentality. Thus, 'holding back emotion that might disturb him, Jules knows how to bring out the sensitivity within him that must create something' ['arrêtant l'émotion qui le troublerait, [Jules] sait faire naître en lui la sensibilité qui doit créer quelque chose' (OC 1 370)]. In this sense, what is often perceived as an apparent lack of emotion or sympathy in Flaubert is, in fact, a more refined manner of sifting through and expressing the intensity, the depth and the particular qualities of human experience. It is a point that Flaubert was to make in various ways in his correspondence with George Sand, and which led to the writing of *Un cœur simple*, a text which would, he hoped, show that he was eminently capable of tenderness and compassion. It is, indeed, this 'contemplative tenderness' that gives some of Flaubert's minor characters such a strong emotional appeal to the reader (one thinks of Justin, in *Madame Bovary*, or Dussardier in *L'Education sentimentale*). Flaubert maintained that the uniqueness of every emotion, every sensation, even every physical object should be apprehended by the writer who was alert and attentive. It was a lesson that his protégé Maupassant was to remember well, when he described in 'Le Roman', the preface to his 1888 novel *Pierre et Jean*, how Flaubert had taught him to contemplate his subject long and hard, until every tiny facet of it was apparent to him.[7] Such a lesson was as true of people as it was of ideas or objects. Everything and everyone, in Flaubert's view, had unique qualities that it was the artist's duty to seek out. And as Michael Tilby will point out in the next chapter, Maupassant's view – though it may not have corresponded precisely to the reality of Flaubert's practice – did much to promote the image of 'Flaubert the Master' which became common currency by the end of the nineteenth century.

Given the contemplative, ascetic dimension to Flaubert's approach, it is hardly surprising that we find throughout his writing a monastic and mystical quality. His fascination with religion and the discipline it imposes is evident, and if he cannot himself believe in God, the transfer of mystical contemplation into the writing process provides the logical alternative. The nineteenth century, for Flaubert as for so many thinkers and artists, was truly an era of the twilight of the gods. In 1875 he writes: 'The nineteenth century is destined to see all religions perish. Amen! I weep for none of them' ['Le XIXe siècle est destiné à voir périr toutes les religions. Amen! Je n'en pleure aucune' (Cor. IV 997)]. And yet, his work is full of saints, monks and mystics, and the history of religion is a subject of which he came to have a profound knowledge, as we see in *La Tentation de saint Antoine*, *Salammbô* and *Hérodias*. But for Flaubert, modern life has replaced the quest for God by the quest for the eternal, indeed transcendent, truth of art itself. The theme recurs frequently during the years he is writing *Madame Bovary*, though we should be aware that it may sometimes be a strategy to maintain his ivory-tower seclusion when faced with the demands of Louise Colet. In September 1852 he states: 'I am turning towards a kind of aesthetic mysticism' ['Je tourne à une espèce de mysticisme esthétique' (Cor. II 151)], and in December: 'Had it not been for the love of form, perhaps I would have been a great mystic' ['Sans l'amour de la forme, j'eusse peut-être été un grand mystique' (Cor. II 218)]. So the writer is himself the modern mystic, a lonely hermit wearing his hair shirt and tormenting himself with his discipline. He writes on 24 April 1852: 'I love my work with a frenetic and perverted love, as the ascetic loves the hair shirt that scratches his belly' ['J'aime mon travail d'un amour frénétique et perverti, comme un ascète le cilice qui lui gratte le ventre' (Cor. II 75)]. The writer's lot, like the lives of saints, is a painful one that involves unremitting tribulation as his faith is challenged by the jealous God of Art. Yet there are rare moments of artistic joy as the hermit of Croisset senses himself dissolving into his own creation, escaping from the burden of his individuality and the suffering that goes with it. These moments may have their root in genuinely mystical experiences at various stages in Flaubert's life outside of his writing. In the paragraph following his evocation of the hair shirt, he writes: 'On my great days of sunshine, I have sometimes glimpsed a state of the soul superior to life itself, and for which glory would be irrelevant and happiness itself of no consequence' ['J'ai entrevu quelquefois (dans mes grands jours de soleil) [. . .] un état de l'âme ainsi supérieur à la vie, pour qui la gloire ne serait rien, et le bonheur même inutile' (Cor. II 76)]. The great days of sunshine are there in the writing too. On 23 December 1853, after an afternoon spent working on the scene of Emma's seduction in the forest by Rodolphe, Flaubert declares: 'It is a delicious thing to write, no longer to be oneself, but to circulate in the whole creation one speaks of' ['C'est une délicieuse chose que d'écrire! que de ne plus être *soi*, mais de circuler dans toute la création dont on parle' (Cor. II 483)] – though interestingly, a few lines earlier he had suggested, pre-empting this intuition of the sublime with characteristic earthiness, that he now felt 'like a man who has done too much fucking' ['comme un homme qui a trop foutu'].

According to one exuberant biographer in the 1980s, Flaubert was indeed a man who massively over-indulged his sexual appetite. Jacques-Louis Douchin, author of a prurient account of Flaubert's sexual liaisons, set out to destroy a number of long-held myths about the hermit of Croisset.[8] One of these myths was that Flaubert had a single lifelong passion for Elisa Schlésinger, an older woman encountered during a family holiday in Trouville in 1836, and often considered to have been the model for Madame

Arnoux in the 1869 *Education sentimentale*. Though the importance of Elisa Schlésinger in Flaubert's biography is beyond all doubt, the theory of the 'single passion' is by now largely discredited, and on this point Douchin was no doubt right. But Douchin went much further, maintaining that the standard image of Flaubert as a recluse, working day and night to hone his sentences in the silence of his study, was pious nonsense that been passed down through the literary manuals. The 'hermit of Croisset' is a fake, a historical fabrication. Certainly, if Douchin's chronology of the author's sexual activities were to be taken at face value, we might be tempted to conclude that Flaubert could not have had enough time to write! In fact, as is so often the case when the orthodox view is challenged, the argument was grossly exaggerated, especially when Douchin resuscitated the long-discredited myth that Flaubert was also the father of Maupassant. A much more balanced and objective view of Flaubert, writer and man, can be found in the well-informed and readable recent biography in English by Geoffrey Wall.[9] Be that as it may, Douchin's contribution did have the merit of reminding us that Flaubert also had a life outside of his writing, and that alongside the literary 'mystic' there was a man of earthly and earthy appetites. Biographers have long been aware of the existence of a secret, long-term relationship with his niece's English governess, Juliet Herbert, though the information about this liaison is tantalisingly elusive.[10] Elsewhere, there is abundant evidence of Flaubert's sexual encounters, his lifelong frequenting of prostitutes, and his experiments with same-sex relationships. We should not forget either that the hermit of Croisset was one of the best travelled men of his generation (a full assessment of the importance of Flaubert's travels and of his writings about them will be found in Adrianne Tooke's chapter here); or indeed that the notes and letters documenting his hedonistic travels in the Middle East in 1849–51 give a picture of an early practitioner of sexual tourism. During this journey, Flaubert contracted syphilis. It was to make him go prematurely bald, and the mercury treatment would blacken his teeth. For some biographers it was the latter stages of syphilis that caused Flaubert's death in 1880 at the comparatively young age of 58, though the standard explanation remains that it was a recurrence of the epilepsy that had first struck him in January 1844.

In his letters to his closest friend Louis Bouilhet, Flaubert often talks of intimate matters with a coarseness that should remind us that his view of life is also shot through with a sense of the grotesque, the carnal, and the physical. This writer of legendary finesse could also be a man of staggering vulgarity. But then, at some level, that might too have been in the name of art, for Flaubert always resolutely refused to put his own quest for the ideal into some germ-free environment. Like his own character saint Antoine, whose closest companion is a pig which wallows in the mud, he accepts the cohabitation of opposites as one of the ironies of the writer's lot. It is therefore important to modify the view of Flaubert as the uniformly reclusive artist who spent his life in solitary aesthetic contemplation. He did, of course, spend long hours and days and weeks at his desk, painfully working through the drafts of his novels, and he did raise the stakes very considerably when it came to the writer's vocation. But he was also a man who carried within him all the contradictions that he saw in life itself. After all, as he had written of his writer-hero in the 1845 *Education sentimentale*, 'he arrived at this axiom: inconsequence is the ultimate consequence, and the man who is not absurd today is the one who was absurd yesterday and who will be tomorrow' ['il en arrivait à cet axiome: l'inconséquence est la conséquence suprême, l'homme qui n'est pas absurde aujourd'hui est celui qui l'a été hier et qui le sera demain' (OC 1 361)].

In the 1860s Flaubert frequently left Croisset to spend time in Paris, where he made many friends, led a busy social and amorous life, and indulged his lifelong passion for the theatre (the crucial importance of which is discussed by Alan Raitt later in this collection). As a celebrated author, he moved in high circles and enjoyed the esteem of the Parisian *literati*. He also became friendly with the Emperor's cousin, Princesse Mathilde, who in collaboration with the critic Sainte-Beuve arranged for him to receive the Légion d'Honneur on 15 August 1866. Flaubert meekly and proudly accepted this award, even though he was forced to share the honour of the occasion with the popular author Ponson du Terrail whom he despised. For a man who railed throughout his life against decorations and honours (see for example the entry under 'Décoration' in the *Dictionnaire des idées reçues*) this is a contradiction to savour. But it is in the end heartening to find that the writer's writer is after all a man with his foibles and weaknesses, that the mystic and the ascetic bears within him a creature of flesh and blood, and is on occasions prone to staggering and startling *bêtise*. It may indeed be that Flaubert's writing ultimately fed off the absurdities of which he was aware in his own life; or that the unexpected and sometimes surprising warmth of his style had its origin in the contradictions of his own character.

NOTES

1 Henry James, 'Gustave Flaubert' (1914), in *Literary Criticism. French Writers, Other European Writers* (Cambridge: Cambridge University Press, 1984), pp. 314–46, p. 329.

2 See also Woody Allen's short story 'The Kugelmass Episode', in *Side Effects* (New York: Random House, 1980), pp. 59–78, in which humanities professor Sidney Kugelmass steps into the fictional world of *Madame Bovary* and turns up in Yonville.

3 Julian Barnes, *Flaubert's Parrot* (London: Cape, 1984); *Something to Declare* (London: Picador, 2002).

4 Roland Barthes, *Le Degré zéro de l'écriture* (Paris: Seuil, 1972 [1953]), pp. 45–8.

5 Honoré de Balzac, preface to *La Peau de chagrin*, in *La Comédie humaine*, vol. X (Paris: Gallimard, 1979), p. 52.

6 See the recent study by Alan Raitt, *The Originality of 'Madame Bovary'* (Bern: Peter Lang, 2002).

7 See the preface to *Pierre et Jean* in Guy de Maupassant, *Romans* (Paris: Gallimard, Bibliothèque de la Pléiade, 1987), pp. 703–15, and especially the remarks on Flaubert, pp. 713–14.

8 Jacques-Louis Douchin, *La Vie érotique de Flaubert* (Paris: Carrère, 1984).

9 Geoffrey Wall, *Flaubert: A Life* (London: Faber, 2001).

10 See Hermia Oliver, *Flaubert and an English Governess: The Quest for Juliet Herbert* (Oxford: Clarendon, 1980).

2

MICHAEL TILBY

Flaubert's place in literary history

For Flaubert, the nineteenth century was 'l'Hénaurme siècle'. This distortion of the epithet *énorme* admirably conveys not only his ironical attitude towards the misplaced self-confidence and pretension of the age, but also his frank enjoyment of the grotesque figures who, for him, embodied these quintessentially bourgeois characteristics. As the novelist Milan Kundera would later put it, with only minimal recourse to hyperbole: 'Flaubert discovered stupidity. I dare say that is the greatest discovery of a century so proud of its scientific thought.'[1] In Flaubert's eyes, *bêtise* ['stupidity'] contaminated even the highest reaches of intellectual endeavour. Writing to George Sand after reading Lamennais's *Essai sur l'indifférence en matière de religion*, he boasted: 'I am now thoroughly acquainted with all those monumental jokers who have had such a calamitous influence on the nineteenth century' ['Je connais maintenant, et à fond, tous ces immenses farceurs, qui ont eu sur le 19e siècle une influence désastreuse' (Cor. IV 758)].

Yet in all Flaubert's writings, even when the ostensible subject matter was ancient Carthage or the life of a third-century Egyptian saint, the society of which he purported to be such a reluctant denizen constituted his overriding concern. This is true, for example, not only with regard to the way *Salammbô* can be read as a commentary on Second Empire France, but also in the very opacity of his representations which, to a greater or lesser extent, clashed glaringly, but intentionally, with the assumptions of the nineteenth-century reader. Small wonder that the reception of *L'Education sentimentale* encompassed both hostility and bewilderment, since that novel's undermining of belief in purposeful action, the individual's capacity for self-fulfilment and the inherent meaningfulness of the external world went beyond mere literary categories. Henry James pronounced it a failure, while reserving his bewilderment for *La Tentation de saint Antoine*.[2] But even in the case of the more accessible *Madame Bovary*, it is sufficient to imagine the bafflement Flaubert's detached and ambiguous narration would have caused its 'heroine' to appreciate the challenge it presented to the assumptions on which traditional romantic fictions were founded.

Flaubert's cult of impersonality likewise ran counter to the contemporary expectation that a work of literature would reveal its author's opinions and personality. Still more disconcertingly, his celebrated irony extends beyond his characters to spare neither reader nor author himself as writing subject. The result is an ambivalent text that deprives the reader of any fixed position. For Flaubert, writing represented an attempt to maintain diametrically opposed implications in an unresolved state of tension, thereby illustrating his conviction that in all things opposites meet.

Bêtise is as touched by this cultivation of paradox as everything else in Flaubert. In mounting an attack on such nineteenth-century shibboleths as progress and education, and in directing his incisive irony at the bourgeois citizen, Flaubert may give the impression that his work was a pretext for a demonstration of his own superior intelligence. But the reality is significantly more complex, and often for contrasting reasons. A fundamental ambiguity, for example, informs his relationship with his readership. For while the latter can only be drawn from the class he most commonly satirises for its stupidity, the writing presupposes an ability to be awakened to an appreciation of the author's insights. A contrasting ambiguity exists in the way, in *Madame Bovary*, the intellectually limited know-all Homais (whose name irresistibly recalls *homo sapiens*) professes to be a disciple of Voltaire, Flaubert's reverence for whom he inherited from his father. On the other hand, Félicité's simple-mindedness in *Un cœur simple*, while inclining the reader to gentle mockery, is no less readable as an indication of her saintliness. The most profound source of this ambiguity, however, derives from the acknowledgment that *bêtise* was truly universal and, as such, something from which not even its merciless anatomist was exempt, though his own entrapment in the phenomenon inevitably widens and deepens the term, depriving it of the banality that attaches to it in everyday discourse. His ambiguous position in relation to this universal *bêtise* would find its fullest embodiment in his *Dictionnaire des idées reçues* and, above all, in the unfinished *Bouvard et Pécuchet*, a work which simultaneously denounces and celebrates a pair of exemplary case-studies of stupidity.[3]

Flaubert's writing was thus a strategic activity designed to accommodate the ambiguity of his own position, without which his satire would have been confined to the surface and his works rendered both ephemeral and innocuous. While his compositions are almost ludicrously diverse for an age that was moving towards uniformity and standardisation, they are a reflection of each other in respect of their shared commitment to the simultaneous presentation of both sides of every coin. Their resonance is inseparable from the radical hesitation that characterises the reader's experience in the face of constant *aporia*, the manifestations of which are not only internally consistent with each other and with Flaubert's larger picture, but chime with lived experience, while deepening it as a result of the way contradictions give way to similarities and parallels open up to reveal contrasts. Each of Flaubert's compositions contains within it not only the perspective of its own critique, but a potential alternative or contrary act of writing. *L'Education sentimentale* is, for example, perpetually poised between its banal surface narrative and description and the rich suggestiveness teasingly contained within the details themselves; between a sense of emptiness and the feeling that life has been encompassed in its totality; between an intimation of sincerity and one of parody. The banality of everyday events is never abandoned as a redundant springboard. Instead, it remains as a constant reaffirmation of a discredited, but nonetheless unanswerable, reality.

Writing for Flaubert was still less the straightforward celebration of artistic form it has so often been made out to be. This is revealed most clearly by *La Tentation de saint Antoine* and *Bouvard et Pécuchet*, works which, despite their superficial differences of subject matter, are profoundly linked through their shared response to the quest for totalisation that was the dominant epistemological obsession in mid-nineteenth-century France. Both works demonstrate by their very eccentricity, not to say absurdity, the way writing for Flaubert was, for all its obvious external concerns, a profoundly personal enterprise. Both can be seen to reflect their creator's struggle between his commitment to Art and his acknowledgment of the monstrosity of the products of both the imagination and the intellect. Not for nothing did Henry James describe Flaubert as 'almost insanely excessive' (James, *Literary Criticism*, p. 297).

The significance of the deceptively straightforward *Bouvard et Pécuchet* is glimpsed when the reader registers surprise that the eponymous figures who embody inadequacy (whether intellectual, emotional, sexual or with regard merely to the practical aspects of daily living) are not the butts of authorial contempt. Not only are the forms of their ambition determined by the blinkered materialism and positivism of the age, their failure is somehow honourable. At one level, they retain an innocence reminiscent of Félicité and display an embryonic saintliness that is enhanced by their naïveté. Characteristic of Flaubert, however, is the adoption of a stance poised, almost unbearably, between ridicule and respect. As a result of their comic presentation, there is clearly much to differentiate Bouvard and Pécuchet from their supremely self-aware creator, but their all-important ambiguity is lost if one fails to note the parallels they present with Flaubert's own authorial activity: they are by profession pen-pushers engaged in an act of copying, while their vast programme of reading confers on them the status of the author's scapegoats in relation to his own compulsive documentation.

Only slightly less paradoxical, given Flaubert's indefatigable opposition to dogma, is his readiness to identify with saint Antoine. *La Tentation de saint Antoine* is, however, no conventional hagiography. The emphasis is not on the saint's resistance to the grotesque temptations placed before him, but on the reality of the suffering they cause him and on the greater humanity he acquires as a result of his acknowledgment of their powerful and perverse attraction. The work is imbued with a syncretism that deals a crippling blow to any form of orthodoxy. Biblical inconsistencies are a starting point for a more widespread undermining of religious authority. There is a compelling demystification of illustrious martyrs, with Antoine's standing enhanced by his insistence on his own failures and inadequacies, just as it is the lack of conventional respect shown in the depiction of Iaokanann in *Hérodias* that affords John the Baptist a greater realism. Nevertheless, there is, in the wake of Flaubert's reading of Spinoza and Ernest Renan, a respect for the religious perspective in general, for the way it offers entry into a world that complements everyday reality.

What justifies an identification of Antoine and Flaubert the artist is their shared capacity for heightened imaginary experience, an experience simultaneously glorious and monstrous, and one highlighted again in *La Légende de saint Julien l'Hospitalier*. In both his evocations of Christian saints, the workings of the imagination are pursued into the realm of dream, and more especially nightmare. If the susceptibility of Antoine and Julien to fantastic depictions and narratives marks them out as artist figures, and if in *La Tentation* the Word ['le Verbe'] is said to occupy the pinnacle, their identification with their creator is only completed by the anguish that accompanies the reception of their visions.[4]

The uniquely paradoxical nature of Flaubert's writings, together with his emphasis on the solitary nature of artistic activity, thus sets him apart from his age. Yet his uncompromising attempt to raise creative writing to a higher plane inevitably intersected with existing literary practice, both intertextually and in more basic ways, though he always maintained the ambivalence that was the defining characteristic of his stance as writer. From such a perspective, he emerges as both idiosyncratic and representative.

On its first appearance, *Madame Bovary*, being contemporaneous with the manifestos and fictional output of Champfleury and Duranty and with the paintings of Courbet, was inevitably seen as an exemplar of the new Realist school. Yet Flaubert admired the work of neither Realist writer and objected to the painter's doctrinaire dimension. If Zola is to be believed, he wrote his novel in order to annoy ['embêter'] Champfleury and his fellow Realists, presumably by showing up the narrowness of the notion they had made their own.[5] He vehemently rejected the designation 'Realist', just as he would subsequently profess abhorrence for the programmatic dimension of Naturalism and, to a lesser extent, for the work of the early Impressionist painters, whom he not unreasonably associated with Naturalism. Had he lived to a more advanced age, he might well have come to appreciate the ironic and enigmatic dimensions of the work of Manet, Degas and Caillebotte, together with their stark use of juxtaposition and their unconventional exploitation of space, just as, in due course, he came to admire certain 'non-realist dimensions' of the photographic image. As it was, in a letter he wrote to Maupassant in 1876, he dismissed both 'Naturalism' and 'Realism' as 'meaningless' and observed that the caricaturist Henry Monnier was 'no truer' than Racine (CHH xv 516).

This insistence on the independent status of his art was matched by his comparative detachment from mainstream Parisian literary and artistic life, though he formed a number of literary friendships. According to the writer and critic Arsène Houssaye in his memoirs, it was the poet Théophile Gautier who suggested the subject of *Salammbô* to him. The celebrated Magny dinners brought him into contact with the Goncourt brothers and the critic Sainte-Beuve, while in his later years he would be sought out by Zola, and, above all, Maupassant. His most faithful correspondents included George Sand and Tourgueniev, but also such writers as Louise Colet and Louis Bouilhet, whom history has deemed minor.

In other respects, too, Flaubert remained detached from the life of the nineteenth-century man of letters. He was one of the few major writers of his generation not to engage in regular journalism. His forays into that other coveted passport to financial stability, the theatre, were both few and unsuccessful, though he retained an attraction to writing for the stage until the end of his career.

In line with many of his contemporaries, Flaubert was drawn to the visual arts, both for themselves and for the stimulus they provided for his writing. In spite of his celebrated passion for *le mot juste*, he remained in awe of the immediacy and purity of the painted image and saw it as something to emulate in his writing. His finely wrought compositions may accordingly be seen as the product of a 'denaturalisation' of language, in which the latter's discursive function is largely eliminated in favour of a materialisation of the word, admired principally for its colour and solidity. But for the most part (and with the notable exception of the paintings of Gustave Moreau), it was the work of the Old Masters that exerted the greatest fascination upon him, just as, from an early age, it was Rabelais, Montaigne and Cervantes who provided him with greater stimulus than the writings of his own century. He was, moreover, suspicious of art criticism and, unlike Baudelaire, Gautier and a host of writer-journalists, never wrote a guide to the annual Paris Salon.

In contrast to Balzac, Flaubert the novelist steered clear of depicting contemporary literary life in any detail. (In *L'Education sentimentale*, it is with Hussonnet's political ambitions for his journal that he is principally concerned.) His preferred focus is on reading, with Emma and Bouvard and Pécuchet being the most obvious examples. Of Sénécal in *L'Education*, it is said: 'he sought in books the justification for his dreams' ['il cherchait dans les livres de quoi justifier ses rêves' (OC II 57)], just as the tomes strewn across Jules's table in the first *Education sentimentale* provoke the comment that he had not read them all but used them as material for his daydreams. This might seem an instance of 'bad reading', yet other details Flaubert provides in illustration of Jules's voracious reading reveal it to echo his own, prompting the realisation that reading may legitimately be seen as a multifaceted activity, in which the acceptance of an invitation to daydream has a part to play. On the other hand, those examples of 'bad reading' that test negative for ambiguity should not blind us to the instances of inadequacy connoted by a reluctance to read (e.g., the hero of the early story *Bibliomanie*; or Charles Bovary, the pages of whose reference volumes have remained uncut).

Jules is the exception in Flaubert's novels in being primarily a man of literary ambitions. Although in the 1869 *Education sentimentale* Frédéric Moreau entertains, like Balzac's Lucien de Rubempré, an ambition to be the Walter Scott of France, literature is only one of several potential arenas he considers. He is, moreover, distinguished from his creator by both his lack of aesthetic precepts and his non-productivity (and that in an age when all and sundry had written, and often published, at least some kind of pamphlet, poem, article or play); in each case, he fails to progress beyond the stage of a self-indulgent daydream. It is easy to imagine why the mature Flaubert was disinclined to depict a writer at work. Implicit in his aesthetic is the assumption that a questioning of literary precepts and achievement is productive only if it takes the form of a radical self-questioning.

Such a viewpoint may explain in part Flaubert's relative reluctance, uncharacteristic of nineteenth-century French writers, to engage in literary criticism, though Zola claimed that he was ready to take apart in private a page of Mérimée's *Colomba* or to express a profound dislike of Stendhal's writing, which was at the opposite end of the stylistic spectrum from his own. But he was also reluctant to theorise publicly with regard to his own work. His temperament was unsuited to the literary manifesto, and there was clearly no place in his work for a counterpart to Balzac's preface to the *Comédie humaine*. Yet there are no important prefaces to his individual works, either. As for the numerous isolated comments he made on the subject of his art, their fragmented nature should incline us to caution. Although they may seem to add up to a conscious and coherent aesthetic, they are mostly off-the-cuff comments made in response to remarks by his correspondents. They undoubtedly highlight his emphases and inclinations, but throw surprisingly little light on the specificity of his writing, as a result, paradoxically, of the ease with which, in their generality, they fit his compositions. They can even acquire a disconcerting resemblance to the *idées reçues* of which Flaubert was the incomparable compiler. It is safe to suppose that he would have been astounded by the frequency with which such oracular phrases as his 'Madame Bovary, c'est moi' ['Madame Bovary is me'] or 'un livre sur rien' ['a book about nothing'] have been picked apart.

Flaubert's semi-detachment from the contemporary world of letters also translated into a political non-alignment that some admirers have found troubling. The legal proceedings taken against him as the author of *Madame Bovary*, alleging both blasphemy and obscenity, left a lasting rancour, in spite of the 'not guilty' verdict. Yet it was the same author who, notwithstanding his low opinion of Napoleon III, took pride in his intimacy with the more cultivated Prince Napoleon and Princesse Mathilde and cherished his invitations to the Imperial château. In one of his frequent misanthropic outbursts to George Sand, he characterised the worker as 'ignoble' (Cor. IV 372), and in the twilight years of the Second Empire he repeatedly bemoaned, in letters to the same correspondent, the stupidity of the masses. His portrayal of the 1848 Revolution in *L'Education sentimentale* was accordingly negative, though he not unreasonably held that he had been even-handed.

In *Qu'est-ce que la littérature?* (1948), Jean-Paul Sartre felt duty-bound to expose the way Flaubert sought refuge in terms of reference that were psychological and idealist in nature, rather than adopting a position of political 'commitment' ['engagement']. Yet he later accepted that his writing presented an authentic denunciation of the imprisoning structures of bourgeois culture. Roland Barthes, in his early 'Sartrean' essay *Le Degré zéro de l'écriture* (1953), duly championed Flaubert as the exemplary modern writer torn between his social condition and his intellectual vocation, with bourgeois ideology shown to be merely one among many possible others.[6] He identified in Flaubert a new mode of writing that represented a radical break with the previous 'classical' phase by embodying the irreversible loss of faith in the transparency of language that occurred around 1848. In characterising it as 'writing as craft' ['écriture artisanale' (*Le Degré zéro*, pp. 46–8)], he succeeded, moreover, in releasing Flaubert's texts from hallowed idealist conceptions of the author's 'style'. Yet when all is said and done, Flaubert's writings remain deeply rooted in his age, not least as a result of his concern with beauty, which, although in his case it interested him principally in relation to truth, constituted an aesthetic direction he shared with both Gautier and Baudelaire.

Like many of his contemporaries, he was drawn to the genre of travel writing, and, like them, saw it as an opportunity to explore the attractions of Orientalism, though neither his travels in Egypt with Maxime Du Camp nor his earlier trip through Anjou and Brittany with the same friend led to a completed publication in his own lifetime.

Though in their own way idiosyncratic, the fictions he wrote in his youth have in common an inclination towards the extremes of the Romantic imagination. Several of these stories display either his predilection for Byron or the love of Rabelais he shared with many early nineteenth-century French writers. To his friend Ernest Chevalier he declared: 'there are only two men I esteem: Rabelais and Byron, the only two to have written out of an intention to spite humanity and laugh in its face' ['je n'estime profondément que deux hommes: Rabelais et Byron les deux seuls qui aient écrit dans l'intention de nuire au genre humain et de lui rire à la face' (Cor. 1 28)]. The taste for the macabre displayed in *Un parfum à sentir* was as much the influence of Jules Janin's novel *L'Ane mort et la femme guillotinée* (1829) as of his youthful exposure to the Rouen dissecting room, while *Bibliomanie* and *Quidquid volueris*, which depicts a brutal rape by an alleged ape-man who had been conceived as a scientific experiment, betray an attraction to Petrus Borel's collection of 'immoral tales', *Champavert* (1833).

In one important respect, Flaubert was an undoubted man of his age. This was in his fascination with the Marquis de Sade, a fascination that followed naturally from his reading of Janin and Borel and embroiled him in controversy with Sainte-Beuve. As Mario Praz has famously documented,[7] the later French Romantics and their Decadent offspring perpetuated a tradition that indulged widely in erotic fantasies rooted in sadistic impulses. Both Flaubert's youthful writings and his later 'orientalist' fictions abound in examples of gratuitous cruelty. In *La Tentation de saint Antoine*, the most emphatic sadism is accompanied by an equally histrionic masochism that is also manifested by Julien. The grammatical mood characteristic of the sado-masochistic is the imperative. The power of the scenes evoked by Flaubert duly stems from the subordination of the individual to a relentless and unquestionable command, the perversity of which is ensured by its essentially intellectual, and therefore unnatural, nature. Antoine might be regarded as tormented by the sheer proliferation of the accounts of heresy with which he is familiar. In his way he is, like Emma Bovary, an impressionable reader who has read too much. The evocations of the Queen of Sheba (in *La Tentation*) and Hérodias, which emphasise their luxuriant hair and their malevolent fingernails (phantasmic details already apparent in Flaubert's juvenilia), indicate that the power of such figures derives from the way the voluptuousness of woman is enhanced by the threat she represents.

The sadistic dimension is necessarily attenuated in the compositions set in contemporary France. The latter tend to emphasise the victim's lot rather than the tormentor's calculated cruelty, which is commonly replaced by a congruence of circumstances possessing the outward appearance of Fate. In a universe that looks forward to Darwin, the least fit to survive are guaranteed to suffer. Flaubert is also careful to give the victims names that contrast ironically, or problematically, with their status or lot: the bemused farm-servant in *Madame Bovary* is named Catherine (from the Greek for 'pure'); in the same novel, the ostler Hippolyte, whose name is inherited from Greek tragedy, is subjected to a botched operation on his club-foot; in *Un cœur simple* Félicité (see the entry Félicité in the *Dictionnaire des idées reçues*) loves a young man named Théodore (or 'gift of God'). In the 'French' novels, it is invariably the women who are tormented: Emma, but also Madame Arnoux, punished, as she sees it, as a mother following her avowal of adulterous feelings. Here, as well as in the 'exotic' compositions, disturbance of the established order is frequently expressed through an ambiguity of gender or sexual identity. Julien murders his mother, having mistaken her for the wife he wrongly assumes to have been unfaithful. Antoine's physical contact with the leper is homoerotic in its notation. Catherine Leroux's surname emphasises her masculinity ('Leroux' rather than 'Larousse'). Emma, whose independent behaviour put Baudelaire in mind of a man, exhibits a perverse refusal of motherhood; her unimpeded manipulation of Charles duly feminises him. Sexual impotence is a muted component of Frédéric's overall passivity; he is said to exert on Deslauriers 'an almost feminine attraction' ['un charme presque féminin' (OC II 97)].

It is, however, in his relationship to Balzac that Flaubert the novelist most notably reveals both his dependence and his originality. When, in *L'Education sentimentale*, Deslauriers famously enjoins Frédéric to heed Balzac's most celebrated *arriviste* – 'Keep in mind Rastignac in the *Human Comedy* and you'll be a success, I'm sure of it' ['Rappelle-toi Rastignac dans la *Comédie humaine*! Tu réussiras, j'en suis sûr!' (OC II 14)] – it is difficult to be certain whether this is intended as tribute to Balzac's gift for memorable characterisation, or as snide denigration of both writer and his reader, Deslauriers, for confusing the boundaries between Art and Life. Deducing Flaubert's literary allegiances from references in his fictional compositions is, moreover, a hazardous activity. Emma's liking for Walter Scott and the initial delight Bouvard and Pécuchet take in the same author's historical novels should not, for example, be taken as evidence that Flaubert disdained the *Waverley Novels*. He reread Scott as an adult, and expressed gratitude to George Sand for recommending that he read *The Fair Maid of Perth*. Scott was the author he chose to help him while away the time in 1870 as he waited for the Prussians to advance as far as Rouen, and was the only 'English' novelist he considered to possess a sense of structure.

Flaubert, in fact, held a far more nuanced view of Balzac than did his character Hussonnet, who dismissed the author of the *Comédie humaine* as 'overrated' ['surfait' (OC II 59)]. From comments made to various correspondents, it may seem that he considered him ignorant, vainglorious, provincial and devoid of any idea of how to write. He nevertheless waxed lyrical to Louise Colet on the depiction of youthful genius in *Louis Lambert*. His tribute, in *Par les champs et par les grèves*, to Balzac's discovery of 'the woman of thirty' ['la femme de trente ans'], though hyperbolic, was in essence sincere, and he counted *La Cousine Bette* among the great masterpieces of the novel. He professed himself greatly affected by Balzac's death and objected to Sainte-Beuve's lack of indulgence towards him as a writer, though, according to Zola, his attraction to Balzac's work became diminished over time as a result of his quest for artistic perfection. If many of the parallels of character, plot and theme advanced in support of Flaubert's indebtedness to Balzac are superficial or inconclusive, there is much to suggest a critical reflection on Balzac's compositional practice.[8]

The first *Education sentimentale*, completed in 1845, is reminiscent of Balzac's depiction of both Rastignac and some of the most prominent characters in *Illusions perdues*. The form itself may be considered 'Balzacian' in its fundamental orthodoxy. The narrative is presented by a 'voice' instantly recognisable as that of a conventional storyteller, and employs mock-serious digressions and addresses to the reader that betray the passion for Rabelais the young Flaubert shared with Balzac, though rather than presenting a continuation of the 'self-conscious tradition' for its own sake, it is part of an ironic counterpoint to stereotypical depictions of the *mal du siècle*. The narrative is direct and expansive in a manner reminiscent of Balzac and much other Romantic writing, so much so that the early twentieth-century critic Albert Thibaudet not unreasonably charged it with being 'verbose'. Significantly, in view of Flaubert's later claim to detest the presence of dialogue in novels, there is extensive direct speech.

The 1869 *Education* continues the exploitation of the same key texts from *La Comédie humaine*, together with Balzac's account of Félix de Vandenesse's love for the married Henriette de Mortsauf in *Le Lys dans la vallée*. All four categories represented by the objects of Frédéric's desire derive from Balzac's depiction of contemporary Paris, while the group of

Pellerin, Regimbart and Hussonnet clearly refers back to the Cénacle featured in *Illusions perdues*. But whereas in the first *Education*, Henry and Jules remain individuals in the Balzacian manner, *L'Education sentimentale* is relentless in its insistence on the uniformity and monotony of the contemporary world. It represents an implied critique of Balzac's reliance on dramatic contrast and of his endowment of his characters with superlative powers. With its emphasis on mediocrity, error, and failure to connect, the mature *Education sentimentale* is an implicit condemnation of Balzac's distortion of the real through his readiness to allot genius to all and sundry. The passage from Henriette de Mortsauf to Marie Arnoux is in the direction of mundane reality, while the obvious shortcomings of Rosanette represent an attempt to demolish the romantic myth of the prostitute redeemed by love.

In the second *Education*, dialogue is not only pared to a minimum, it takes on an appropriately stylised appearance as a result. We do not really 'hear' the characters in the novels of the author's maturity, any more than the narrator communicates his personality through the manner in which he speaks. Already in *Madame Bovary*, Flaubert had striven to remove any resemblance between his narrative and the familiar idioms of storytelling. The text gains its prestige from its emphatic status as writing, from the fascination it exerts by virtue of its conscious association of artifice and artistry (what Nathalie Sarraute would refer to as Flaubert's 'trompe-l'œil' effect), and from the way it eschews fluency or spontaneity. The principal motivation for Flaubert's exploitation of free indirect discourse may well have been to cultivate an ambiguity of point of view, but it should also be seen as a means of avoiding the need to incorporate more than the occasional snatch of the philistine language of the *bourgeoisie*. In the second *Education*, the calculated abruptness that is the product of Flaubert's insistence on juxtaposition without explicatory connections purposefully interrupts a fluent reading and stimulates the reader to reflect upon the implications of what are deceptively matter-of-fact formulations.

In both Balzac and Flaubert, the 'realist' enterprise is characterised by materialist descriptions that feature an accumulation of particularised objects. But there the similarity ceases. The Balzacian description is characterised by a proliferation of disparate information and is presented in terms of a challenge to the onlooker's sense-making activity. Order, in the form of interpretation, can never be more than a partial, or temporary, accommodation of an intrinsic plurality, not to say chaos, of potential meanings. The celebrated generalisations that so frequently intrude upon the mimetic project are never the definitive interpretations they might seem, merely part of an ongoing process that results in a kaleidoscopic relativism in which meanings are proposed, only to be thrown into question. Contrary to the popular stereotype, the Balzac novel is a composition that opens up, rather than closes down, interpretative possibilities.

Flaubert's compositions may be still more obviously open-ended, and an exemplification of the author's belief that 'stupidity consists in the wish to conclude' ['la bêtise consiste à vouloir conclure' (Cor. I 680)]. In contrast to those of Balzac, however, they exemplify a much more controlled cultivation of ambiguity, an ambiguity that is both quintessentially ironic and incomparably more radical. It is only to be expected that the fastidious artist Flaubert should have sought to distinguish his writing from the discursive and anarchic Balzacian creation, which posterity has so often felt necessary to explain away as the product of an over-hasty compositional procedure. But it was not merely a matter of aesthetics. Still more important is the radical disjunction between text and world Flaubert sought to maintain. Even in works that were manifestly 'realist' in intention, it was not the function of the Flaubert text to mirror the multidimensional nature of the world it sought to represent. Instead, the text was to assume the very opposite quality, in order to highlight not the fidelity of the representation but the order of a demonstration. Flaubert's 'Balzacian' compositions are thus characterised by an underlying sense of direction, one that is all the more effective in the absence of an author or narrator with a developed identity or personality, and when the demonstration itself is, as most obviously in *L'Education sentimentale*, of a fundamental lack of direction. In other words, the composition not only develops a logic and coherence of its own but ensures, through its single-mindedness, that it consistently calls attention to its own nature as text.

In Balzac's world, meaning is everywhere present, to the extent that it is legitimate to talk of an 'embarrassment of meanings'. In the world of the *Comédie humaine*, meaning is closely related to both desire and will ['volonté']. Notwithstanding his recognition that clashes of self-interest will invariably intervene to threaten an individual's success, Balzac's vision of the new bourgeois era is predicated on the possibility of endless material acquisition and the satisfaction of desire. Contemporary history is unmasked in terms of rapid change, epitomised by fashion. The present is characterised by both its transitory nature and its capacity to evolve, under the pressure of various individual wills, into a new order. In contrast, Flaubert, the novelist of the stagnant Second Empire, pointedly denies his characters any kind of influential willpower, with the result that his tightly controlled compositions do not merely obey an aesthetic imperative but both reflect and reinforce a profoundly pessimistic view of the potential available to the individual. In his work, the present, and, above all, the individual's material surroundings, possess a dead weight.

The way Flaubert's descriptions thwart the expectation that each detail will be meaningful imbues them with a fascination that has no parallel in Balzac. Barthes's celebrated designation of the barometer in Madame Aubain's house in *Un cœur simple* as an example of the 'reality effect' ['effet de réel'] usefully curtails fanciful over-interpretation, but is itself an act of recuperation, insofar as it endows the object with a reassuring function it does not possess.[9] On the contrary, as so often in Flaubert's descriptions, the object continues to fascinate, to be an irritant or even a hostile presence by virtue of its material independence and the way it resists interpretation.

In the Balzacian world, the world of objects is never a threat to the hegemony of the individual. Material surroundings are an extension of the individual's identity, their significance subordinated, for better or worse, to his character or status. In Flaubert's novels, the highly specific details that make up the external descriptions have an unquestionable presence that is the result not only of the communication of a sense of careful selection (the reader is aware that many other such details will have been omitted) or of their non-recuperability at the level of interpretation, but of their independence both of each other and of the individual who shares the space in question. The organising principle is that of juxtaposition. A favourite adverbial expression employed in both *L'Education sentimentale* and *Salammbô* is 'çà et là' ['here and there'], a telling indicator of random distribution, and thus, like juxtaposition, an indication of a lack of inherent order or design. The phrase occurs twenty-eight times in *Salammbô* and thirty-six times in *L'Education sentimentale*. The fact that it appears on only twelve occasions in *Madame Bovary* points to its association with the evolution of Flaubert's 'realism'.

This emphasis on material reality does not merely trigger recognition on the part of the reader. Flaubert's 'real', while seeming to acknowledge its conventionally banal status, offers a novel experience in which the material world of objects is more real, or at least more solid, than the human beings whose story it is. It is perhaps permissible to talk of a hyper-real, characterised by a combined impression of the banal and the extraordinary. What allows this impression is Flaubert's unprecedented recognition of the nature of his medium, his invitation to the reader to enjoy the fact that the novel is a linguistic artefact. Traditionally, Flaubert's concern with language was regarded as a matter of style. Modern critical theory has, however, taught us to be sceptical of critical absolutes, and there is indeed a limit to what the notion of stylistic perfection can reveal about the nature of Flaubert's achievement. Rather than embodying 'beauty', the Flaubert text is perhaps more likely to strike the modern reader as highlighting artifice and, more specifically, endowing the word with its own unique and irresistible appeal. For while Flaubert's work undeniably offers a series of (related) judgments on the age, the author's overriding concern with form leads him to give precedence to establishing a new kind of relationship with the word, seen ultimately as an end in itself.

Relieved of its purely referential function, the word takes on a prestige that neither it nor the object that is its referent had previously enjoyed. Insofar as this prestige is dependent on the non-significance of the referent, one may speak of a certain fetishism of language. That is to say, the word is able to become an object of desire as a result of its superficiality, understood literally as the qualities of its external surface. Small wonder that the diegesis of *Madame Bovary* contains a number of examples of literal fetishism involving clothes, footwear and Rodolphe's cigar case and which unites across any distinction of status Emma and Homais's assistant, Justin. But what is dangerous, or at least an impoverishment, at the level of the individual's emotional life is fundamentally positive in the unnatural world of art. It is the means by which the reader is bound to the text in a relationship of desire that is nonetheless held in check by the pervasive self-conscious awareness of it as artifice. It is this fetishism of the word and the text that may be considered responsible for the reader's experience of a contradictory conjunction of involvement and detachment, meaning and emptiness, banality and suggestiveness, worthlessness and value. It also determines the teasing impression of symbolism in *Madame Bovary*, the irresolvable tension between the frequent encouragement of a symbolic interpretation and the suspicion that these are traps for the reader desperate to participate in a world in which everything has its explanation. One is reminded of Samuel Beckett's enigmatic aphorism in *Molloy*: 'No symbols where none intended.'

In the end, the most striking contradiction experienced by the reader of Flaubert is that between the impression of the text as a closed system in which everything has its place and derives its significance from the whole, and a sense that the meaning of the work lies in what is left unstated, in its silences. *Madame Bovary*, for example, represents an attempt to achieve suspension in a limbo between alternative readings, allowing multiple interpretations to exist in embryo. Morality, intelligence, authenticity, free will and fate, to say nothing of the direction of the reader's sympathy, are all questions to which no conclusive answer is proposed. Flaubert's most widely read masterpiece demonstrates, moreover, the impossibility of the tragic in the new bourgeois age, its place having been usurped by the grotesque, a quintessentially ambiguous category. But this cultivation of ambiguity is matched by a teasing openness to partial, dogmatic readings that preserve intact any propensity the reader has to read judgmentally or with the aim of receiving sentimental gratification. It is as if Flaubert sensed the perverse pleasure to be gained from the idea of his novel being misread by the 'bourgeois' (defined by him, according to Maupassant, as 'anyone who thinks ignobly' ['quiconque pense bassement']). The fact remains that in *L'Education sentimentale* he would be concerned to produce a text that operated a still more radical thwarting of inherited reading habits.

The most striking aspect of *L'Education* is its unprecedented elasticity of form. The most obvious example of the unorthodox economy of the composition is provided by the celebrated concatenation of parodically short paragraphs in the penultimate chapter. By this stage in the novel the familiar sense of cliché, stereotype and commonplace allows the reader to appreciate the appropriateness of these mega-compressions, rather than inclining him towards taxing the author with losing interest in his protagonist. But Frédéric's vapid and vacuous character also allows the equally parodic expansion of incidental description at moments that would seem to require the emphasis to be on his inner reflections or emotions. Throughout *L'Education*, the contrived rhythm, which can in part be defined in terms of an interplay between the past historic and the imperfect tenses, has less to do with style as an absolute quality than with operating a constant and provocative shift in the reader's distance from the narrative, making it the discreet counterpart of the free indirect discourse of *Madame Bovary*. It can lead to the paradox of the most matter-of-fact statement becoming the most disconcerting at the level of interpretation. But the most profound challenge to the reader comes from a still more widespread ambiguity that is the product of the systematic avoidance of any fixed criterion. The statement: 'Frédéric, a man possessed of every weakness, was overcome by the universal dementia' ['Frédéric, homme de toutes les faiblesses, fut gagné par la démence universelle' (OC II 117)] is an apt illustration of Flaubert's creation of a new epistemological order, one that ceases to find a path towards meaning in terms of contrasting positions or characteristics.

In the slightly earlier *Salammbô*, Flaubert had been concerned to experiment with a different kind of writing that provided the reader with a correspondingly different, though related, kind of experience. Difference is, indeed, enshrined in *Salammbô*, since it is set in neither the Christian nor the Greco-Roman world. But its crucial distinctiveness stems from the fact that the narrative is not presented from a Western point of view. It emphatically does not offer the stereotypical encounter with the seductive Oriental other. At the basic level of plot, *Salammbô* is a demanding text. In contrast to the norms of the historical novel derived from Scott, there is, at least in the final version, no introductory account of the complex historical situation to which the individual characters' personal and political endeavours relate. Flaubert employs an anonymous, impersonal narrator who resists identification in terms of historical or cultural origin. In spite of featuring antagonism and partisanship, the tale is told with apparent indifference. (Indifference, significantly, is a stance explicitly attributed to Spendius, a Greek and therefore a token Westerner, and is a response said to defy the Libyan Mâtho's understanding.) Still more strikingly, there is no sense of the narrator as an artist for whom the real is a pretext for the creation of beauty, though there may be formulations that arouse the reader's intense admiration.

Instead, the reader is offered a real that comes close to Alain Robbe-Grillet's ideal of a real that 'simply is'. The latter's descriptions are, indeed, prefigured in Flaubert's frequent recourse to geometrical terms. The lack of resonance or suggestiveness of the descriptions is symptomatic of a text that thwarts the reader's response. It is writing that disarms the reader of not only his emotions but also his beliefs and knowledge-systems, thereby delivering a blow to a self-confidence born of the assumption of occupying a central social, geographical and metaphysical vantage point. *Salammbô* is, thus, a painful novel, not merely in respect of the graphic scenes of violence, but because the relationship the text entertains with the reader is essentially sado-masochistic.

In his major compositions, Flaubert succeeds in turning the Balzac novel inside out. Rather than contriving a mode of realist writing that sought to make form subservient to content, he boldly affirmed the formal dimension of his compositions in all its idiosyncrasy, to the point of experimenting with the paradoxically ideal goal of unreadability. In view of the radical nature of this uncompromising reflection on the act of writing itself, it was inevitable that those nineteenth-century admirers who wrote in his wake should turn their backs on the self-questioning dimension of his practice and extract from his work a single strand that was then pursued more or less straightforwardly. In other words, the movement would be towards specialisation rather than retaining Flaubert's ambition of universality.

For all the negative assessments Flaubert's work attracted from his contemporaries, and for all his hostility to the notion that he had originated a new school of writing, a number of writers were inspired by his example. Ernest Feydeau's novel, *Fanny* (1858), was immediately compared by critics to *Madame Bovary*.[10] The Goncourt brothers' *Charles Demailly* (1860), a *roman à clef* that included a brief anonymous portrait of Flaubert, has been seen as a reversal of the same novel. But it was on the Naturalists that Flaubert's writing left its most enduring mark, and nowhere more so than on Zola, Maupassant and Joris-Karl Huysmans, even if it is Henry Céard's novel *Une Belle Journée* (1881) that has been described as 'the most explicit [Naturalist] homage to Flaubert'.[11] In his 1903 preface to *A rebours*, Huysmans declared that, for the Naturalist authors of *Les Soirées de Médan* (1880), *L'Education sentimentale* had been their bible and remained the only true Naturalist novel, since Zola had taken things in the wrong direction. As for Zola himself, even after the publication of *L'Education sentimentale*, he professed that *Madame Bovary* was the quintessential Naturalist novel, exhibiting, as it did, the latter's three defining characteristics: the exact reproduction of life; the abolition of the conventional hero; and the concealment of the author. Unsurprisingly, he emphasised Flaubert's commitment to documentation. By the time he came to review the second edition of *L'Education sentimentale* in 1879, he was, however, ready to affirm the new orthodoxy that it constituted the true Naturalist model (Zola, *Œuvres complètes*, XII, pp. 606–9).

Zola's novels likewise reveal a retentive reader of Flaubert. The scene in *Son Excellence Eugène Rougon* (1876) featuring the inauguration of the Niort-Angers railway line has, for example, been seen as a 'remake' of the Comices Agricoles episode in *Madame Bovary*. *Pot-Bouille* (1882) bristles with reminiscences of the same novel, albeit in the form of an arguably parodic banalisation of the theme of adultery. Zola himself described it as 'mon *Education sentimentale*', and it indeed also presents an ironic rewriting of a number of key scenes from that novel.[12] More generally, the Rougon-Macquart novels derive from Flaubert much of their descriptive manner, notably the incorporation of a self-conscious aesthetic dimension. With the aid of an uncontroversial vocabulary taken from painting, Flaubert's descriptions are highlighted for their efficacy in Zola's essay, *Du roman* (1880). Although he acknowledged that most of Flaubert's successors, himself included, had been less restrained in their descriptions, his own demonstrate a commitment to balance and selectivity that shows that these qualities are not in themselves what makes Flaubert's compositions so remarkable. When placed alongside ostensibly similar passages in Flaubert, Zola's descriptions are much more straightforwardly pictorial. They draw attention to the fact that they are carefully composed tableaux and seek recognition of their artistic status. In contradistinction to Flaubert's descriptions, where one's reading frequently 'snags' on one or more of the details, each detail is instantly 'readable' and contributes to a unified cumulative impression, the ambiguity of which is never radical. Entirely absent is Flaubert's crucial 'undecidability'. For all their finesse, Zola's descriptions are functional in a way that Flaubert's could never be. Their purposefulness is betrayed by the persistent use of adverbs and conjunctions that link and explain. Zola's self-imposed mandate is to convince rather than challenge. It is therefore difficult to gainsay Barthes's view of Naturalist writing as an incomplete by-product ['une sous-écriture'] of Flaubert.

It was Maupassant who gave currency to the view of 'Flaubert the Master'. In his essay 'Le Roman' (1888), he recounted a lesson in the art of description he had allegedly received from the author of *L'Education sentimentale* and which had taken the form of an injunction to describe a grocer or *concierge* in a way that made him stand out from all other examples of the species. It is questionable whether the advice corresponded to Flaubert's own practice. That said, in his own fictional compositions, Maupassant's adherence to Flaubertian principles is visible not only in his conception of the text as a closed unit structured internally by recurring semantic components, but in a sharply focused use of irony that exploits the fact that the narrative is aimed at a reader. Leaving aside the parallels deriving from a similarly cynical judgment on humanity, stories such as *Boule de suif* (1880) present carefully contrasted characters together with contrived descriptions, the apparently incidental details of which are part of signifying patterns that confer on the text both shape and meaning.

Flaubert's function as reference point in the second half of the century is further illustrated by the evolution of Naturalism in the person of one of its most original representatives, Huysmans. The latter's defection from the orthodox Naturalism of his early novels to the ambivalent characterisation of a Decadent aesthete in *A rebours*, and his ultimate embracing of a Catholicism coloured by the precepts of Symbolism, could be seen as a more complete prosecution of the Flaubertian heritage than was possible through the Naturalist novel alone. Flaubert's fascination with later Roman history and the history of the Early Church is paralleled in the Decadent taste of Des Esseintes, the 'hero' of *A rebours* (1884). The obsessive collector's approach to texts and artefacts also suggests the influence of *Bouvard et Pécuchet*, published just three years before. The extended example of *ekphrasis* (a verbal description of a painting or sculpture) with regard to Moreau's *Salomé* provides an additional link with Flaubert. As Praz observes: 'this Salome is sister of the Queen of Sheba in [Flaubert's] *Tentation*' (*The Romantic Agony*, p. 326). Flaubert's fixation with the sadistic and the perverse is indeed continued in Huysmans's immediate post-Naturalist phase, albeit in a form the ambivalence of which invites a reading in terms of parody.

The lack of prestige accorded the novel by the Symbolists, and the readiness of late nineteenth-century critics to proclaim the genre to be in a state of crisis, may similarly be seen as a logical extension of the Flaubertian heritage. For the alternative to the partial reading adopted by Zola and the Naturalists was the recognition that Flaubert had discredited mimesis and obliged narrative prose to pursue a reflection on its status as writing. In his own reflexive masterpiece, Proust, undoubted admirer of Flaubert that he was, would show deftness in opting for a rewriting of Balzac. Meanwhile, Remy de Gourmont's *Sixtine* (1890), arguably the most accomplished example of a Symbolist novel and a work which incorporates its own reflection on Flaubert's art, continued the breakdown of generic categories begun in *A rebours* and, through its incorporation of extracts from the novel the protagonist is writing, looks forward to André Gide's *Les Faux-Monnayeurs* (1925). All Gide's ironic fictions betray not only the seminal influence of Symbolist aesthetics, but also the lesson of Flaubert, which in his case took the form of viewing literary composition as a knowingly contrived activity in which each word was strategically positioned to disabuse the reader of any sense that the representation was natural or unproblematic. It was, however, the *nouveau roman* that allowed Flaubert to preside over a renewal of the genre. In *L'Ere du soupçon* (1956), Sarraute may have been content to bracket Flaubert with Balzac as supreme creators of a by then obsolete notion of literary character, but twenty years later she would be in no doubt that he was the precursor of the modern novel. It was, however, Robbe-Grillet in *Pour un nouveau roman* (1963) who first claimed for the *nouveau roman* an affinity with Flaubert through a shared obsession with description. It was, he argued, the *nouveau romancier*'s task to seek engagement with Flaubert's writing at a moment prior to its enrolment in a naturalist project.

Yet such a position represents no more complete a reading of Flaubert than that proposed by the Naturalists. Tacit acknowledgment of the fact is provided by Sarraute's curiously revisionist reading in *Flaubert le précurseur*.[13] In the end, the debate 'master realist or first of the non-figuratives?' is incapable of resolution. Flaubert's texts quite simply allow powerful alternative readings. The intrinsic impediment to resolution invites us, however, to focus on the hesitation between such readings, and to identify the 'pleasure of the text' with those fleetingly glimpsed moments at which the text reveals the limitations of the reading pursued. To revert, in appropriately circular fashion, to our starting point, the 'pleasure of the text' may similarly be equated with our exposure to the irresolvable conflict between the straight and the parodic, between a sense of Flaubert's work as a pæan to the intelligence and a sense of it as a monstrous embodiment of *bêtise* itself.

NOTES

1 Milan Kundera, *The Art of the Novel* (London and Boston: Faber, 1988), p. 162.
2 See James, review of *La Tentation de saint Antoine* in *Literary Criticism. French Writers, Other European Writers* (Cambridge: Cambridge University Press, 1984), pp. 289–94, p. 293.
3 For the uncomprehending Henry James, *Bouvard et Pécuchet* was 'a work as sad as something perverse and puerile done for a wager' (James, review of *Correspondance de Gustave Flaubert* in *Literary Criticism*, pp. 295–314, p. 306). For a more illuminating view, see Leslie Hill, 'Flaubert and the Rhetoric of Stupidity', *Critical Inquiry*, 3 (1976), 333–44.

4 Flaubert wrote to his mother on 15 December 1850: 'It is my view that the artist is a monstrous creature, quite outside the realm of nature' ['L'artiste, selon moi, est une monstruosité, – quelque chose de hors nature' (Cor. 1 720)].

5 See *Les Romanciers naturalistes* in Zola, *Œuvres complètes* (Paris: Cercle du livre précieux, 1968), XI, pp. 97–155.

6 Roland Barthes, *Le Degré zéro de l'écriture* (Paris: Seuil, 1972 [1953]), pp. 44–5.

7 See Mario Praz, *The Romantic Agony* (London: Oxford University Press, 1933).

8 See Graham Falconer, 'Le travail de "débalzaciénisation" dans la rédaction de *Madame Bovary*', *Revue des Lettres Modernes*, 865–72 (1988), 123–56; Richard D. E. Burton, 'The Death of Politics: The Significance of Dambreuse's Funeral in *L'Education sentimentale*', *French Studies*, 50 (1996), 157–69; and André Vial, 'Flaubert, émule et disciple émancipé de Balzac: *L'Education sentimentale*', *Revue d'Histoire littéraire de la France*, 48 (1948), 233–63.

9 Roland Barthes, 'L'Effet de réel' (1968), reprinted in Roland Barthes et al., *Littérature et réalité* (Paris: Seuil, 1982), pp. 81–90.

10 On these two novels of adultery, see Hans Robert Jauss, *Toward an Aesthetic of Reception* (Minneapolis: University of Minnesota Press, 1982), pp. 27–8; and Bill Overton, *The Novel of Female Adultery. Love and Gender in Continental European Fiction, 1830–1900* (Basingstoke: Macmillan, 1996), chapter 4.

11 See David Baguley, *Naturalist Fiction. The Entropic Vision* (Cambridge: Cambridge University Press, 1990), pp. 91–4; and Nicholas White, *The Family in Crisis in Late Nineteenth-Century French Fiction* (Cambridge: Cambridge University Press, 1999), pp. 13–14.

12 See Robert Lethbridge, 'La pot-bouille des genres: adultération et originalité chez Zola', *Les Cahiers naturalistes*, 74 (2000), 17–32; Bill Overton, *Fictions of Female Adultery, 1684–1890* (Basingstoke: Palgrave-Macmillan, 2002), chapter 7; and Jacques Noiray, '*Pot-Bouille* ou "L'Education sentimentale" de Zola', *Les Cahiers naturalistes*, 69 (1995), 113–26.

13 Nathalie Sarraute, *Paul Valéry et l'enfant d'éléphant; Flaubert le précurseur* (Paris: Gallimard, 1986).

3

TIMOTHY UNWIN

Flaubert's early work

'Louis XIII being aged only nine, Parliament gave the regency to his mother Marie de Médicis. Intrigue and ignominy were rife at the court . . .' ['Louis XIII n'ayant que neuf ans, le Parlement donna la régence à Marie de Médicis sa mère. L'intrigue et la bassesse régnaient à la cour . . .' (OJ 3)]. So wrote the nine-year-old Gustave Flaubert, no doubt identifying with the boy king, in a text dedicated to his own mother for her name-day on 28 July 1831. With this, the first text in the new Pléiade edition of Flaubert's early works, begins a lifelong passion for history and historiography. Encouraged from 1835 onwards by his teacher Chéruel, Flaubert devotes much of his early writing to historical subjects, with a preference for the Middle Ages, and an obvious fascination too for Ancient Rome.

Yet what strikes any reader of the early work is the sheer range of subjects and styles to which this extraordinarily precocious writer turns his pen. Alongside the historical stories and dramas, we find philosophical and moral tales, journalistic and critical essays, tales of the fantastic, mystery plays, and realist or psychological stories. To a scatological early piece on constipation, we can add the bilious humour of an 1837 sketch, owing much to Balzac, in which the young writer derides the habits and the clichés of the office clerk (*Une leçon d'histoire naturelle: genre commis*). Then there are the philosophical speculations of the *Cahier intime de 1840–1841*, or the travel writings of 1840 (the Pyrenees and Corsica) and 1845 (Italy). It is a time of experiment and self-definition, a time also of reflection on art and its possibilities. We see the artist in his raw state, and while there are obvious moments of crisis and self-doubt which both undermine the writing and become one of its themes, these texts differ from the mature works by virtue of their spontaneity and their ease. The young Flaubert writes fast and he writes fluently, as we know from the manuscripts (most of which are conserved in the Bibliothèque nationale de France and elsewhere). Dominating the rich output of these early years are three longer narratives, to which we shall return, showing the writer honing the skills he was later to develop: *Les Mémoires d'un fou* (1838), *Novembre* (1842) and *L'Education sentimentale* (1845).

For all their variety and interest, the early writings occupy an uncomfortable space in the Flaubertian corpus. Famously and lengthily analysed by Sartre in the first two volumes of *L'Idiot de la famille* (where much of the emphasis is on Flaubert's early psychodrama), brilliantly and painstakingly explicated by Jean Bruneau in a seminal study of Flaubert's developing years,[1] these texts are still overlooked by some critics, or cursorily dismissed by others as the errors and misjudgments of youth. Though there are notable textual and thematic studies of the early work,[2] the great bulk of Flaubertian criticism remains focused on the later texts. True, these are more complex and more refined, and we know that Flaubert himself certainly did not consider his youthful writings to be publishable. Referring to *Novembre* on 28 October 1853, he writes to Louise Colet: 'Ah! what good judgment I showed not to publish it! How it would embarrass me now!' ['Ah! quel nez fin j'ai eu de ne pas le publier! Comme j'en rougirais maintenant!' (Cor. II 460)] However, if we are to aspire to a full understanding of the writer, we must not overlook this rich early archive, where we glimpse the great Flaubertian themes and modes at the moment of their inception. For those readers unable to approach Flaubert in the original, there are translations of most of these early works (see the main Bibliography) with the notable exception of the 1845 *Education sentimentale*. For readers of French, the 2001 Pléiade edition now offers for the first time a complete and authoritative compendium of the early texts accompanied by copious scholarly notes and background material. There has never been a better moment to read the early Flaubert.

Critics will no doubt remain divided on the question of whether the early works should be approached as a separate corpus or as an integral part of the Flaubertian canon. It is true, on the one hand, that they show all the hesitations and errors of apprenticeship. On the other hand, they foreshadow much of what is to come, and adopt an early focus on the question of literature itself, heralding a self-conscious mode of writing that will be characteristic of Flaubert. To that extent, these early works are the building blocks upon which Flaubert will construct the aesthetic monument of his mature novels, and whilst we can and should see in them the failings that will later be overcome, it would be folly to overlook them on the grounds of their aesthetic inferiority. Besides, they have much about them that is intrinsically interesting. As a voracious reader of French and world literature, the young Flaubert is highly attuned to the themes and preoccupations of his century. A true Romantic at the outset, he attempts to follow in the footsteps of Goethe,

Byron, Rousseau, Chateaubriand and many others, and like his contemporary Baudelaire he expresses the *ennui* and world-weariness of his generation. He will write memorably to his friend Maxime Du Camp at the still tender age of twenty-five: 'It's strange that I was born with so little faith in happiness. From an early stage I had a complete intuition about what life would hold. It was like a foul stench of cooking escaping through a ventilator' ['C'est étrange comme je suis né avec peu de foi au bonheur. J'ai eu tout jeune un pressentiment complet de la vie. C'était comme une odeur de cuisine nauséabonde qui s'échappe par un soupirail' (Cor. 1 261)]. The task of the early works will be to find a way of turning this despondency into something meaningful and readable. To read the early Flaubert is to witness his struggle with burgeoning misanthropy and despair, and to discover that despite his pessimism he succeeds spectacularly well on occasions in finding meaning in art where life itself had failed him. In an 1837 story entitled *Quidquid volueris*, he describes the inner torments and soul-searching of a creature who is half-man, half-ape. Brought back to France from Brazil by a cynical and materialistic master, the ape-man Djalioh struggles in vain to express the poetry and the beauty of his innermost feelings. Despite his inability to articulate himself, he experiences pantheistic effusions and reveries that are magnificently verbalised by the sixteen-year-old author. Not for the last time in Flaubert's work, the writer steps in to express what a character is unable to put into words. In one scene, Djalioh picks up a violin and produces a strange, discordant music on it – noise to the ears of the listeners, but oddly indicative of the distant and bizarre poetry in his soul:

> The sounds were at first soft and slow; the bow touched the strings lightly and moved along them from the bridge to the pegs almost without producing any sound. Then gradually Djalioh's head started to move; as he bent it progressively over the wood of the violin, his brow furrowed, his eyes closed and the bow skipped across the strings like an elastic ball, in jagged leaps. The music was jerky, filled with sharp notes and rending cries.

> [Les sons étaient d'abord lents, mous; l'archet effleurait les cordes et les parcourait depuis le chevalet jusqu'aux chevilles sans rendre presque aucun son. Puis peu à peu sa tête s'anima; l'abaissant graduellement sur le bois du violon, son front se plissa, ses yeux se fermèrent et l'archet sautillait sur les cordes comme une balle élastique, à bonds précipités. La musique était saccadée, remplie de notes aiguës, de cris déchirants. (OJ 259)]

Thus begins a thread in Flaubert's work about the language of music, whose strange resonances will more than once be seen as offering a privileged but perhaps indecipherable insight into human emotions – as in the moving but, as ever, deeply complex description of Madame Arnoux singing in the second *Education sentimentale* (OC II 26). And through Djalioh, Flaubert is also expressing his own dilemmas as an artist, confronting that acute discrepancy between his turbulent inner life and the inadequate resources of language.

The roll-call of Flaubert's early themes is, it is true, decidedly apocalyptic. We are repeatedly confronted with decay, despair, destruction, misery and unhappiness. Prostitution, adultery and death are regular bedfellows. The Satanic litany is livened up with murders, suicides, acts of wanton violence and scenes of horrifying agony. The 1836 story *Rage et impuissance* describes the death of a village doctor who wakens from an opium-induced dream to find himself in a coffin, buried by his fellow-doctors after they had wrongly pronounced him dead. Going through the gamut of hope, religious conversion and philosophical despair, the doctor finally causes his own death when he breaks the lid of the coffin and is crushed by the weight of the earth that engulfs him. In another story from the same year entitled *Un parfum à sentir*, a rejected and beaten wife first attempts to turn to prostitution, then drowns herself in the Seine. Flaubert, who had been brought up in the Hôtel-Dieu de Rouen where his father was surgeon-in-chief, had a keen eye for physical decay and knew a thing or two about rotting corpses: 'A few flies came buzzing around and licked the dried blood around her half-open mouth. Her swollen arms were bluish and covered in small black spots' ['Quelques mouches venaient bourdonner à l'entour et lécher le sang figé sur sa bouche entrouverte, ses bras gonflés étaient bleuâtres et couverts de petites taches noires' (OJ 111)]. His close observation of physical symptoms will famously be brought into play years later when he describes another suicide, that of the heroine of *Madame Bovary*. Indeed, the heroine of *Un parfum à sentir* has more than one characteristic in common with Emma Bovary, as she contemplates the gulf between her dreams and the reality of her existence. At least one other early character, Mazza in *Passion et vertu* (1837) – one of the few early texts whose importance has been amply acknowledged – is also a clear prototype of the adulterous heroine. Mazza, a wife and mother, falls passionately in love with a man who decides that he must rid himself of this clinging and possessive mistress. He writes Mazza a farewell letter and leaves for Mexico. Abandoned by her lover, Mazza poisons her husband and her children, but on receiving a further letter from her lover she finally accepts the truth that he does not, perhaps never did, love her. So she poisons herself too, and at the moment of her death we are invited to reflect – as we shall be in *Madame Bovary* – on the charms and seductions of the heroine's body:

She removed her clothes, and remained for several minutes looking at her beautiful body which nothing covered, thinking of all the pleasure it had given, and of the wonderful sensations that she had bestowed upon her lover.

What a treasure the love of such a woman is!

[Elle ôta ses vêtements, et resta quelques minutes à regarder son beau corps, que rien ne couvrait, à penser à toutes les voluptés qu'il avait données, aux jouissances immenses qu'elle avait prodiguées à son amant.

Quel trésor que l'amour d'une telle femme! (OJ 301)]

This brief account of *Passion et vertu* is enough to suggest many parallels with the later work – the heartless lover, the goodbye letter, the theme of poison and suicide, and of course that very Flaubertian cohabitation of sex and death. On other occasions in the early work – notably in *La Femme du monde* (1836) and *La Danse des morts* (1838) – sex and death will be allegorised, thus heralding a technique that Flaubert will use in the three versions of *La Tentation de saint Antoine*. But the parallels with later works often occur in surprising places, and the more we read the writings of these apprenticeship years, the more it becomes apparent that Flaubert is doing a 'dry run', constructing the first drafts of texts and ideas that will come to their full fruition much later. All through his life he will work in this manner, sometimes allowing ideas to gestate for years in brief notes before they are used. Here and there in the early work, we find a phrase or a thought that has striking resonance and suggests unexpected connections between the different strands of later Flaubertian inspiration. In the 1839 mystery play *Smar*, clearly a forerunner of the *Tentation*, we find this reflection placed in the mind of a dissatisfied wife: 'If fate had willed it, however, I would be different. My husband would be handsome, tall, a fine horseman, with dark eyebrows and white teeth' ['Si le sort avait voulu pourtant, je serais autre, mon mari serait beau, grand, joli cavalier, aux sourcils noirs et aux dents blanches' (OJ 545)]. These are the yearnings of Emma Bovary, right down to the importance she attaches to teeth, so what *Smar* tells us very clearly is that the aspirations of the adulteress are not so distant from the metaphysical themes that the allegorical works deal with. Elsewhere, we find a word or a phrase that will reappear in modified form years later. Thus a sentence in *Novembre* – 'There is an instant during departure when, in the anticipation of sadness, the loved one is already no longer with you' ['Il y a un instant, dans le départ, où, par anticipation de tristesse, la personne aimée n'est déjà plus avec vous' (OJ 815)] – will turn up after a gap of twenty-seven years in the following form at the end of *L'Education sentimentale*: 'There is a moment, during separations, when the loved one is already no longer with us' ['Il y a un moment, dans les séparations, où la personne aimée n'est déjà plus avec nous' (OC ii 161)]. Elsewhere in the early work, we find many prototypes of characters of the later works. In *Rage et impuissance*, the story about the doctor buried alive, we see for the first time a character resembling Félicité of *Un cœur simple*. The doctor's servant, Berthe, is described as 'one of those good, honest maids who are born and who die in a family, who look after and bring up the children' ['une de ces bonnes et honnêtes filles qui naissent et meurent dans les familles, [. . .] prennent soin des enfants et les élèvent' (OJ 175)]. To this the narrator adds that Berthe's life, within its restricted compass, 'had also had its passions, its anguish, its pain' ['avait eu aussi ses passions, ses angoisses, ses douleurs' (OJ 176)]. The loaded use of 'also' here ushers in Flaubert's lifelong championing of the character who is a limited register of human experience. Given Flaubert's belief in the impossibility of achieving higher intelligence or a value-free standpoint on the world, the partial reflector becomes for him a privileged means of studying how we distort or reconstruct our reality. The much-hyped 'impersonality' of Flaubert's technique is not only about standing back from his characters, of 'treating the human soul with the impartiality that is applied to the study of matter in the physical sciences' (Cor. ii 451). It is also about entering into the character's subjective viewpoint on the world and seeing it as a possibly valid alternative to the supposed objectivity of the narrator. Flaubertian irony, with its unnerving capacity to undermine everything including itself, is born of such oppositions.

Irony is also founded on a sense of the grotesque and a belief in the omnipresence of human stupidity (*bêtise*). In *Smar*, the grotesque is allegorised in a figure called Yuk. A descendent of the Garçon, a character invented by Flaubert and his school friends to personify and ridicule representatives of authority,[3] Yuk is both the symbol of the grotesque and its active embodiment. His laugh, a cynical reaction to the events he perceives, itself becomes the subject of the work as it 'invades' the text: 'And after that he laughed the laugh of the damned, but a long, Homeric, inextinguishable laugh, a laugh as indestructible as time, a laugh as cruel as death, a laugh as large as the infinite, as long as eternity – for it was eternity itself' ['Et il riait après cela d'un rire de damné, mais un rire long, homérique, inextinguible, un rire indestructible comme le temps, un rire cruel comme la mort, un rire large comme l'infini, long comme l'éternité, car c'était l'éternité elle-même' (OJ 575)]. The grotesque is also closely allied to the omnipresent *bêtise* of the bourgeois which was to dismay yet fascinate Flaubert throughout his life. From 1837 onwards, with the writing of *Une leçon d'histoire naturelle: genre commis*, he will ridicule his fellow-citizens for their pomposity and their platitudes, while ironically recognising that such characters may have something to say back to the novelist. For language is a treacherous instrument which constantly seduces us into simplistic formulae, and no one more so than the novelist himself. Thus does Flaubert's representation of *bêtise* become an invasive and double-edged presence in his work. *Bêtise* may be ridiculous, but it reveals a genuine human need to communicate through banal utterances or empty assertions. If Rodolphe is incapable of recognising the true sentiments beneath the trite formulae in Emma's letters (OC I 639), the novelist implicitly recognises that he too is in permanent danger of underestimating the real emotions that may lurk beneath the surface of cliché. Yet cliché is also, by definition, language that has become fixed and automatic, and for Flaubert it must be flushed out and shown for what it is. In the 1838 *Les Mémoires d'un fou*, he describes in these terms the conversations that are struck up in small seaside towns such as Trouville then was:

> In seaside resorts, in the country and on journeys, conversations are struck up more easily, for people wish to get to know one another. The slightest circumstance can lead to an exchange, and the weather seems to assume much greater importance than usual. People complain about the discomfort of the accommodation, and the appalling food in the inns. This latter subject, above all, is considered very *chic*. 'Oh! isn't the table-linen dirty! There is too much pepper; it is too spicy! Oh! my dear! how terrible it is!'

> [Aux bains de mer, à la campagne ou en voyage, on se parle plus facilement – on désire se connaître. – un rien suffit pour la conversation; la pluie et le beau temps bien plus qu'ailleurs y tiennent place. On se récrie sur l'incommodité des logements, sur le détestable de la cuisine d'auberge. Ce dernier trait surtout est du meilleur ton possible: 'Oh! le linge – est-il sale! C'est trop poivré, c'est trop épicé! Ah! l'horreur, ma chère!'   (OJ 489)]

Clearly the young author is here relishing his power as a novelist to mock and to undermine the language of the bourgeois, though there is irony in the fact that his own work is thus contaminated by it. But the focus on the clichés and commonplaces of modern life will, as any reader of Flaubert knows, be a constant in the works of his maturity. It leads ultimately to the *Dictionnaire des idées reçues*, that compendium of laughable yet familiar absurdities that Flaubert wanted to arrange 'in such a way that the reader is unsure if he is being ridiculed or not' ['de telle manière que le lecteur ne sache pas si on se fout de lui, oui ou non' (Cor. I 679)]. The early works, too, are full of waspish and darkly humorous ridicule that, for all its misanthropy, remains one of the delights of Flaubert's writing. When champagne (see the entry in the *Dictionnaire des idées reçues*) is served in a scene in the 1845 *Education sentimentale*, the narrator observes that it is 'an essentially French wine, which has had the misfortune of bringing about so many verses, as French and as tedious as itself' ['vin essentiellement français, qui a eu le malheur de faire naître tant de couplets, français comme lui et ennuyeux comme lui' (OJ 858)]. Later in the same novel, the father of Henry, one of its main characters, turns out to be a man who thinks in clichés: 'His ideas were made up on every possible subject. For him, every young lady was *pure*, every young man a *joker*, every husband a *cuckold*, every poor man a *thief*, every policeman a *bully* and every countryside scene was *delightful*' ['Il avait ses idées faites sur tous les sujets possibles. Pour lui, toute jeune fille était *pure*, tout jeune homme était un *farceur*, tout mari un *cocu*, tout pauvre un *voleur*, tout gendarme un *brutal* et toute campagne *délicieuse*' (OJ 982)]. The italics, capturing the character's utterances in free indirect mode, suggest that the character of Homais, one of Flaubert's greatest ironic creations, is already present in this early figure.

For all their macabre, misanthropic or sometimes blasphemous content, the early works nonetheless show an unshakeable belief in one thing, and that is art itself. In *Les Mémoires d'un fou*, Flaubert writes: 'If there is a single hallowed belief on the face of the earth and in the midst of all the nothingness, if there is something holy, pure and sublime, something which complements the immoderate desire for the infinite and the vagueness that we call the soul, it is art' ['S'il y a sur la terre, et parmi tous les néants, une croyance qu'on adore, s'il est quelque chose de saint, de pur, de sublime, quelque chose qui aille à ce désir immodéré de l'infini et du vague que nous appelons âme, c'est l'art' (OJ 503)]. Above all else, the young Flaubert wants to be a writer, and there is a progressively sharper focus throughout the 1830s and early 1840s on the importance of writing itself. Certainly, there are many passages that attest the daunting difficulties of writing. In an uncharacteristic invocation to the God he does not believe in, Flaubert will write in the *Cahier intime de 1840–1841*: 'Oh my God, my God, why did you cause me to be born with so much ambition?' ['O mon Dieu, mon Dieu, pourquoi donc m'avez-vous fait naître avec tant d'ambition?' (OJ 732)] Yet, alongside the laments or the damning self-criticisms that themselves get incorporated into the final stages of texts like *Smar* or *Novembre*, there is also the occasional pæan to the joys of the artist's lot, such as the one we find at the end of *Un parfum à sentir*: 'To write! Oh, to write! It is to take hold of the world, of its prejudices and its virtues, and to sum it up in a book. It is to feel one's thoughts take shape, grow, live, stand up on their pedestal and remain there for good' ['Ecrire, oh! écrire, c'est s'emparer du monde, de ses préjugés, de ses vertus et le résumer dans un livre. C'est sentir sa pensée naître, grandir, vivre, se dresser debout sur son piédestal, et y rester toujours' (OJ 112)]. The latter stages of the 1845 *Education sentimentale* will be dominated by this belief in the power of writing both to change the individual who practises it and to change the world itself for the better. At the end of that novel art becomes a modern equivalent of Spinoza's intellectual love of God,[4] the one true value in an otherwise meaningless world dominated by absurdity, death, evil and disintegration. By entering into the artistic contemplation of reality, the novelist submits himself to the requirements of a new form of asceticism, transcending the boundaries of his own personality and feelings, and trying by every means available to expand his perception of the world. Thus does art have a mystical function, and Jules, the writer-hero, is at one with his vocation: 'Moving outwards to all the elements, he brings everything back to himself, focusing entirely on his vocation, on his mission, on the fatality of his genius and his labour, in this vast pantheism that passes through him and reappears in art' ['Ramifié à tous les éléments il rapporte tout à lui, et lui-même tout entier il se concrétise dans sa vocation, dans sa mission, dans la fatalité de son génie et de son labeur, panthéisme immense qui passe par lui et réapparaît dans l'art' (OJ 1074)]. We should not be surprised, then, to find the later Flaubert so frequently referring in ascetic or mystical terms to his vocation as a writer. For him, writing means abandoning normal engagement with life and learning to experience the world in an entirely different way. The early works show him progressing towards this form of literary mysticism, and it is consistent with this approach that we should also find in them descriptions of 'genuine' mystical states which no doubt feed into both his writing and his sense of artistic mission. In Corsica in 1840, he describes one such state as he heads along a seaside track towards the town of Sagone: 'there are happy days on which, like the countryside, the soul too opens itself out to the sun and gives off the fragrance of hidden flowers that supreme beauty has brought into bloom' ['il est des jours heureux où l'âme aussi est ouverte au soleil comme la campagne et, comme elle, embaume de fleurs cachées que la suprême beauté y fait éclore' (OJ 694–5)]. Later such passages in *Novembre* and the 1848 *Par les champs et par les grèves* will reinforce the impression that Flaubert may, as Georges Poulet once suggested, envisage for art the same kind of epiphanic experience that he finds in nature.[5]

But the glorious sensation of transcendence is one thing; putting it into words is quite another. The three early novels, *Les Mémoires d'un fou*, *Novembre* and *L'Education sentimentale*, spanning the years 1838 to 1845, show Flaubert struggling with his medium and working his way painfully towards his own particular mode of writing. In these texts he begins, among other things, to deal seriously with the nuts and bolts of the writer's art. Each contains passages of description and dialogue that show him practising and experimenting with different registers. In varying measure, we will find irony and humour, philosophical generalisation, shifts of focalisation, psychological analysis and social realism. For all that, the term 'novel', though generally used to describe these texts (the highly reputable 1964 Seuil edition grouped them together under the rubric 'First Novels'), is something of a misnomer. At times heavily overlaid with autobiography – *Les Mémoires d'un fou* recounts the searing 1836 encounter with Elisa Schlésinger in Trou-ville, and *Novembre* the sensual awakening in the arms of Eulalie Foucaud de Langlade in 1840 – they are of heterogeneous and fragmented inspira-tion. The writer occasionally steps right out of his text, either breaking the contract with his reader altogether or stretching it to its very limits. Thus, in *Les Mémoires d'un fou*, after describing the Trouville episode, he bla-tantly inserts a text written two years earlier about his encounter with two English sisters. In *Novembre*, when the first-person narrator runs out of steam towards the end of the text, a second narrator blandly steps in and takes over. And in *L'Education sentimentale*, where two heroes (Henry and Jules) compete for the narrator's attention, the novelist opts in the final stages to write his own aesthetic manifesto through the medium of his second hero, Jules. But for all their structural flaws, each of these texts shows Flaubert focusing on the question of writing itself, and asking the questions that will be present throughout his career as a writer. What is a novel? What can it truly say or express? How can the constructions of fiction represent the truths of the world? How can language capture the richness and depth of reality? How can a writer wrest his words free of the already written, the already spoken? And what does it ultimately mean to be a writer in the nineteenth century, when so much great literature is already available? It is because they both ask and attempt to answer such questions within a broadly fictional compass that these three texts are so interesting. Seldom before had fiction been so highly aware of the difficulties or the contradictions of its own undertaking.

We should not be surprised, then, to find sharp and sometimes awkward variations of point of view in these texts. But shifts of stance are not a sudden innovation at this point in Flaubert's development, nor by any means will they disappear from his subsequent work. From the earliest, Flaubert shows both characters and narrators engaging in abrupt changes of perspective. The process has both a philosophical and an aesthetic basis. Since every feeling, every philosophical position, every intellectual or emotional vantage point can be replaced by another one in the infinite kaleidoscope of life, Flaubert comes swiftly to the conclusion that there is no ultimate, value-free, objective standpoint from which to view reality. This being so, the novelist must be everywhere and nowhere, both inside and outside his characters' 'minds' and, indeed, both inside and outside his own novelistic stance. Variation of point of view will therefore become a key feature throughout his work, an essential means of showing up the relativity of different perceptions and standpoints. We need only think of the narrator who opens the second part of *Madame Bovary* with his judgments about this region of Normandy, or of the sudden switch of focalisation that occurs in the famous cab scene with Léon. But there, variations between one perspective and another will be made acceptable by the smooth patina of Flaubert's style, which covers over the cracks and fissures, sometimes concealing the moment of transition. In the three early novels we find a similar process, but usually in a much less refined state.

Les Mémoires d'un fou is undoubtedly the least constructed and the least even of these texts. But although it grinds to a halt on more than one occasion, there are central questions, raised early, whose echoes reverberate throughout: 'By what steps can we return from the infinite to the concrete? By what processes can poetry bow down without allowing itself to be broken? How can we scale down that giant who embraces the infinite?' ['Par quels échelons descendre de l'infini au positif? Par quelle gradation la poésie s'abaisse-t-elle sans se briser? Comment rapetisser ce géant qui embrasse l'infini?' (OJ 470)] Flaubert here begins to develop a truly self-conscious mode of writing, a style which works intensely on itself and its own methods. Though the framework of this text is largely autobiographical – it recounts the narrator's school years and early dissatisfactions, his meeting with Elisa Schlésinger (named Maria here) and his earlier encounter with two English sisters – it also presents itself as a workshop and a series of experiments in language and writing. Even the artificially inserted episode of the English sisters shows a high degree of stylistic self-consciousness, as when the narrator pauses to describe the surrounding scene during a walk: 'Fog shrouded the town and, from the vantage of our hill, we could see the tight jumble of rooftops covered in snow, then the silent countryside, with the distant sounds of the steps of a cow or a horse as its hoof sank into the furrow' ['Un brouillard ensevelissait la ville et, du haut de notre colline, nous voyions les toits entassés et rapprochés couverts de neige – et puis le silence de la campagne, et au loin le bruit éloigné des pas d'une vache ou d'un cheval, dont le pied s'enfonce dans les ornières' (OJ 496)]. Elsewhere, certain techniques familiar to readers of Flaubert's mature novels will be given their first airing as the writer experiments with new forms. One of these is the characteristic sequence of deadpan sentences or phrases. When Maria departs from Trouville, we read: 'It was necessary to leave. We parted without being able to say farewell. She left the resort on the same day as we did. It was a Sunday. She left in the morning, we in the evening' ['Il fallut partir. Nous nous séparâmes sans pouvoir lui dire adieu. – Elle quitta les bains le même jour que nous – c'était un dimanche – elle partit le matin, nous le soir' (OJ 492)]. (It should be borne in mind that in the early manuscripts Flaubert makes very frequent use of dashes in the place of a full stop.) The characteristic Flaubertian rhythms have not quite been found, but Flaubert is clearly working his way towards a style that will look and sound his own.

Most important of all in *Les Mémoires d'un fou* is the constant shift of point of view. Each stance that the narrator adopts, each moment of the 'story', is superseded as he strives to review it from a new vantage point. Thus the lofty descriptions of his inner poetic life are counterbalanced by passages of dark philosophy, while dithyrambic descriptions of Maria alternate with cynical reflections on the nature of love. There is, it is true, something quite unplanned and unpredictable about all this, as Flaubert admits in the dedication of the text to his friend Le Poittevin. Yet it becomes clear as well that one of the necessities of his art is that it can never maintain the same perspective for very long. Flaubertian 'impersonality' begins here, unexpectedly perhaps, in what might seem to be the most emotional of texts. For 'impersonality' is less a question of remaining emotionless than of passing through and balancing out a range of different possible emotions.

Common to both *Les Mémoires d'un fou* and *Novembre*, and bearing out the self-conscious mode in which Flaubert now writes, is a sustained reflection on world literature. In the course of these years, Flaubert's reading covers the history of French literature – with a special preference for Rabelais and Montaigne – and a huge variety of world authors from antiquity through to his own time. Shakespeare, Byron and Goethe, all of them mentioned in these texts, will be early favourites, though Flaubert's first and most enduring literary love was Cervantes's *Don Quixote*, with its famous hero steeped in the literature of chivalry. But we find references too to a wide variety of French authors: Marot, Molière, Rousseau, Lamennais, Musset, Dumas *père* and a host of others. Above all, we have the sense of a developing awareness that the body of world literature is an archive to be plundered and exploited, and, most importantly, to be reread and rewritten. Thus does Flaubert begin to write himself into the intertexts of literary history. He may be painfully aware that everything has been said before, but he seems in *Les Mémoires d'un fou* and *Novembre* to sense that his task is essentially about reworking and reconfiguring literature in his own mould. Echoes of Byron, Lamennais and Chateaubriand abound. Added to the blend is a hint of Rousseau ('There is the true school of style' ['Voilà la vraie école de style'] writes Flaubert of Rousseau's *Confessions* to his friend Ernest Chevalier on 11 October 1838 (Cor. 1 29)) and a *soupçon* of Montaigne. As for Shakespeare, two plays (*Romeo and Juliet* and *Hamlet*) are singled out for explicit mention, but the Hamlet theme is, almost inevitably, present throughout both texts where a world-weary central figure spends so much time investigating his own existential gloom and his inability to participate actively in life. At least one passage in *Les Mémoires d'un fou* explicitly echoes Hamlet's famous 'What a piece of work is a man!' speech, opening with the line: 'What follies there are in man!' ['Que de folies dans un homme!' (OJ 498)] Clearly, Flaubert's writing is already far from 'innocent', as it uses and exploits the resonances of known texts.

But where we find the presence of a large corpus of literary works, we will also find the danger of imitation and repetition, and nobody is more aware of such a danger than Flaubert himself. This might, indeed, be considered the central issue of *Novembre*, a text which is haunted, it seems, by the fear of echo and cliché, but which explores the artistic possibilities of that realm. In so far as there is a plot, it is the story of a young man who is consumed and overwhelmed by an abundant inner life, and loses the will to live. The hero constantly stresses the unexceptional nature, indeed the sheer banality, of his daily life, in contradistinction to the vivid dream-world he inhabits. In the central stages of the story he encounters the prostitute Marie, who has attempted to discover through sensuality what the narrator has attempted to discover through his reveries: the presence of some alternative to banal reality. Yet Marie, herself struggling against the commonplaces of everyday life, is in another sense the very symbol of the 'common place'. Her body is in the public domain, used and forgotten by the men who visit her. But so too is her language, itself a body of clichés. The narrator's encounter with her is as much a meeting with cliché as with a body craving the novelty that does not exist. His sense of being overwhelmed by cliché and repetition remains long after their encounter, and the mould cannot be broken. 'Try as one might to sow new passions over the old, they reappear' ['On a beau, par-dessus les passions anciennes, vouloir en semer de nouvelles, elles reparaissent toujours' (OJ 816)], he writes of his subsequent attempts at finding love. This image will then develop into a description of a Roman road, reappearing under fields and paths, never to be obliterated. As Victor Brombert pointed out in a remarkable study of this text,[6] the road, the body and human language itself are for Flaubert the symbols of monotony and overuse. *Novembre* is both a coming to terms with this unpalatable truth, and an attempt to write his text into and through the very space of cliché. Far from resisting the inadequacies of language, the novelist is now accepting its limitations and sensing that he must work self-consciously from within its constraints. When his narrator dies and is replaced by a second narrator, the first narrator's own clichés are initially held up to ridicule. But, as the second narrator proceeds, his debunking of the first turns into admiration. Having distanced himself from cliché, the second narrator enters back into it, so that his damning description of his predecessor's style might equally well apply to himself.

It is another of those about-turns that we are beginning to recognise as so typically Flaubertian, but on this occasion the shift is smoothly managed – smoothly enough, at least, to have bamboozled Sartre, whose reading of this episode (*L'Idiot*, II, pp. 1711–56) as a consistent attempt by Flaubert to 'kill off' his old self and achieve a new identity takes no account whatever of its extraordinary ambivalence.

If there is one thing that is apparent in *Novembre*, however, it is the novelist-narrator's urge to enter into and understand world-views which initially he does not comprehend or share. The early pages of the text show him imaginatively identifying with a wide range of human experiences, sensing the infinite variety of history, literature and the human condition. He tries to adopt an Olympian perspective, expanding the sphere of his own feelings to contain the whole of human life. He writes: 'In the variety of my being I was like an immense Indian forest, where life palpitates in every atom and appears, monstrous or adorable, in every ray of the sun' ['J'étais, dans la variété de mon être, comme une immense forêt de l'Inde, où la vie palpite dans chaque atome et apparaît, monstrueuse ou adorable, sous chaque rayon de soleil' (OJ 773)]. This is an early version of the artistic pantheism that will be developed at the end of the 1845 *Education sentimentale*, where Jules enters into a systematic programme of reading and study, by way of breaking out of the confines of his own limited personality. It is in the 1845 novel, however, that Flaubert fully develops his aesthetic of detachment or *impassibilité*, showing his artist-figure living out the aesthetic contemplation of life and devoting himself entirely to his artistic mission. For some readers, the writer Jules, like the first narrator of *Novembre*, comes across as a dry, emotionless figure. What is significant, though, is that Flaubert does not use these characters to deny the value of feeling or personal experience. On the contrary, he seems to be saying that the unique qualities and the real intensity of personal experience can best be understood when contemplated from the vantage point of the artistic imagination. Jules will come to see that aesthetic distance is the best means of understanding and sensing the complex realities of experience, for 'wine has a taste unknown to those who drink it, woman offers pleasures overlooked by those who frequent her, and love has a resonance unfamiliar to those who are full of it' ['le vin [a] un goût ignoré de ceux qui en boivent, la femme des voluptés inaperçus de ceux qui en usent, l'amour un lyrisme étranger à ceux qui en sont pleins' (OJ 1072)]. Where previously Jules had hoped, with all the illusions of youth, that the world would conform to his idea of it, he comes to accept that it is now his task, as an artist, to accept the world as otherness, to discover its unexpected qualities and unhoped-for treasures wherever they may be. So the novel ends as a surprising and fascinating hymn to the wonders of art, and it stands as a unique mission statement in the Flaubertian corpus, perhaps the only time where this author is at one with his fictional character.

The final pages of the 1845 novel are for many readers – most especially, and understandably, to admirers of Joyce's *Portrait of the Artist as a Young Man* – its most memorable ones. Flaubert himself was somewhat cooler when, in a letter to Louise Colet who read the novel in January 1852, he wrote: 'The pages that struck you (about Art, etc.) don't seem to me to be difficult to do. I won't redo them, but I think I could do them better. It's passionate, but it could be more synthetic' ['Les pages qui t'ont frappé (sur l'Art, etc.) ne me semblent pas difficiles à faire. Je ne les referai pas, mais je crois que je les ferais mieux. C'est ardent, mais ça pourrait être plus synthétique' (Cor. II 29–30)]. On the other hand, he says, there is a section of the novel which Louise does not mention, and which seems to him to have been well done. It is chapter twenty-four, dealing with the first hero, Henry, who absconds with his mistress Emilie to New York only to discover, slowly but surely, that the relationship is failing. It is, indeed, a wonderful demonstration of psychological finesse and sharp observation, and shows Flaubert now achieving mastery in an area which Balzac had placed firmly at the centre of the novelist's art. Henry's experiences and ultimate disillusionment in love are, of course, a parallel to the later disillusionment of Jules in art. Each character undergoes a sentimental education, in which the hard lessons of life, love and art are learned. This notion of education is the unifying aspect of an otherwise structurally flawed novel, which starts out with Henry as its main character, only to replace him in the later stages by Jules. But sentimental education is not reserved to the two heroes alone. There is a minor character, a former slave and convict named Itatoè, who is present on board the ship that takes Henry and Emilie to New York. He it is who gives the novel its title:

His father had sold him for a packet of nails; he had come to France as a servant. He had stolen a scarf for a chambermaid with whom he was in love, and had been sentenced to hard labour for five years. He had returned on foot from Toulon to Le Havre to see his mistress again. He had not found her. He was now returning to the country of the black people.

He too had undergone his sentimental education.

[Son père l'avait vendu pour un paquet de clous; il était venu en France comme domestique. Il avait volé un foulard pour une femme de chambre qu'il aimait – on l'avait mis cinq ans aux galères. – Il était revenu de Toulon au Havre à pied pour revoir sa maîtresse; il ne l'avait pas retrouvée. – Il s'en retournait maintenant au pays des Noirs.

Celui-là aussi avait fait son éducation sentimentale. (OJ 978)]

In this moving passage, the more forceful for its being so understated, the young Flaubert succeeds in conveying the sense of a lifetime's emotions and drama, lived out on an individual scale. Here too he finds and expresses one of his key themes, one which will give the text its title and which will return with the more famous novel of 1869.

The 1845 *Education sentimentale* spans the crucial period of Flaubert's first nervous attack on the road to Pont-l'Evêque in January 1844, an event that forced him to abandon his law studies in Paris and to return to the family home in Croisset. Sartre argues lengthily, in *L'Idiot de la famille*, that January 1844 was a psychosomatic event that Flaubert had secretly willed and produced, turning himself into the 'family idiot' in order to avoid having to confront the realities of the professional life that was expected of him. Sartre's diagnosis is not consistent with medical research, which generally considers Flaubert's ailment to have been epilepsy. Be that as it may, the event did give Flaubert the leisure to become the hermit of Croisset, more especially after his father's death in 1846. The writing of the 1845 *Education sentimentale* no doubt shows the impact of those major changes that took place in his life from January 1844 onwards, and critics have long sought to identify the moment in the text which marks the break. The manuscript, conserved at the Fondation Bodmer in Cologny and described by the editors of the Pléiade edition (OJ 1537–41), in fact shows the signs of several breaks. However, it should also be underlined that the shift from one hero to another in this novel is a fairly gradual process, and the sign more of a general refocusing of the project on Flaubert's part than of an abrupt and sudden decision to take the writing in a different direction. For all that, the novel remains eminently readable and provides fascinating insights into Flaubert's work and his ideas. Like many of the early works, it repays close study and allows us to understand more fully what makes Flaubert the writer he is.

The *Education sentimentale* of 1845 is the first text from Flaubert's pen which, despite its transformation into an aesthetic tract in the final stages, might properly be considered a 'realist' novel, as it depicts a variety of characters against the backdrop of a particular society. Certainly, its debt to Balzac is significant, but in it, we also find the novelist in the final phase of his apprenticeship, experimenting with a range of styles and techniques. As he breaks beyond the stylistic and the thematic limits that he had set himself in earlier texts, Flaubert both sets the scene for the works that are to come and intimates that a vast programme of work awaits him. Although he once proclaimed that *Novembre* had marked the closure of his youth ['la clôture de ma jeunesse' (Cor. 1 410)], in the corpus of his works that role belongs more strictly to the 1845 novel. Indeed, it is at once a fitting finale to the early writings, and a fascinating and revealing overture to his life's work. With the writing of the first *Education sentimentale*, Flaubert completes his self-imposed rites of passage and enters the mature phase of his artistic life.

NOTES

1 Jean-Paul Sartre, *L'Idiot de la famille: Gustave Flaubert de 1821 à 1857*, 3 vols. (Paris: Gallimard, 1988 [1971–2]), translated by Carol Cosman as *The Family Idiot, Gustave Flaubert 1821–1857*, 5 vols. (Chicago and London: University of Chicago Press, 1981–93); Jean Bruneau, *Les Débuts littéraires de Gustave Flaubert, 1831–1845* (Paris: Armand Colin, 1962).

2 Among others: Eric Gans, *The Discovery of Illusion: Flaubert's Early Works, 1835–1837* (Berkeley: University of California Press, 1971), Marie J. Diamond, *Flaubert: The Problem of Aesthetic Discontinuity* (London and New York: National University Publications, 1975), and Timothy Unwin, *Art et infini: l'œuvre de jeunesse de Gustave Flaubert* (Amsterdam: Rodopi, 1992).

3 The first mention of the Garçon in Flaubert's correspondence is in a letter to Ernest Chevalier on 24 March 1837. Flaubert tells his friend that the school's *censeur* has been caught in a brothel. He writes: 'Quand je pense à la mine du censeur surpris sur le fait et limant, je me récrie, je ris, je bois, je chante ah ah ah ah ah ah et je fais entendre le rire du Garçon, je tape sur la table, je m'arrache les cheveux, je me roule par terre, voilà qui est bon. Ah! Ah! voilà qui est Blague, cul, merde' (Cor. I 23) ['When I think of the *censeur*'s expression as he's caught in the act thrusting in and out, I start up, I laugh, I drink, I sing ha! ha! ha! ha! ha! ha! and I let out the laugh of the Garçon, I thump the table, I pull out my hair, I roll on the ground. Oh! It's good! What a joke! Arse! Shit!'] For more on the Garçon, see Bruneau, *Les Débuts littéraires*, pp. 150–60.

4 On Flaubert's interest in pantheism and his reading of Spinoza, see Timothy Unwin, 'Flaubert and Pantheism', *French Studies*, 35 (1981), 394–406.

5 Georges Poulet, 'Flaubert', in *Etudes sur le temps humain* (Edinburgh: Edinburgh University Press, 1948), pp. 318–31, translated by Elliott Coleman as *Studies in Human Time* (London and Baltimore: Johns Hopkins University Press, 1956) ('Flaubert', pp. 248–62).

6 Victor Brombert, 'De *Novembre* à *L'Education*: communication et voie publique', *Revue d'Histoire Littéraire de la France*, 81: 4–5 (1981), 563–72.

4

ADRIANNE TOOKE

Flaubert's travel writings

Flaubert is now recognised as one of the greatest travel writers. His travels may not have been of the same order of magnitude as those of, for example, the mighty Humboldt, whose accounts of South America, distilled into the *Tableaux de la nature*, Flaubert found so captivating.[1] Yet he travelled far more widely and intensively than other major writers of the period who drew on travel as generously as he did for inspiration, writers such as Baudelaire, Fromentin, Gautier and Nerval. However, unlike most travel writers of the time, Flaubert did not publish any of his accounts, with the exception of one fragment from *Par les champs et par les grèves*, which does not look like travel writing at all. He held the genre in very low esteem: it was 'triste' (Cor. II 327), 'facile' (Cor. III 96), a poor, shabby sub-species of literature, which he had learned from his own experience was also almost 'impossible' (Cor. III 561). According to his friend and travelling companion, Maxime Du Camp, Flaubert wrote travel accounts only in order to toughen up his style ['corser le style']; 'there was no difference in his mind between writing a travel account and reporting on some trivial event: both were low-grade literature' ['écrire un voyage ou rédiger un fait divers, pour lui c'était tout un, c'était de la basse littérature'].[2] This, though – if we take a broader view of what constitutes 'style' than Du Camp did – is precisely what makes them the masterpieces they are. Even when Flaubert confines himself to note form, as in the *Voyage en Italie*, the *Voyage en Orient* and *Carthage*, the notes are so suited to their subject and to the writer's project, they are so acute, subtle and evocative, that they put apparently more 'finished' accounts by other writers in the shade.

Flaubert produced five travel accounts, as shown in the table below.

Flaubert's travel accounts: dates and places

Title	Locations	Dates	First significant publication	Recommended edition
Pyrénées-Corse (narrative)	SW France, Fontarabie (frontier with Spain), via Marseilles to Corsica	22 August–1 November 1840	*Œuvres complètes*, Conard, 1910	OJ (ed. C. Gothot-Mersch)
Voyage en Italie (notes)	Provence; Marseilles; via Riviera to NW Italy (Genoa, Turin, Milan), Switzerland	3 April–12 June 1845	As above	OJ (ed. C. Gothot-Mersch)
Par les champs et par les grèves (narrative, odd chapters (six) by Flaubert, even by Du Camp; notes (Flaubert only), *Carnets de voyage*, nos 2–3)	Touraine, Brittany, Normandy	1 May–28 July 1847	Fragment, 'Des pierres de Carnac', *L'Artiste*, 18 avril 1858; fragments in *Œuvres complètes* (Quantin, 1885); Flaubert's chapters in Conard, 1910; complete text CHH vol. x	Droz, 1987 (ed. A. Tooke)
Voyage en Orient (notes in *Carnets de voyage*, nos 4–9; expanded notes for Egypt, Rhodes, part of Turkey only)	Egypt, Palestine, Syria, Rhodes, Turkey, Greece, Italy	October 1849–June 1851	Fragments in *Œuvres complètes* (Quantin, 1885); complete text Conard, 1910	*Voyage en Egypte*, Grasset, 1991 (ed. P.-M. de Biasi); *Voyage en Orient*, CHH vols. x–xi
Carnet de voyage à Carthage (notes)	Algeria, Tunisia	12 April–6 June 1858	Conard, 1910	University of Rouen, 1999 (ed. C.-M. Delavoye)

Flaubert's travel writing is not confined to these five texts, however. Wherever he went, to London, for the Great Exhibition of 1851, or to visit Juliet Herbert (1865), to Fontainebleau (1868) to prepare for the great set piece which appears on it in *L'Education sentimentale*, or to Normandy (1874) to find a home for Bouvard and Pécuchet, or explore the area on their behalf (1877), Flaubert recorded what he saw, for its own sake, for pleasure, over and above anything he thought would feed directly into a book.[3] Writing about travel spills over also into brilliant, lively letters to friends and family. Above all, travel and writing about travel pervade his major works of fiction. Travel on the grand scale is represented, significantly, by only a few phrases at the end of *L'Education sentimentale* at whose brevity Proust would be the first to marvel:

> He travelled.
> He grew to know the sadness of steamboats, the cold awakenings in tents, the dizzying spectacle of landscapes and of ruins, the bitterness of friendships cut short.
> He came home again.
>
> [Il voyagea.
> Il connut la mélancolie des paquebots, les froids réveils sous la tente, l'étourdissement des paysages et des ruines, l'amertume des sympathies interrompues.
> Il revint.   (OC II 160)]

But travel on a small scale is everywhere. In all the walking and riding and contemplation of conveyances, from carriages and boats, trains and horses to elephants and strange closed sedans, Flaubert's characters experience the motions and emotions of travel on a grander scale. Travel is in the mind as much as in the real world. Writing itself, for Flaubert, is a form of travel.

This area of Flaubert's writing is extraordinarily rich and complex. Each travel account is unique in its way, geared to a particular geographical space and to a particular stage in Flaubert's thinking and practice. Recent critical approaches have tended to focus on either the aesthetic or the ideological aspects of Flaubert's travel writing. Few have tackled the tricky area of connections between the two. This chapter will attempt to fill that gap to some extent, by highlighting some key elements in the process by which travel and writing about travel contributed to the development of Flaubert's aesthetic and led directly to the writing of his major works of fiction.

Travel and art go hand in hand for Flaubert: 'travel must be a serious business' ['voyager doit être un travail sérieux' (Cor. I 226)]. Flaubert's first and only systematic statement of aesthetic theory appears as the culmination of his artist-hero Jules's artistic apprenticeship in the *Education sentimentale* of 1845 (OJ 1031–43). Though travel as such does not figure in the aesthetic, it is the ideal medium for testing its two basic principles: that 'Self' and 'Other' are not discrete unities; and that differences in general are not irreducible. Thanks in part to Flaubert's appreciation of the work of the great natural scientist, Geoffroy Saint-Hilaire, 'that great man who legitimised the existence of monsters' ['ce grand homme qui a montré la légitimité des monstres' (Cor. II 450–1)], even what appears to escape the norm, even monsters and freaks, are still seen to be manifestations of the laws of nature. In Geoffroy Saint-Hilaire's words, 'Monsters are normal creatures like any other; or, rather, there are no Monsters and nature is one' ['les Monstres sont d'autres êtres normaux; ou plutôt: il n'y a pas de Monstres, et la nature est une'].[4] Armed with the aesthetic, Jules focuses on what links rather than what divides humanity. In a 'vast pantheism, which passes through him and reappears in the form of art' ['panthéisme immense, qui passe par lui et réapparaît dans l'art' (OC I 370)], Jules finds that differences are only superficial, masking a constant equality.

Two and a half years later, *Par les champs et par les grèves* put these principles into practice. The traveller is introduced as a 'monade' (OC II 473). The monad, according to the philosopher Leibniz who invented the concept, is 'a perpetual living mirror of the universe',[5] containing the Other in himself, as the Other contains him. Travel consists of a continual interplay of contrast and similarity, which the travel account itself seeks to mirror ('unite a mass of disparate things into a whole' ['faire un tout d'une foule de choses disparates' (Cor. II 66)]): 'And that's how a day passes when you're on the road [. . .]: a river, vegetation, the fine head of a child, some tombstones [. . .]; and the next day you see other men, other places, other traces, you set up contrasts, you make analogies. That's the pleasure of it' ['Ainsi se passe une journée en voyage [. . .]: une rivière, des buissons, une belle tête d'enfant, des tombeaux [. . .]; et le lendemain on rencontre d'autres hommes, d'autres pays, d'autres débris; on établit des antithèses, on fait des rapprochements. C'est là le plaisir' (OC II 509)]. Echoes of the aesthetic recur again and again in the pages of *Par les champs*, sometimes in serious, sometimes comic mode. There are a great many figures of the artist enacting some version of the aesthetic – a performing seal, a dentist polishing and arranging sets of false teeth. The travelling dog showman is the most developed. In a gruesome parody of the creative act, 'Self' unites with 'Other' as he eggs his poor demented animals on, to the point at which all the disparate elements of his show come together into an 'harmonie discordante', an ecstasy of biting and barking, controlled (but only just) by himself as their 'chef d'orchestre':

Gripping them between their legs, their masters turned the dogs' heads towards their adversaries, and shook them violently about; the thin man, especially, put his whole heart into it; he tore from his chest a hoarse, rough, ferocious cry in a brutal spasm which whipped the excited group into a state of fury. As serious as a conductor at his rostrum, he drew into himself this dissonant harmony, directing and enhancing it; but when the dogs had been unchained and were howling and tearing each other to bits, he could not contain his enthusiasm, he was ecstatic, nearly out of his mind: he barked, applauded, twisted about, stamped with his feet, made as if to attack like a dog, hurling his body forward as they did, shaking his head like them; he would have liked to bite too, and be bitten, be a dog, have a muzzle, so that he could roll around with them, in all the dust, yelping and blood, to feel his fangs sink into the hairy skin and the warm flesh, to wallow in this maelstrom with all his heart, and writhe about in it with his whole body.

[Les maîtres, les tenant dans leurs jambes, leur tournaient la tête vers leurs adversaires et la leur hocquesonnaient avec violence. L'homme maigre surtout travaillait de tout cœur; il tirait de sa poitrine, par une secousse brutale, un jet de voix rauque, éraillée, féroce, qui inspirait la colère à toute la bande irritée. Aussi sérieux qu'un chef d'orchestre à son pupitre, il absorbait en lui cette harmonie discordante, la dirigeait, la renforçait; mais quand les dogues étaient déchaînés, et qu'ils s'entre-déchiraient tous en hurlant, l'enthousiasme le prenait, il se délectait, ne se reconnaissait plus, il aboyait, applaudissait, se tordait, battait du pied, faisait le geste d'un chien qui attaque, se lançait le corps en avant comme eux, secouait la tête comme eux; il aurait voulu mordre aussi, qu'on le mordît, être chien, avoir une gueule pour se rouler là-dedans, au milieu de la poussière, des cris et du sang; pour sentir [entrer] ses crocs dans les peaux velues, dans la chair chaude, pour nager en plein dans ce tourbillon, pour s'y débattre de tout son [corps].

(OC II 529–30, text corrected, as in the Droz edition)]

Flaubert never reneged on the aesthetic of 1845, which is expounded at length in the first *Education sentimentale*. But when, in 1852, Louise Colet gave her highest praise to that section of the work, he acknowledged its value but pointed out also that he now knew better what he was about: '*Je sais comment il faut faire*' (Cor. II 30, Flaubert's emphasis). The major part of that invaluable practical experience was provided by travel writing, which proved to be a very hard school. The 1845 aesthetic was admirable as far as it went, but it was above all a touchstone, a statement of faith rather than a scientific explanation of life and the universe. It needed the challenge of real life, and challenged it was. Flaubert's 'mania', as he calls it at the beginning of the *Voyage en Orient*, for imaginatively entering other people's lives

(OC II 554) is not always satisfied. Sometimes, Self and Other are united only in their sense of each other's differences:

> This idiotic amazement which takes hold of us when we see people living where we don't, and passing their time differently from us, is impossible to resist. Do you remember how, often, passing through a village in the morning, just as the day was breaking, you would catch a glimpse of some local inhabitant, opening his shutters or sweeping his doorstep, and who would stop open-mouthed to see you go by? He was hardly able to make out your face or you his, and yet in that one brief moment you were both, simultaneously, stunned with an immense feeling of amazement; he wondered as he watched you fly past: 'Where can that chap be going and why is he on the road?', and you, as you sped on your way: 'What's he doing there?' you asked. 'Does he never go anywhere else?'

> [C'est une chose dont on ne peut se défendre que cet étonnement imbécile qui vous prend à considérer les gens vivant où nous ne vivons point, et passant leur temps à d'autres affaires que les nôtres. Vous rappelez-vous souvent, en traversant un village le matin, quand le jour se levait, avoir aperçu quelque bourgeois ouvrant ses auvents ou balayant le devant de sa porte, et qui s'arrêtait bouche béante à vous regarder passer? A peine s'il a pu distinguer votre visage ni vous le sien, et dans cet éclair pourtant tous les deux, au même instant, vous vous êtes ébahis dans un immense étonnement; il se disait en vous regardant fuir: 'Où va-t-il donc celui-là et pourquoi voyage-t-il?', et vous qui couriez: 'Qu'est-ce qu'il fait là? disiez-vous, est-ce qu'il y reste toujours?'
> (OC II 493–4)]

This sense of the impenetrability of other people is amply demonstrated later, in Flaubert's *Voyage en Orient*, where the traumatic encounter with the dancer and courtesan Kuchouk-Hânem convinces him that she will never be anything but a closed book, which even the artist cannot open.

The fact that life runs athwart human designs is an essential feature of Flaubert's writing: 'I like there to be a bitterness to everything, an eternal blowing of the whistle in the midst of our triumphs, and for desolation even to be present in enthusiasm' ['Je veux qu'il y ait une amertume à tout, un éternel coup de sifflet au milieu de nos triomphes, et que la désolation même soit dans l'enthousiasme' (Cor. II 283)]. The shock of the new is a major feature of Flaubert's travel writing, and is sometimes so great that integration into any system, however flexible, seems out of the question. An early example occurs in the *Voyage en Italie*, when the traveller's appreciation of a sublime Alpine landscape is rudely shattered by the abrupt appearance of a very ugly head, thrusting itself through a carriage window: 'we meet the stagecoach; hideous man sticking his head through the window; grotesque in the midst of the sublime' ['rencontre de la diligence; homme dégoûtant passant sa tête par la portière; grotesque au milieu du sublime' (OJ 1113)]. This image recurs in the figure of the hideous blind man in *Madame Bovary*, who haunts Emma as persistently as such apparitions haunted Flaubert – only she, unlike Flaubert, averts her eyes and tries to get rid of the unwelcome sight by throwing him a coin.

Both sides, the sense of recognition, and the shock of the new, play a role in Flaubert's first encounter with Egypt. Soon after his arrival, Flaubert writes in a letter to Louis Bouilhet that Nature is a rediscovery, whereas people have turned out to be a complete surprise (Cor. 1 538): 'I would never have suspected this aspect to Travel' ['Je n'aurais jamais soupçonné ce coté au Voyage' (Cor. 1 707)]. Eventually, as Flaubert travels farther and farther up the Nile and into the heart of Egypt, closer to Africa, he finds that Nature too loses its appearance of familiarity and turns into something he could not possibly have anticipated, 'a terrible landscape' ['paysage terrible' (OC II 570)], 'enormous' ['énorme' (OC II 572)], where the sun bites into his skull as if it were an animal (OC II 580). Looking back, in 1853, what Flaubert remembers of Egypt is not its surface glitter, which is not in fact new at all (he calls it Byronic), but a deeper 'harmonie de choses disparates' (that phrase again) where contrasts are shocking but where even the vermin 'form golden arabesques in the sun' ['fait au soleil des arabesques d'or' (Cor. II 283)].

Flaubert's aesthetic is certainly more at home with monsters and the irreducibly Different than with sameness and homogeneity. 'Leave my country' ['Quitter mon pays' (OJ 818)]: travel for Flaubert is an attempt at escape, from France, from the clichés of contemporary French culture and his old caged self, to a broader way of being, to alternative cultures whose external and internal differences have not been homogenised or ironed out: 'I hate Europe, and France my own country' ['Je hais l'Europe, la France mon pays' (Cor. 1 76)]. Flaubert is 'a barbarian', 'as much Chinese as French' ['barbare' (Cor. II 123), 'autant Chinois que Français' (Cor. 1 300–1)], more attuned to the Arabs of Algeria than to the French who have defeated them. Hence his enthusiasm for Corsica and its bandits, or the crude exuberance of Cairo street life, and his delight at the often unwelcome realities of foreign travel, from bedbugs to beggars to the absence of toilets as we know them (see *Par les champs* (OC II 523) for a fine example of the latter). But the search for the new is bedevilled by the *idée reçue*. Flaubert is one of the generation of 'belated travellers' referred to by Ali Behdad, condemned perpetually to walk in the footsteps of their too many and too illustrious predecessors.[6] His journeys coincide with the first wave of mass tourism, which began in France in the 1830s and 1840s. *Pyrénées-Corse* is already unusually sensitive to the growing homogenisation of cultures, and clearly foresees, as early as this, the era of the *tristes tropiques*, the degradation of tropical countries through Western exploitation, commercial and otherwise, as defined by Lévi-Strauss. Flaubert may long to escape from France, but France goes with him, or gets there first. Corsica is already beginning to cave in: Bastia is more French than France (OJ 720); Breton peasants are in the process of being absorbed; in Cairo and Alexandria the signs of French influence are everywhere, even in the lithographs people hang on their walls. Worst of all, perhaps, is that as a tourist Flaubert contributes to the destruction of the very things he has come to admire. Clambering over the ruins of a charming old abbey at Landévennec, in Brittany, he notes that he has dislodged some stones and worn away the cement: 'Are we then destroyers too? And what neither time, nor humankind, nor good taste, nor industry have been able to knock down, along comes the innocent viewer, in the very act of admiring curiosity, unwittingly to destroy it completely' ['Est-ce que nous détruirions aussi nous autres? Et ce que n'ont pu abattre ni le temps, ni les hommes, ni le bon goût, ni l'industrie, voilà que l'achève, sans le savoir, le contemplateur naïf, dans l'exercice même de sa curiosité admirative' (OC II 523)].

Travel writing is no less jaded, constrictive and cliché-ridden than travel, different only in degree from carving one's name in letters three feet high on Pompey's column, like the egregious 'Thompson of Sunderland' (OC II 558). From *Pyrénées-Corse* to the *Voyage en Orient*, Flaubert's travel writing is a series of attempts to reinvigorate the genre, to infuse it with freshness and life. Writing *against* the genre, as much as within it, he finds a voice of his own, which will eventually take him away from travel writing entirely. Flaubert's journey is also a textual one, from travel writing to writing as travel, a journey on which we will now attempt to follow him.

Flaubert's first travel account, *Pyrénées-Corse* (1840), makes every effort to conform to the rules of the genre. The narrator's intention, from the outset, is to write spontaneously, as if he were merely shaking the dust of his travels off his clothes directly onto the paper with his pen ['avec ma plume, jeter sur le papier un peu de la poussière de mes habits' (OJ 648)]. This may look like the claim of the average *voyageur enthousiaste* of the time to be tossing off his impressions on the corner of the nearest inn table, but in Flaubert's case it is a genuine attempt to turn the fiction into a reality. If it failed, as it did, this was for two reasons: first, because he was travelling in a family-endorsed group, and therefore not free to follow his own emotional and intellectual itinerary (Spain, notably, was accorded only half a day); second, because writing as he went did the exact opposite of what was intended, and drained his account of all colour and vitality:

There is nothing so tiring as to be constantly describing your travels, and taking note of the tiniest impressions that you feel; by the very act of rendering everything and expressing everything, there is nothing left inside you; every feeling you translate gets weaker in your heart, and duplicating every image in this way means that the original colours become corrupted on the canvas which has received them.

[Il n'y a rien de si fatigant que de faire une perpétuelle description de son voyage, et d'annoter les plus minces impressions que l'on ressent; à force de tout rendre et de tout exprimer, il ne reste plus rien en vous; chaque sentiment qu'on traduit s'affaiblit dans notre cœur, et dédoublant ainsi chaque image, les couleurs primitives s'en altèrent sur la toile qui les a reçues.   (OJ 669)]

The resulting account is distinctly edgy. The young traveller would like to be somewhere else (the text is peppered with the names of places which are neither in the Pyrenees nor in Corsica), to be doing something else (riding a mule, spending more time in the fresh air and less in churches, making love), to be someone else (a mule-driver, a gentleman of the road, a bandit), and, above all, to be *writing* something else. The reader feels that, left to himself, Flaubert might have aimed at producing something akin to the little carvings which he notes in the church of Saint-Bertrand de Comminges, playful, droll, and created for the sheer love of creation ('anything at all, provided that it is something' ['n'importe quoi pourvu que ce soit quelque chose' (OJ 671)]), or something which would give the same kind of pleasure as that which he feels when walking over rocks which are like red and black bronze and whose sharp edges sparkle in the sun (OJ 716). This continual sense of constraint, of unfulfilled desire, is, paradoxically, what 'lifts' the prose, imparting a kind of sparkle, like the halo which appears on one occasion through some trick of the light around himself and his perfectly ordinary companions (OJ 674). His pleasure at the splendour of Corsica is enhanced, not spoiled, by his awareness of an invisible Italy, signalled on the horizon by a 'ligne blanche' (OJ 716), a white line which is like a 'memory of things he has never seen' ['souvenir de choses que je n'avais pas vues'], or, it could be added, a line of prose waiting to be written.

Pyrénées-Corse is the first step in the process of 'mulching down' which Flaubert, like other travelling artists of his time, considered essential. The raw first impression needs to be worked on by time and memory.[7] Giving up the attempt to write as he travels, Flaubert completes *Pyrénées-Corse* as a retrospective account, infused with all the magic of memory: 'I like repeating these details to myself' ['J'aime à me redire tous ces détails' (OJ 715)]. Even then, it is not finished: 'I shall frequently add to these notes' ['je reprendrai souvent ces notes [. . .]' (OJ 704)]. In the event, it is left to other travel accounts to pick up the baton.

The *Voyage en Italie* (1845), fruit of yet another family outing, settles for the note form and simple *reportage*.[8] *Par les champs et par les grèves* (1848), however, is Flaubert's first and last serious and sustained attempt to create a recognisable travel account which is also a work of art.

Flaubert is now at last free to travel according to his lights. If not completely alone, he is at least alone with his friend, Du Camp, so 'completely free and alone' ['*totalement libres et seuls*' (Cor. I 353, Flaubert's emphasis)]. Brittany would not have been his first choice, or even an obvious choice. It was Du Camp's idea, originally, as he had thought of writing a novel about the Vendée.[9] The yearning to be *somewhere else* is still apparent, from the very beginning: 'For some other time, for later, great voyages through the whole world' ['A d'autres temps, pour plus tard, les grands voyages à travers le monde [. . .]' (OC II 473)]. Flaubert's health, after the devastating nervous attack of 1844, is not yet up to more than this still fairly modest excursion; and his mother comes to join them in Brest (Cor. I 459). However, this time, Flaubert, following Jules's example, throws himself resolutely into his subject, with the greatest good will. 'Beauty is everywhere' ['Le beau est partout'], he writes to his best friend, Le Poittevin, thus incurring his mockery, 'the point is to see it' ['il ne s'agit que de l'y voir'].[10] It is by now irrelevant whether or not Flaubert is interested in Brittany: 'I'm looking to describe the thing in itself, not my feelings about it' ['je cherche [. . .] non pas la *vibration* mais le *dessin*' (Cor. I 489)]. Flaubert is here anticipating the ideological position he will take up later during the writing of *Madame Bovary*, 'that there aren't good subjects for art in literature, and that Yvetot, therefore, is as good as Constantinople; and that therefore you can write anything at all quite as well as any other subject you may think of' ['qu'il n'y a pas en littérature de beaux sujets d'art, et qu'Yvetot donc vaut Constantinople; et qu'en conséquence l'on peut écrire n'importe quoi aussi bien que quoi que ce soit' (Cor. II 362)]. Resolutely conforming to the rules of the genre, the narrator will omit nothing: 'Think what it means to write a travel account where you've decided in advance to tell *everything*' ['Songe ce que c'est que d'écrire un voyage où l'on a pris le parti d'avance de *tout* raconter' (Cor. II 66)]. All the diverse subjects thrown up by the basically random twists and turns of the road will be left to suggest their own connections and interweave to form a complex tapestry, which will depend for its unity not on the usual linking device of the traveller's *moi*, but on the fact that everything is necessarily of itself potentially related to everything else. There is to be no selection or forcing the note. The result, unsurprisingly, was that the writing of *Par les champs* was a nightmare.

Par les champs is a conscientious attempt to give a picture of the real Brittany, with all its nuances. Without ever seeming to do so, it manages to provide a complete course of Breton history and archaeology, and a complete range of Breton landscapes, from the prehistoric rocks of the island of Belle-Ile to the flat potato-fields of Roscoff. Thanks to his new aesthetic, Flaubert was able to find harmony and therefore beauty even in the poor, neglected little churches, which sat so well in their rustic natural surroundings, and in the Bretons themselves, often presented as figures of fun in contemporary culture: 'They were beautiful, these men, beautiful because they were real, both in the simplicity of their costumes, moulded to their shape, suited to their bodies, with creases reflecting their life's labour, and in the integrity of their religious faith which breathed easily in this church which was made for it' ['Ils etaient beaux ces hommes, beaux parce qu'ils etaient vrais et dans la simplicité de leurs costumes faits à leur taille, aptes à leurs corps, pliés selon le travail de leur vie, et dans la bonne foi de leur croyance qui s'exhalait à l'aise dans cette église faite pour elle' (OC II 509)]. But this is not the only view of them. At other times, in other moods, the emphasis is rather on their stuntedness, their dourness and general unloveliness, which are accounted for, in turn, by the fact of their crippling poverty. And Flaubert does not lose his sense of humour. 'Brittany' is also revealed in its very ordinariness as much as in its breathtaking coastal views, in the conversations of the *table d'hôte* of Pont l'Abbé (OC II 533) or the dourly respectable little brothel of Brest (OC II 528) or the insignificance of the little town of Landerneau, about which there is nothing to be said except that a dog is running through the streets half demented with a saucepan attached to its tail (OC II 531). As had happened in the case of Corsica, *Par les champs* brilliantly catches the reality of a place which is on a cusp, in the process of losing its traditional identity. Anticipating the figure of Catherine Leroux in *Madame Bovary*, a peasant woman in her traditional clothes stands submissively before a French tax inspector with gold-rimmed spectacles, on whom she is waiting at table: 'the ancient portrait humbles itself before the modern caricature' ['le vieux portrait s'humilie devant la caricature moderne' (OC II 511)]. There is no doubt where the narrator's sympathies lie in this confrontation. But, lest the reader should become sentimental, (s)he is treated, shortly afterwards (OC II 517) to the strange spectacle of Bretons dancing, one behind the other in a straggling line, mechanically but with little sense of rhythm, to the sounds of the bagpipe. Here already, in *Par les champs*, Flaubert is adhering to one of the fundamental literary precepts of his maturity: 'to write about ordinary life as you write history or the epic (without inflating the subject)' ['écrire la vie ordinaire comme on écrit l'histoire ou l'épopée (sans dénaturer le sujet)' (Cor. II 287)].

Clearly, more has to be at stake than the recording of surface detail. The hardest task in the writing of *Par les champs* was to 'render the *Idea*' ['rendre *l'Idée*' (Cor. I 475, Flaubert's emphasis)]. This sense of an extra dimension beyond the surface impression, of great patterns dimly glimpsed, is present in all the writing of Flaubert's maturity. One example among many in *Par les champs* is that of the description of a simple boat-trip, which taps into something extraordinary, to do with the passing of time, and with the beauty and precariousness of language and art in the context of Nature as a whole, as the song of the cabin boy comes and goes, half blown away on the wind:

> Leaning on its side, the boat sliced through the waves which slid along past the planking with a twist of sea-spray. The three sails, billowing in the wind, rounded their gentle curves. The masts creaked, the air whistled in the pulleys; at the prow, his face lifted to the breeze, a cabin-boy was singing; we couldn't hear the words, but it was a slow, tranquil, monotonous melody, repeated over and over again, never getting any louder or softer, and seeming never to end as it died away in a series of lingering modulations.
>
> It stole away gently and sadly over the sea, like the passage of a dim memory in somebody's soul.

> [Incliné sur le flanc, le bateau coupait les vagues qui filaient le long du bordage en tordant de l'écume. Les trois voiles bien gonflées arrondissaient leur courbe douce. La mâture criait, l'air sifflait dans les poulies. A la proue, le nez dans la brise, un mousse chantait; nous n'entendions pas les paroles, mais c'était un air lent, tranquille et monotone qui se répétait toujours, ni plus haut, ni plus bas, et qui se prolongeait en mourant, avec des modulations traînantes.
>
> Cela s'en allait doux et triste sur la mer, comme dans une âme un souvenir confus qui passe. (OC II 502)]

The fact that this text turned out to be, by Flaubert's own recognition, a tough assignment and the first he found difficulty in writing stems primarily, I would suggest, from the fact that Flaubert is here at grips for the first time with the external world in all its awkwardness. Blending with the Other turns out to be very hard work. The 'book about nothing' which Flaubert longed to write was only ever an ideal. In practice, Flaubert never lost the habit of referring his writing first to reality, as the 'tremplin', the trampoline from which his style would touch the stars.

The *Voyage en Orient* (1849–51) is still not everything Flaubert would have wished. He would have liked to push on further: after Egypt, Palestine, Syria, on to a series of places whose very names spell magic to Flaubert: 'Baghdad, Basra, Persia as far as the Caspian Sea, the Caucasus, Georgia, Asia Minor along the coasts' ['Bagdad, Bassora, la Perse jusqu'à la mer Caspienne, le Caucase, la Géorgie, l'Asie Mineure par les côtes . . .'

(Cor. 1 506)]. He still chafes at convention: 'Doing what you feel you have to; being always what a young man, a traveller, an artist, son or citizen etc. ought to be' ['Faire ce qu'il faut faire; être toujours [. . .] comme un jeune homme, comme un voyageur, comme un artiste, comme un fils, comme un citoyen, etc. doit être!' (OC II 581)]. He is still not travelling alone (he will have to wait for *Carthage* for that), and relations with Du Camp, at first good, begin to deteriorate, irrevocably, as their paths begin to diverge, Du Camp's continuing upwards and onwards towards the achievement of clear literary and material goals, and Flaubert's, to all appearances, sliding downhill into sadness and stagnation. The negative reactions of Du Camp and Louis Bouilhet to what Flaubert had thought of at the time as his *magnum opus*, the *Tentation de saint Antoine* of 1849, had made a huge dent in his self-confidence; and in the presence of Du Camp, busily taking photographs, proud to be making writing redundant, Flaubert returns continually in his notes and letters to the question of his own abilities and of whatever it is, if anything, he should write.

In fact, though, this trip is taking Flaubert further along the path he thinks he has lost. The impact on his art of Egypt, in particular, cannot be exaggerated. The *Voyage en Orient*, at last, moves away from the idea of 'finish', still paramount in *Par les champs et par les grèves*. Incompletion is now a positive choice. Had Flaubert published an account of his travels, he would have produced something entirely new in the art of travel writing, a series of discrete, short prose texts, written on the spot and with no ambition to 'faire un tout': 'I'd intended to write my travel account in the form of short chapters, as I went along, whenever I had the time' ['J'avais l'intention d'écrire [. . .] mon voyage par paragraphes, en forme de petits chapitres, au fur et à mesure, quand j'aurais le temps' (OC II 552)]. An idea of how this would have worked can be gleaned from the section entitled 'la Cange' (OC II 552–5), which abandons direct description in favour of the tentative and the oblique. However, the idea proved impracticable. The desert storm which provided the pause for writing came to an end, and Flaubert moved on. The series of fragments remains itself a fragment.

In the *Voyage en Orient*, the note comes into its own. No longer a makeshift or *aide-mémoire*, its lack of completion and lightness of touch denies the possibility of any authoritative overview. Egypt is revealed quite as powerfully through tiny images as through its usual 'sights': three folds of waves rippling over the Nile (OC II 573), moonlight gleaming on a white sock (OC II 580), two dogs standing in the dark on a roof,[11] the intricate pattern caused by the sun shining through slats (OC II 576), the gesture of an ancient camel driver as he takes hold of a woman (OC II 568). This minimalist style reflects not only Egypt itself but the extent to which Flaubert was disorientated by it. Already in *Pyrénées-Corse* there is the sense that certain impressions are taboo: 'One must not write all that' ['Il ne faut pas écrire tout cela' (OC II 710)].

Naturally, the whole of the *Voyage en Egypte* does not operate in this way. There is plenty of straightforward description and *reportage*. Bored Flaubert may have been, eventually, by the plethora of temples (OC II 581), but he was still quite happy to describe a monument in minute detail, for the record. His eye for detail was indeed very acute. Even so, monuments and landscapes speak also for more than themselves. Monuments are not just tourist sights to be described, but signs, pointing a way forward: the Sphinx, the Pyramids, the colossi of Abu-Simbel shook him to the core. Egypt created the space for writing.[12]

If Egypt often appears as one great studio in the travel notes, if the spectacle of the streets is as vivid and 'unrealistic' (or not) as the numerous puppet shows he saw while there, if the Nile looks like a huge stage-set and the palms look like painted trees, if objects are obscured as in a mirage, and black looks like white, or landscapes turn into slabs of primary colour and caravans of camels appear to be walking in the clouds, this is because Egypt has already become part of Flaubert's *imaginaire*. Egypt pervades his style, not just in the *Voyage en Orient*, but, as Jeanne Bem has argued, in all his writing.[13] In the *Tentation de saint Antoine*, the goddess Isis applies this idea to the creation of Egyptian hieroglyphs: 'The animals of its zodiac reappeared in its pastures, and filled its mysterious writing with their shapes and colours' ['Les animaux de son zodiaque se retrouvaient dans ses pâturages, emplissaient de leurs formes et de leurs couleurs son écriture mystérieuse' (OC I 557)].[14] The Orient goes underground, and flickers through Flaubert's writing like a veil.

In Constantinople, on 14 November 1850, Flaubert still longs to go to India, or California. He settles for Croisset and the internal voyage of writing. As for the notes of the *Voyage*, they become the half-finished building blocks of Flaubert's own Pyramids. The end of travel writing is writing itself.

With the exception of *Carthage* (1858), Flaubert's travels and travel works are confined to the period of his apprenticeship. The plethora of short journeys which replace travel on the grand scale perhaps underlines the point that travel is always in the mind, whether on the banks of the Nile or the banks of the Seine, at Nogent ('Niagara', for Louise Roque (OC II 99)). Travel henceforth is contained in its signs: small exotic objects such as those which fill Félicité's bedroom, which have the capacity to 'faire rêver'; and the hieroglyphs of writing, which perform the same function.

In a letter of 1860, Flaubert tries to dissuade his friend Ernest Feydeau from writing up an account of his recent journey to Algeria: 'Do you need to prove that you know how to do descriptions?' ['As-tu besoin de prouver que tu sais faire des descriptions?' (Cor. III 96)] Flaubert's travel writing did give him ample opportunity to refine his descriptive styles, but it also taught him a great deal more about style than that. Part of Flaubert's admiration for Humboldt stems undoubtedly from the latter's style which, in accordance with his stated aim in the Preface to his *Tableaux de la nature*, was precise and poetic, combining scientific fact with beauty and art. This is what Flaubert wanted his own prose to be: as 'rhythmic as poetry, as precise as the language of science, and yet quivering and throbbing like the cello, with diadems of flashing lights' ['rythmé comme le vers, précis comme le langage des sciences, et avec des ondulations, des ronflements de violoncelle, des aigrettes de feux' (Cor. II 79)]. Flaubert greatly admired the painter Gleyre, less for his paintings, however, than for his narrative style, which was both precise and poetic, and marvellously evocative. Stopping off to visit him in Lyon, on his way to the East, Flaubert is introduced to the flora and fauna of the banks of the Blue Nile by Gleyre at his narrative best:

> He talks to us about Sennâr and gets us very excited about the monkeys which come at night and lift up the bottoms of the tent flaps to look at the traveller; in the evening the guinea-fowl begin to roost in the tall trees and the gazelles, in herds, approach the drinking holes. There are savannahs of tall grass out there, and elephants which gallop faster than you can catch them. At one o'clock in the morning, all the same, we said goodbye to each other, and all the night we dreamt of Sennâr.

> [Il nous parle de Sennâr et nous monte la tête à l'endroit des singes qui viennent la nuit soulever le bas des tentes pour regarder le voyageur; le soir, les pintades se mettent à nicher dans les grands arbres et les gazelles, par troupeaux, s'approchent des fontaines. Il y a là-bas des savanes de hautes herbes et des éléphants qui galopent sans qu'on puisse les atteindre. A 1 heure du matin, cependant, on se dit adieu, et toute la nuit nous rêvons Sennâr.

> (OC II 554–5)]

It is just such a tantalising combination of precision and poetry, geographical fact and simple formal perfection that makes the travellers' tales of Apollonius and Damis, the Queen of Sheba, and indeed most of the tales recounted in the *Tentation de saint Antoine* so beguiling: they are a *tentation* precisely because of the pact they seem to offer with the real. Travel writing, then, by its very nature, turns on its head an essential principle of Flaubert's aesthetic: 'I must, through Beauty, create nevertheless something alive and true' ['Il faut faire, à travers le Beau, vivant et vrai quand même' (*Voyage à Carthage*, OC II 720)]. In the texts discussed in this chapter, I have argued that much the opposite occurs: that, while discovering the discordant realities of what is alive and true, Flaubert finds himself engaged in a challenge to seek out beauty and harmony in the jarring mess of human lives.

NOTES

1 For Flaubert's reading of Humboldt, see Cor. II 20.

2 Maxime Du Camp, *Souvenirs littéraires* (1882–3) (Paris: Aubier, 1994), p. 358.

3 For accounts of these shorter expeditions, see Jean Seznec, ed., *Flaubert à l'Exposition de 1851* (Oxford: Clarendon Press, 1951) and Flaubert, *Carnets de travail*, ed. Pierre-Marc de Biasi (Paris: Balland, 1988), pp. 362–7, 419–28, 798–800, 857–78.

4 Etienne Geoffroy Saint-Hilaire, *Philosophie anatomique* (Paris: Méquignon-Marvis, 1818), p. 260.

5 Baron Gottfried Wilhelm von Leibniz, *Monadology* (1714), in *Basic Writings* (La Salle, IL: The Open Court Publishing Company, 1968), p. 263.

6 Ali Behdad, *Belated Travelers: Orientalism in the Age of Colonial Dissolution* (Durham, NC: Duke University Press, 1994).

7 See Adrianne Tooke, *Flaubert and the Pictorial Arts. From Image to Text* (Oxford: Oxford University Press, 2000), pp. 12–13 and 18–21.

8 See the excellent 'Notice' on the *Voyage en Italie* by Claudine Gothot-Mersch (OJ 1587–1604), and Tooke, *Flaubert and the Pictorial Arts*, for discussion of paintings and other art works.

9 Maxime Du Camp, *Lettres inédites à Gustave Flaubert*, ed. G. Bonaccorso and R. M. di Stefano (Messina: Edas, 1978), p. 14 (26 May 1844).

10 Flaubert's words are quoted back at him by Le Poittevin in a letter written 'after 22 May 1847', in *Correspondances. Gustave Flaubert – Alfred Le Poittevin, Gustave Flaubert – Maxime Du Camp*, texte établi, préfacé et annoté par Yvan Leclerc (Paris: Flammarion, 2000), p. 130.

11 *Voyage en Egypte*, ed. Pierre-Marc de Biasi (Paris: Grasset, 1991), p. 264 (detail from the description of a visit to a prostitute, omitted in the OC).

12 Luca Pietromarchi, among others, draws attention to this point in *L'Illusione orientale: Gustave Flaubert e l'esotismo romantico (1836–1851)* (Milan: Edizioni Angelo Guerini e Associati s.r.l, 1990).

13 Jeanne Bem, 'L'Orient ironique de Flaubert', in *Le Texte traversé* (Paris: Champion, 1991), pp. 131–41.

14 An earlier version of the same very modern idea – that writing expresses the real world indirectly, through style, regardless of explicit content – occurs in *Par les champs et par les grèves*: 'I hear confusedly in Juvenal the death-rattle of gladiators; some of Tacitus's turns of phrase are like the folds of a tunic, and certain lines of Horace have the loins of a Greek slave woman, with swaying of the hips and short and long syllables which resound like castanets' ['J'entends confusément dans Juvénal des râles de gladiateur; Tacite a des tournures qui ressemblent à des draperies de laticlave, et certains vers d'Horace ont des reins d'esclave grecque, avec des balancements de hanche et des brèves et des longues qui sonnent comme des crotales' (OC II 540)].

5

ROSEMARY LLOYD

Flaubert's correspondence

Writing to Louis de Cormenin in June of 1844, the twenty-two-year-old Flaubert sketches an ideal society of 'good lads, all men of letters, living together and gathering two or three times a week to eat a good meal washed down with a good wine, while savouring some succulent poet' ['bons garçons, tous gens d'art, vivant ensemble et se réunissant deux ou trois fois par semaine pour manger un bon morceau arrosé d'un bon vin, tout en dégustant quelque succulent poète' (Cor. 1 209)].[1] Friendship, the pleasures of the table, the delights of conversation, above all talk devoted to literature: these are all central to Flaubert's personality, all the more important for someone who chose to lead an existence that was primarily solitary. These are also the motifs that run through his correspondence like brightly coloured threads, even when the general fabric grows dark with the pessimism of his later years.

In many ways the letters he wrote and received provided him with that ideal society, for from very early on we find him using his correspondence to discuss love and friendship, politics and art, the seductive beauty of Northern Africa, to which he travelled in his twenties, and the remorseless challenge of his own creative writing, to which he devoted the whole of his adult life. What makes the letters so attractive and entertaining is partly this wide sweep, partly the sense of seeing what Baudelaire called the strings and pulleys of a writer's workshop, and partly the immediacy of Flaubert's changeable, complex and challenging personality. They provide us with what Julian Barnes has convincingly termed 'Flaubert's best biography'.[2] While his letters are often read primarily for the multifaceted window they offer into his creative writing, its sources, its problems, its delights and its torments, they are also a mirror of his personality, reflecting his enthusiasms, his prejudices, his aspirations, his sense of humour, and above all his values.

As with all mirrors, its reflection reveals varying degrees of distortion, since Flaubert tailors the image he is willing to disclose according to the nature of his correspondent and the quality of his relationship with him or her. Reading the correspondence, we need to be aware of its context, and avoid overlooking the tenor of the letter as a whole or the personality of its recipient. Nevertheless, it remains the case that the strict control Flaubert exercised over whatever he wrote for publication is set aside here for a style that is often more spontaneous and less guarded, the kind of writing he reserves for late at night, when the work of the day is set aside, and he lowers the barriers and restraints he has kept so firmly in place. Flaubert uses his letters as others might a diary, with this difference, that he is always aware of his correspondent, creating, despite his determined isolation, the sense either of a quiet and intimate conversation, or of a raw and uncontrolled outpouring of emotions or boasting or invective directed at the bourgeois, republicans, or anyone else who had aroused his passions. The personality of the author may be something he works at eliding from his novels, but it is strongly present in the letters, an essential part of their considerable charm.

That charm has been strong enough to fuel a variety of different editions of Flaubert's letters, ever since the letters between him and George Sand were published in 1884, together with a study by Guy de Maupassant. Flaubert's niece, Caroline, published the first edition of the collected correspondence, in four volumes, the first of which appeared in 1887, the last in 1893. In addition to watering down Flaubert's often salty prose, she removed from this collection the letters her uncle had sent her, publishing them in a separate volume in 1906. In 1921, René Descharmes published a centenary edition of the correspondence, to which he could add many of the letters to Louise Colet, which Caroline had been unable to acquire. By 1926, the publishing house Conard, now in possession of over a thousand new letters, produced a nine-volume edition, drawing largely on the editorial skills of Descharmes. From 1973 to his death in June 2003, the great Flaubert specialist Jean Bruneau had been publishing a revised edition for Gallimard's Pléiade collection, enriched by numerous additional documents, especially those associated with Louise Colet. Four of the envisaged five volumes have appeared to date, bringing the correspondence up to December 1875. Responsibility for the fifth volume, due out at the end of 2004, has been undertaken by Yvan Leclerc, who had already been working with Bruneau. With its additional documentation, its impeccable notes, and its numerous clarifications, as well as its publication of various letters to Flaubert, notably by Colet and Sand, the Pléiade edition is an exceptionally fine resource both for the general public and for researchers. There have also been publications of specific exchanges, those with Maupassant for instance, that reveal more sharply the ways in which Flaubert created a series of conversations and voices for certain of his friends.[3]

Building those conversations, making each correspondent aware that he is not just using them as a sounding board but has them clearly in mind, is an art in itself. We can hear his voice changing as he writes to different people, idiosyncratically summing them up in a series of striking and often amusing epithets: Louise Colet is the Muse, George Sand the dear master, Edmond Laporte 'my old solid one' (CHH XVI 52), Tourgueniev a 'dear and gigantic personage' (CHH XVI 24). 'Hello, old rat', he greets his dearly loved sister Caroline, who he knows is eager to hear of his meeting with Victor Hugo at the house of their mutual friends, the Pradiers: 'You're expecting me to send you details about Victor Hugo. What can I say? He's a man who looks like any other, with a fairly ugly face and a fairly common appearance. He has splendid teeth, a superb forehead, no lashes or eyebrows. He doesn't talk much, seems to watch himself, doesn't want to let anything escape' ['Tu t'attends à des détails de V. Hugo. Que veux-tu que j'en dise? C'est un homme qui a l'air comme un autre, d'une figure assez laide et d'un extérieur assez commun. Il a de magnifiques dents, un front superbe, pas de cils ni de sourcils. Il parle peu, a l'air de s'observer et de ne vouloir rien lâcher' (Cor. I 193)]. Aware of how much his mother will be missing him during his travels in North Africa he writes frequently, often inscribing into his letters vivid verbal sketches of what he sees, sketches moreover that invite her to look too, as if over his shoulder:

> Imagine a large square courtyard, surrounded on three sides by buildings painted white with great horizontal bands of red, green, blue and black. From the top of the terrace hang plants that dangle down like hair. And vines as thick as trees climb up from below. Before my eyes is an enormous bunch of oleander and all its open flowers cast red patches in the green.
>
> [Figure-toi une grande cour carrée, entourée sur trois faces de bâtiments peints en blanc avec de grandes bandes horizontales rouges, vertes, bleues, noires. Du haut de la terrasse de la maison pendent des plantes qui tombent en chevelures. – Et des vignes grosses comme des arbres montent d'en bas. J'ai devant moi sous mes yeux une énorme touffe de lauriers-roses dont toutes les fleurs épanouies font des taches rouges dans la verdure.   (Cor. I 687)]

Knowing that she wants to be able to picture him in the setting from which he is writing, he tells her: 'I'm writing, dear old lady, in full dress, white waistcoat, court shoes, etc. like a man who has just paid a visit to a prime minister. We have just this moment left the home of Artin-Bey, minister for foreign affairs' ['Je t'écris, chère vieille, en grande tenue, habit noir, gilet blanc, escarpins, etc., comme un homme qui vient de faire une visite à un premier ministre. Nous sortons à l'instant de chez Artin-Bey, ministre des affaires étrangères' (Cor. I 530)]. We will meet this side of his personality often, later on, when he becomes a pillar of the Second Empire, but it is already present here in that only mildly self-mocking portrait of himself dressed up to the nines, and loving it.

The tone is entirely different in letters to Mademoiselle Leroyer de Chantepie, a minor writer, given to religiosity and deep depressions, for whom he formulated advice such as the following: 'Do you know Dr Strauss's *The Life of Jesus*? Now there's a book that makes you think and is substantial! I recommend this reading to you – it's dry but it's interesting in the highest degree' ['Connaissez-vous *La Vie de Jésus* du docteur Strauss? Voilà qui donne à penser et qui est substantiel! Je vous conseille cette lecture aride, mais intéressante au plus haut degré' (Cor. III 352)]. This is Flaubert attempting to enter into a mentality in many ways remote from his own, although whether out of sheer pity or for more practical writerly reasons remains open to conjecture. There was always the possibility that his correspondents could find themselves translated into his novels.

The letters to George Sand let us hear another and more complex voice, sometimes more controlled, hiding his feelings and judgments from her, sometimes bursting out with opinions he knows will scandalise or irritate her, indeed that he puffs up in order to infuriate her. Central to their relationship was a tension built of profound differences in aesthetics and politics, differences that each at times seems to intensify, as if their friendship depended not on feeling at ease together but on knowing that at any moment they risked destroying it through furious arguments. Thus Flaubert snorts in rage when Sand recommends he spend more time with Hugo, as though there could be anything in common between them, either as individuals or writers:

> You advise me, in one of your latest letters, to spend time with old Hugo! Well, he filled me with *despair* the last time I saw him! You can't imagine what stupid things he said about *Goethe*, believing for instance that he wrote *The Camp of Walstein* and attributing *Elective Affinities* to Ancillon! He's never heard about Goethe's *Prometheus* and considered *Faust* a feeble work! The visit literally made me sick!

> [Vous me conseillez, dans une de vos dernières lettres, de fréquenter le père Hugo! Eh bien! il m'a *désolé* la dernière fois que je l'ai vu. Ce qu'il a dit de sottises sur *Goethe* est inimaginable, croyant par exemple qu'il a fait *Le Camp de Walstein*, et attribuant *Les Affinités électives* à Ancillon! n'ayant jamais entendu parler du *Prométhée* et trouvant *Faust* une œuvre faible! Cette visite m'a rendu littéralement malade! (Cor. IV 916)]

She even took it into her head at one point to advise him to get married. Maybe she preferred him cross to lethargic.

He is perhaps at his least guarded in writing to his niece Caroline, late in his life, after most of his closest male friends have died. To her alone perhaps could he have written this confession, in which she may well have recognised a complaint that to be eased needed merely to be expressed: 'I've spent my life depriving my heart of the most legitimate nourishment. I've led a hardworking and austere existence. Well, I can't bear it any more; I feel I'm at the end of my tether!' ['J'ai passé ma vie à priver mon cœur des pâtures les plus légitimes. J'ai mené une existence laborieuse et austère. Eh bien! je n'en peux plus! je me sens à bout!' (Cor. IV 932)] But of course, as his letters reveal, that hardworking and austere existence was not just what he chose, but also what delighted him, and however much he may grumble and protest about it, such complaints are also part of a pleasure that was for him the most essential of nourishments. Writing, fiction or letters, is fundamental to his sense of self and to his interpretation of existence.

It seems certainly to have been the case that sharing the specific delight of reading, for example, is not just a means of discussing what is most central to his personality but also the most satisfying way to reveal it to himself. Indeed, the desire to communicate with friends is often conveyed in terms of reading, of writers he and his correspondent admire or despise, or of newly discovered works. He gives his correspondent not just tips about whom to read but above all insights into what these writers and these works mean to Flaubert himself. Despite the grumbles to his niece, books remain throughout his life the most legitimate of nourishments. An early letter to his friend Ernest Chevalier is typical in this regard: 'I've almost finished Rousseau's *Confessions*. I encourage you strongly to read this admirable work. That's where you'll find the true school of style' ['J'ai presque fini les *Confessions* de Rousseau. Je t'engage fort à lire cette œuvre admirable, c'est là la vraie école de style' (Cor. I 30: cf. Cor. I 29)], and a few lines later: 'My Rabelais is bursting with notes and commentaries – philosophical, philological, bacchic, erectile etc.' ['Mon Rabelais est tout bourré de notes et commentaires philosophiques, philologiques, bachiques, bandatiques, etc.' (Cor. I 30-1)]. Books are read not just for pleasure – although they clearly provide that – but as stylistic models and as stimulators of thought. His bedside books, he tells Louis de Cormenin in the 1840s, include Montaigne, Rabelais, Régnier, La Bruyère and Le Sage, above all Homer and Shakespeare ('Homer and Shakespeare – everything's there!' ['Homère et Shakespeare, tout est là!' (Cor. I 210)]) In 1852 we see him recalling very early experiences with books when he tells Louise Colet that he rediscovers all his origins in 'the book I knew by heart before I could read, *Don Quixote*' ['le livre que je savais par cœur avant de savoir lire, *Don Quichotte*' (Cor. II 111)]. A decade later, Don Quixote is still riding through the plains of Flaubert's imagination, as he writes to the Russian novelist Tourgueniev: 'Just as, when I read *Don Quixote*, I would like to ride along a road that is white with dust and eat olives and raw onions in the shade of a cliff, so your *Scenes of Russian Life* make me long to be shaken along on a telega through fields covered with snow, the howls of wolves in my ears' ['De même que quand je lis *Don Quichotte* je voudrais aller à cheval sur une route blanche de poussière et manger des olives et des oignons crus à l'ombre d'un rocher, vos *Scènes de la vie russe* me donnent envie d'être secoué en télègue au milieu des champs couverts de neige, en entendant des loups aboyer' (Cor. III 310)]. Flaubert's insistence on the concentrated essence of a book's nature and its power to transform the space around him suggests the intense interpenetration of his reading and his experience of existence. While the plastic arts occasionally act on him in similar ways – most notably in the case of Brueghel's painting of the temptation of Saint Anthony – both his temperament and the reclusive life he led made literature his central medium for understanding life, and in writing about books, he is also sharing with his correspondent the central core of his personality.

Situating himself within a chosen intellectual and especially emotional context, created to a large extent by books, is something that both comes naturally to him and that he has deliberately built up, as a letter of 1846 suggests, although it should be added that this letter seems more restrained, less spontaneous than many to closer friends:

> To live, I won't say happily (that aim is a deadly illusion) but calmly, you have to create for yourself outside of the visible existence we all share, another existence which is internal and inaccessible to anything belonging to the domain of the contingent, as the philosophers say. Happy those who have spent their hours pinning insects onto sheets of cork or contemplating through a magnifying glass the rusted medallions of Roman emperors! When you can combine that with a little poetry and enthusiasm, you should give thanks to heaven for making you like that.
>
> [Pour vivre, je ne dirai pas heureux (ce but est une illusion funeste) mais tranquille, il faut se créer en dehors de l'existence visible, commune et générale à tous, une autre existence interne et inaccessible à ce qui rentre dans le domaine du contingent, comme disent les philosophes. Heureux les gens qui ont passé leurs heures à piquer des insectes sur des feuilles de liège ou à contempler avec une loupe les médailles rouillées des empereurs romains! Quand il se mêle à cela un peu de poésie ou d'entrain, on doit remercier le ciel de vous avoir fait ainsi naître. (Cor. I 271)]

Emma Bovary and Frédéric Moreau were to be the insects he pinned on sheets of cork, the medallions on which he gazed with his brilliantly deflating

magnifying glass. In this letter, Flaubert speaks in terms of poetry and enthusiasm, but other letters are more forthright in expressing levels of intensity
well beyond this, an intensity that is profoundly and unmistakably erotic.

What is more, the letters reveal how closely related to the erotic experience
of reading, for Flaubert, is that of writing. As Janet Beizer has pointed out,[4]
Flaubert's letters to the poet Louise Colet, with whom he had a lengthy love
affair at the time he was writing *Madame Bovary*, rapidly shift from expressions of passion for her, to explorations of a passion for writing, a passion,
moreover, frequently conveyed in terms that are not just strongly physical but
also clearly sexual. The gendered nature of his image of style is a dominant
feature of his thinking. 'What I like above anything else is a sentence that
is sinewy, substantial, clear, with bulging muscles and a tanned skin: I love
male sentences and not female ones like those Lamartine very often writes,
or, to a lesser degree, Villemain' ['J'aime par-dessus tout la phrase nerveuse,
substantielle, claire, au muscle saillant, à la peau bistrée: j'aime les phrases
mâles et non les phrases femelles comme celles de Lamartine fort souvent et,
à un degré inférieur, celles de Villemain' (Cor. I 1210)], he records in 1844,
using a terminology so intrinsic to the time in which he was living that he
clearly does not subject it to any kind of critical assessment. He is, after all, a
man of a profoundly misogynistic age, in which what it was to be masculine
or feminine was taken both as axiomatic and immutable, and extended into
every aspect of a person's behaviour and existence. Few writers, however, are
on record as having taken this imagery as far as Flaubert in its application to
writing, pushing the act and process to extreme physiological lengths. This is
partly because his own responses to writing affected him physiologically, or
at least in ways he believed he could express only in such metaphors: 'Style,
which is something I take to heart, shakes my nerves up horribly, it enrages
me and gnaws at me' ['Le style, qui est une chose que je prends à cœur m'agite
les nerfs horriblement, je me dépite, je me ronge' (Cor. I 475)], he complains
to Louise Colet. 'The vulgarity of my subject sometimes makes me want to
vomit' ['La vulgarité de mon sujet me donne parfois des nausées' (Cor. II
382)], he asserts later, again to Colet. Much later still he grumbles to George
Sand, whose physical and emotional struggles to make time for the writing
that was essential to keep her family from poverty Flaubert seems either not
to have known or to have refused to believe: '*You* don't know what it's like
to spend an entire day with your head in your hands squeezing your poor
head to find a word' ['Vous ne savez pas, vous, ce que c'est que de rester
toute une journée la tête dans ses deux mains à pressurer sa malheureuse tête
pour trouver un mot' (Cor. III 566)]. Not living on the rents from land that
she owned, she probably did not, if only because it was a luxury she could
not afford.

Amidst the moaning, there is clearly a sense of choice and satisfaction. In a letter to Colet in 1852, Flaubert insists that ever since his earliest attempts at writing, when he had to ask his nurse how to spell out the sentences he dreamt up, he has pursued a straight line (Cor. II 110), and when he speaks of himself as a clown and acrobat, the image he appears to have most sharply in mind is of the tight-rope walker, sticking through thick and thin to a narrow rope stretched taut before him. 'The basis of my nature, whatever people might say, is the acrobat. In my childhood and youth I was madly in love with the boards. I would perhaps have been a great actor if heaven had ordained that I be born poor' ['Le fond de ma nature est, quoi qu'on dise, le saltimbanque. J'ai eu dans mon enfance et ma jeunesse un amour effréné des planches. J'aurais été peut-être un grand acteur si le ciel m'avait fait naître plus pauvre' (Cor. I 278)]. It is an image he transfers to *Madame Bovary* more specifically when he asserts that 'the whole merit of my book, if it has any, will be to have succeeded in walking straight along a hair, hanging between the double abyss of lyricism and vulgarity' ['toute la valeur de mon livre, s'il en a une, sera d'avoir su marcher droit sur un cheveu, suspendu entre le double abîme du lyrisme et du vulgaire' (Cor. II 57)]. The straight line of his direction is compared, with increasing exasperation, to the curves and arabesques of Colet's style. The representation of Colet's style as physiologically feminine is startling in its intensity and in the implicit value it places on standards consistently judged masculine. 'Pull in, tighten the breasts of your heart, show it as muscle and not as a gland' ['Rentre, resserre, comprime les seins de ton cœur, qu'on y voie des muscles et non une glande' (Cor. II 304)] he exhorts her, in an image whose bad taste might seem to border on the parodic were it not repeated with slight alterations at various points in their correspondence. It should perhaps be said that he was far from alone in expressing such sentiments in such terms: Mallarmé, to give only one example, announces in an early poem that the form of the sonnet gives the writer the same pleasant sense of restriction as the ballerina Camargo felt within her corset.[5]

Flaubert's letters are more interesting in the light they shed on literary productivity when they turn away from this baroquely masculine imagery to focus on specific aspects of his own writing. From as early as 1847 we find Flaubert's famously demanding high standards, even when all he is writing is a travelogue:

> At present we're busy writing our journey and although this sort of work demands neither great refinements in its effects nor the preparation of balances among the various parts, I'm so unused to writing and it makes me so bad

tempered, especially towards myself, that it can't fail to cause me concern. It's as if a man with a good ear played his violin out of tune; his fingers just refuse to produce the right sound although that sound is in his head.

[Nous sommes occupés maintenant à écrire notre voyage et quoique ce travail ne demande ni grands raffinements d'effets ni dispositions préalables de masses, j'ai si peu l'habitude d'écrire et je deviens si hargneux là-dessus, surtout vis-à-vis de moi-même, qu'il ne laisse pas que de me donner assez de souci. C'est comme un homme qui a l'oreille juste et qui joue faux du violon; ses doigts se refusent à reproduire juste le son dont il a conscience. (Cor. I 473)]

Yet however much he might protest and moan about his writing, attacking the style he had to produce for *Madame Bovary* for instance, he leaves us in no doubt that work – by which he means both the necessary preparatory reading as well as the act of writing itself – was also not just a great source of pleasure, but the only imaginable way of giving meaning to life: 'Read and don't dream. Plunge into lengthy studies. There's nothing that's constantly good except for the habit of determined work. It gives off an opium that numbs the soul – I've gone through atrocious moments of boredom and spun to and fro in the wind, overcome with *stupefaction*. The only escape is through constancy and pride: try it' ['Lisez et ne rêvez pas. Plongez-vous dans de longues études. Il n'y a de continuellement bon que l'habitude d'un travail entêté. Il s'en dégage un opium qui engourdit l'âme. – J'ai passé par des ennuis atroces et j'ai tournoyé dans le vide, éperdu d'*embêtement*. On s'en sauve à force de constance et d'orgueil: essayez' (Cor. II 3)]. Certainly the image he consistently seeks to give his correspondents and presumably himself is of a man lost in work that may at times seem mere drudgery but that remains essential to his sense of self-definition. 'I've returned to working like a rhinoceros' ['Je me suis remis à travailler comme un rhinocéros' (Cor. III 29)], he writes early in 1852, in a characteristically unlikely metaphor. As if he wants puritanically to claim for himself the status of a real worker, not just someone doing what gave him particular delight, he tends to insist that his current project is not what he would be really comfortable writing. 'Good or bad, this book will have been for me a prodigious tour de force, the style, composition, characters and the *effect it creates* are so far from my natural manner' ['Bon ou mauvais, ce livre aura été pour moi un tour de force prodigieux, tant le style, la composition, les personnages et l'*effet sensible* sont loin de ma manière naturelle' (Cor. II 194)]. Even this sense of working on something essentially alien is integral to an overall aesthetic policy:

The more personal you are, the weaker you are. That's always been my own failing. The fact is I've always put myself into everything I've done. – Instead of Saint Anthony, for example, you'll find me. The temptation was mine and not my reader's. *The less you feel something, the better you can express it as it really is.* [. . .] But you have to have the skill to *make yourself feel it.*

[Plus vous serez personnel, plus vous serez faible. J'ai toujours péché par là, moi; c'est ce que je me suis toujours mis dans tout ce que j'ai fait. – A la place de saint Antoine, par exemple, c'est moi qui y suis. La tentation a été pour moi et non pour le lecteur. – *Moins on sent une chose, plus on est apte à l'exprimer comme elle est.* [. . .] Mais il faut avoir la faculté *de se la faire sentir.*

(Cor. II 127)]

Writing something that is further removed from your own personality, therefore, releases the power that comes from separating yourself from your characters and your subject. Of course he realises that writers cannot completely excise themselves from their works, that characters and scenes must in part be drawn from experience, but he suggests that the way to proceed is to scatter yourself through the characters: 'If you broadcast yourself in all your characters, they will live, and instead of an everlasting declamatory personality, which cannot even be clearly formed, through lack of precise details which will always be absent because of the distortions which disguise it, your readers will see in your books crowds of humans' ['Toi disséminée en tous, tes personnages vivront, et au lieu d'une éternelle personnalité déclamatoire, qui ne peut même se constituer nettement, faute de détails précis qui lui manquent toujours à cause des travestissements qui la déguisent, on verra dans tes œuvres des foules humaines' (Cor. II 61)].

Many of his letters explore the themes, problems and structural difficulties of his novels, making them justifiably famous for the glimpses they provide of the writer's laboratory. In responding to Louise Colet's suggestion that he excise one of the central characters of the first version of *L'Education sentimentale*, for instance, he justifies the need for two central characters by insisting that each of the two would be weakened if isolated since their characteristics stand out only in contrast to each other. (It is a formula the creator of Sherlock Holmes and Dr Watson would have endorsed.) Unsurprisingly, Flaubert's judgment leads to an affirmation of his duality as writer:

In terms of literature there are in me two separate individuals. One of them is in love with howls, lyricism, great flights of the eagle, all the sonorities of the sentence, the summits of thought. The other sifts and digs out truth as much as he can, loves to stress the little fact as powerfully as the great, wants to make you feel almost *materially* the things he reproduces; this is the one who laughs and delights in humanity's animality.

[Il y a en moi, littérairement parlant, deux bonshommes distincts: un qui est épris de *gueulades*, de lyrisme, de grands vols d'aigle, de toutes les sonorités de la phrase et des sommets de l'idée; un autre qui fouille et creuse le vrai tant qu'il peut, qui aime à accuser le petit fait aussi puissamment que le grand, qui voudrait vous faire sentir presque *matériellement* les choses qu'il reproduit; celui-là aime à rire et se plaît dans les animalités de l'homme.   (Cor. II 30)]

If laughter and delight tend to come across less clearly in his letters to Colet, it is mainly because he wants to present a picture of a writer intensely pre-occupied with the great flights of the eagle, but he is also letting off steam, depressurising, after the intensity of the day's work. There are countless variations on the theme of struggling with the medium: 'In the middle of all this I'm moving painfully forward on my book. I'm wasting a consider-able amount of paper. You should see all the crossings out! The sentences are really slow in coming. What a devilish style I've adopted! A curse on simple subjects! If only you knew how much I torture myself, you'd take pity on me' ['Au milieu de tout cela j'avance péniblement dans mon livre. Je gâche un papier considérable. Que de ratures! La phrase est bien lente à venir. Quel diable de style ai-je pris! Honnis soient les sujets simples! Si vous saviez combien je m'y torture, vous auriez pitié de moi' (Cor. II 16)]. Which she does of course, not realising that what she reads as an invi-tation to come and comfort him is merely the desire to get the com-plaint off his chest, safe in the thought that she will pity him at a suitable distance.

If there are all those crossings out, if the sentences come so slowly, it is in part because of his conviction that 'the entire talent of writing lies only, after all, in the choice of words. It's the preciseness that provides the strength' ['tout le talent d'écrire ne consiste après tout que dans le choix des mots. C'est la précision qui fait la force' (Cor. II 137)]. His sense of searching for, and being satisfied only with, the right word marks his angry reply to the critic Sainte-Beuve's finicky review of *Salammbô*: 'Mâtho prowls *like a madman* around Carthage. Madman is the right word. Wasn't love as the Ancients conceived of it a madness, a curse, an illness sent by the gods?' ['Mâtho rôde *comme un fou* autour de Carthage. Fou est le mot juste. L'amour tel que le concevaient les Anciens n'était-il pas une folie, une malédiction, une maladie envoyée par les dieux?' (Cor. III 277)]

Getting the facts down rather than losing them in metaphors is also prob-lematic, another aspect of the need for preciseness: 'I had to do one of the most nimble, psychologico-nervy passages, and I was continually going astray in metaphors, instead of getting the facts down' ['J'avais à faire un pas-sage psychologico-nerveux des plus déliés, et je me perdais continuellement dans les métaphores, au lieu de préciser les faits' (Cor. II 514)], he chastises himself at one point in almost Gradgrindian tones (Gradgrind is the character in Charles Dickens's *Hard Times* whose obsession with facts rather than feelings leads to tragedy). It is a preciseness, moreover, that arises from showing rather than telling, obliging the reader to extract from the scene the tone, emotion, and suggestions embedded in it. Here he is, attempting to convey to Colet a narrative position radically different from the authorial omniscience of Balzac or Hugo:

> Tonight, using a new plan, I began yet again my wretched page about the Chinese lanterns, which I've already written four times. It's enough to make you beat your brains out on the wall! It's a matter of depicting (in one page) the gradations of enthusiasm felt by a crowd as they watch a chap who is setting up a succession of Chinese lanterns on the façade of the town hall. The reader has to see the crowd yelling with astonishment and joy, and *all this without any element of caricature* or any reflections on the part of the author.

> [Ce soir, j'ai encore recommencé sur un nouveau plan ma maudite page des lampions que j'ai déjà écrite quatre fois. Il y a de quoi se casser la tête contre le mur! Il s'agit (en une page) de peindre les gradations d'enthousiasme d'une multitude à propos d'un bonhomme qui, sur la façade d'une mairie, place successivement plusieurs lampions. Il faut qu'on voie la foule gueuler d'étonnement et de joie; et *cela sans charge* ni réflexions de l'auteur.

(Cor. II 444)]

Despite all his wrestling with this episode, Flaubert, unable to complete it to his satisfaction, abandoned it, making this passage just one of many ghosts that flicker around the edges of his novels, like so many Chinese lanterns.

Added to these questions of style and narrative viewpoint are problems arising from the structure of his novels. Acutely aware of the dual necessities of balance and progress within the narrative, he wrote despairingly to Louis Bouilhet late in 1853 when he had finished rereading the second part of his manuscript of *Madame Bovary*:

> The worst of the matter is that the preparations – psychological, picturesque, grotesque etc. – that pave the way, because they are very long, *demand*, or so I think, a development in the action that would be commensurate with them. The Prologue must not carry the Narrative away with it (however disguised and diluted the Narrative might be) and I'm going to have a real struggle to establish a more or less equal proportion between the Adventures and the Thoughts.

> [Le pire de la chose est: que les préparatifs psychologiques, pittoresques, grotesques, etc., qui précèdent, étant fort longs, *exigent*, je crois, un développement d'action qui soit en rapport avec eux. Il ne faut pas que le Prologue emporte le

Récit (quelque déguisé et fondu que soit le Récit), et j'aurai fort à faire, pour établir une proportion à peu près égale entre les Aventures et les Pensées.

(Cor. II 472)]

And again in August 1866, when he's struggling with the broad canvas of *L'Education sentimentale* with its crowds of students, artists, businessmen and revolutionaries, we find him facing similar difficulties: 'I want to portray a psychological state which I believe to be accurate and which hasn't yet been described. But my characters are placed in a setting so copious and teeming that at every line there's a risk they'll disappear. So I'm forced to push back into the middle distance precisely those things that are the most interesting' ['Je veux représenter un état psychologique – vrai selon moi – et non encore décrit. Mais le milieu où mes personnages s'agitent est tellement copieux et grouillant qu'ils manquent, à chaque ligne, d'y disparaître. Je suis donc obligé de reculer à un plan secondaire les choses qui sont précisément les plus intéressantes' (Cor. III 518)].

Later in life, he would reconsider the overriding importance of the plan. He concludes of *L'Education sentimentale* that it was not as successful as he had hoped because it was too true, its plan so well constructed that it disappeared: 'Every work of art', he concludes, 'has to have a point, a summit, make a pyramid, or else a ray of light striking on a point of the head. Well nothing like that happens in life. But Art isn't Nature. No matter! I believe that no one has pushed integrity as far as I have' ['Toute œuvre d'art doit avoir un point, un sommet, faire la pyramide, ou bien la lumière doit frapper sur un point de la boule. Or rien de tout cela dans la vie. Mais l'Art n'est pas la Nature. N'importe! je crois que personne n'a poussé la probité plus loin' (CHH XVI 258)]. But even for so great a lover of Rabelais as Flaubert, the novel conceived as baggy monster was anathema. Dickens's great, undisciplined, comic novel *The Pickwick Papers* was unable to lighten his spirit in the dark days that followed the defeat by the Prussians, Napoleon III's abdication, and the horrors of the Paris Commune. On 12 July 1872 he gave the following jaundiced view of the novel: 'It has some superb bits, but what a faulty composition. All the English writers are like that, with the exception of W. Scott. They don't have a plan! We Latins can't bear that!' ['Il y a des parties superbes; mais quelle composition défectueuse. Tous les écrivains anglais sont là, W. Scott excepté. Ils manquent de plan! cela est insupportable pour nous autres Latins!' (Cor. IV 547)]

By the time he wrote that response to English literature, he had other matters than writing on his mind. His world was beginning to crumble around him, with the death of friends; the collapse of the Empire, which for all his professions of disdain for the bourgeoisie gave him the esteem he craved;

and the sudden intrusion of financial problems brought about partly by the political situation and partly by injudicious speculation on the part of his niece's husband. Moreover, he was mired in the endless research required for *Bouvard et Pécuchet*, which he would leave unfinished at his death. Writing to his friend Edma Roger des Genettes in 1872, he explained: 'It's the story of those two fellows who copy things out, a kind of farcical critical encyclopaedia. I imagine you get the idea. To do it, I'll have to study a lot of things I know nothing about: chemistry, medicine, agriculture' ['C'est l'histoire de ces deux bonshommes qui copient, une espèce d'encyclopédie critique en farce. Vous devez en avoir une idée? Pour cela, il va me falloir étudier beaucoup de choses que j'ignore: la chimie, la médecine, l'agriculture' (Cor. IV 559)]. In the late autumn of that year, he refers again, in tones of dull discouragement, to the preparation demanded by *Bouvard et Pécuchet*: 'I read things that are very hard, I watch the rain falling and I make conversation with my dog, and then the next day it's the same thing. In a word, I'm becoming a stupid animal' ['Je lis des choses très dures, je regarde la pluie tomber et je fais la conversation avec mon chien, et puis le lendemain c'est la même chose. Bref je deviens un sot animal' (Cor. IV 612)].

The final volumes of the correspondence exude a sadness and a sense of having grown old before his time. Flaubert was, after all, not quite fifty when the Empire collapsed, but his letters are steeped in a world-weariness that suggests someone far older. He was profoundly affected by the death of his dear friend Louis Bouilhet, on whose poetry he had bestowed so much supportive criticism and for whose plays he would spend long days in the theatre in a vain attempt to guarantee success. Their friendship dated from 1846, and Bouilhet's death left him feeling amputated, as though he had lost a large part of himself (Cor. IV 77). His letters to Bouilhet suggest a remarkably close and relaxed friendship, a relationship that reveals none of the tensions that are evident in the letters, say, to George Sand, none of the guardedness that comes across when he writes to such authors as Gautier or Zola, whom of course he knew far less well. A letter written from Cairo in December 1849, full of gusto, puns and tenderness, suggests something of the nature of this friendship, something, too, of the devastating loss that Bouilhet's death would inflict on his long-time friend: 'I'll start, my dear old friend, by embracing your good head and blowing onto this sheet of paper all the *inspiration* that I can to make *your spirit* come towards me. What's more, I'm sure you must be thinking very hard about us because *we* are thinking very hard about you and a hundred times a day we wish you were here' ['Je commence, mon cher vieux, par embrasser ta bonne tête et par souffler sur ce papier toute *l'inspiration* possible pour que *ton esprit* vienne vers moi. Je crois, du reste, que tu penses bougrement à nous, car nous pensons, nous autres, bougrement à toi, et cent fois dans la journée nous te regrettons' (Cor. I 536)].

There had been other painful losses in Flaubert's life, including the deaths of his sister Caroline in 1846 and his close friend Alfred Le Poittevin barely two years later. But the series of deaths in the late 1860s and 1870s found him less resilient, affected him more profoundly, as he felt himself grow old in a world that appeared increasingly alien to him. Writing to Princesse Mathilde on 28 October 1872, after the death of the poet and novelist Théophile Gautier, his sadness seems particularly intense: 'there have been too many deaths, too many one after the other! I've never cared much for life, but the threads that bind me to it are snapping one by one. Soon there won't be any left' ['voilà trop de morts, trop de morts coup sur coup! Je n'ai jamais beaucoup tenu à la vie, mais les fils qui m'y rattachent se brisent les uns après les autres. Bientôt il n'y en aura plus' (Cor. IV 597)].

A few weeks later, Léonie Brainne receives an even more dispirited summary: 'I'm still not feeling joyful. Why? The departure of all my friends, the stupidity of the public, my fiftieth birthday, loneliness and some worries about money, those are probably the causes' ['[Je] continue à n'être pas gai. Pourquoi? Tous les amis disparus, la bêtise publique, la cinquantaine, la solitude et quelques soucis d'argent, voilà les causes, sans doute?' (Cor. IV 612)] It is a formula he finds satisfactory enough to repeat to Princesse Mathilde, slightly more honed this time: 'The isolation building up around me, my discouragement with my literary plans, the disgust I feel towards my contemporaries, my over-stretched nerves, my fiftieth birthday behind me, worries about my future, that's my balance sheet. I'm not joyful, that's all I can say' ['L'isolement qui se fait autour de moi, le découragement littéraire, le dégoût que m'inspirent mes contemporains, les nerfs qui se tendent trop, la cinquantaine sonnée et les inquiétudes d'avenir, voilà mon bilan. Je ne suis pas gai, voilà tout ce que je peux dire' (Cor. IV 617)]. His early letters show that he had always preferred isolation, but an isolation he could choose to break by visiting friends or writing to them, not one enforced by the death of those friends. The intelligence of his contemporaries had never inspired him with enthusiasm, indeed, his dictionary of clichés reveals that he derived considerable pleasure from accumulating examples of their stupidity, but what has changed is his perception of the level of power allotted to the masses with the ousting of the Empire and the inception of the Republic. But then, it's hardly worth protesting about the general stupidity: you may as well rage against the rain, he tells Caroline (CHH XVI 333). Writing to his niece on 24 October 1870, after Napoleon III, defeated in the battle of Sedan, had abdicated, and while Paris was occupied by the Prussian army, Flaubert gloomily predicted, as if what was at issue was not the potential destruction of a nation but a shift of attention away from the finer things of life: 'We are about to enter into a time of darkness. People will no longer think of anything but the military arts' ['Nous allons entrer dans une époque de ténèbres. On ne pensera plus qu'à l'art militaire' (Cor. IV 253)].

As the decade progressed his letters would give vent to political convictions that are increasingly reactionary, as a letter to George Sand suggests, with its demand for a

> . . . government of mandarins, provided that the mandarins know something and even that they know a great many things. The populace is an eternal minor, and will always be (in the hierarchy of social elements) on the lowest rank, because it is number, mass, the unlimited. What does it matter that many peasants know how to read and don't listen to their priest any more? What does matter infinitely is that many men like Renan and Littré should live and *be listened to*. Our salvation now lies only with a *legitimate aristocracy*.

> [. . . gouvernement de mandarins, pourvu que les mandarins sachent quelque chose, et même qu'ils sachent beaucoup de choses. Le peuple est un éternel mineur, et il sera toujours (dans la hiérarchie des éléments sociaux) au dernier rang, puisqu'il est le nombre, la masse, l'illimité. Peu importe que beaucoup de paysans sachent lire et n'écoutent plus leur curé, mais il importe infiniment que beaucoup d'hommes, comme Renan ou Littré, puissent vivre et *soient écoutés*. Notre salut n'est, maintenant, que dans une *aristocratie légitime*.

(Cor. IV 314)]

And yet the final decade of his life did see new friendships develop and brought him closer to old friends. There are rich exchanges with Guy de Maupassant and Ivan Tourgueniev, he is still reading Shakespeare ('that revives you and puts air back into your lungs' ['cela vous retrempe et vous remet de l'air dans les poumons' (CHH XV 429)]), and he can find pleasure in the publications of his contemporaries, works like Daudet's sad tale of childhood, *Jack*, and Zola's fierce political satire, *Son Excellence Eugène Rougon*. George Sand's death in June 1876 made him feel as if he had lost his mother a second time, and yet, as he admits to Tourgueniev, two days after the funeral he was back at Croisset and in fine form, delighting in the greenness, the trees and the solitude (CHH XV 460). And by late July a letter from his attractive and accommodating friend Léonie Brainne, describing the sights that regale her while on her slimming cure, not only prompts a lusty response but unexpectedly points forward to his finest work of short fiction, *Un cœur simple*: 'You send me some terrific descriptions of breasts and backsides! enough to make you want to sit on some and fear being crushed by others! how can it be that people who love fat women don't go and live in Marienbad? [. . .] Do you know *who* I have had before me, on my table, for the last three weeks? A stuffed parrot' ['Vous m'envoyez de chouettes descriptions de poitrines et de derrières! c'est à désirer s'asseoir sur les unes et on a peur d'être écrasé par les autres! comment se fait-il que les gens qui aiment les grosses femmes n'aillent pas s'établir à Marienbad? [. . .] Savez-vous *qui* j'ai devant moi sur ma table, depuis trois semaines? un perroquet empaillé' (CHH xv 476)].

Reading Flaubert's correspondence brings startlingly alive a man of enormous complexity, of remarkable appetites and debilitating lethargies, a knotted network of prejudices, insights, blind spots, passions and ambitions. His fulminations against middle-class hypocrisy and snobbery did not prevent him relishing the lionising he received under Napoleon III's empire. Similarly, his letters suggest that his expressions of disgust and dissatisfaction with his writing are an intricate part of his need to write and the pleasure he took in it. What makes the correspondence so compelling is precisely this complexity, this richness, and above all this sense of vitality. The last letter he wrote to Guy de Maupassant is typical in this regard:

> Next week bring me the list of idiots who do so-called literary reviews, in the papers. Then we'll draw up our 'batteries'. But bear in mind that good Horace's old maxim: *Oderunt poetas.*
>
> And then the World Fair!! Dear me!! I'm already bored to tears. It craps me off in advance. I'm throwing up in anticipation.
>
> [. . .]
>
> You'll see me at the beginning of next week.

> [La semaine prochaine apporte-moi la liste des idiots qui font des comptes rendus soi-disant littéraires, dans les feuilles. Alors nous dresserons 'nos batteries'. Mais souviens-toi de cette vieille maxime du bon Horace: *Oderunt poetas.*
>
> Et puis l'Exposition!! Monsieur!! J'en suis scié déjà! Elle m'em . . . d'avance. J'en dégueule d'ennui, par anticipation.
>
> [. . .]
>
> Tu me verras au commencement de la semaine prochaine. (CHH xvi 361)]

Who but Flaubert can get so much enjoyment out of the mere anticipation of tearing critics to shreds and being bored to tears by an event the mass of humanity looks forward to?

Alas, by the beginning of the following week, Flaubert was dead.

NOTES

1 Among the numerous studies of the correspondence, either considered separately or as part of Flaubert's overall production, see Albert Thibaudet, *Gustave Flaubert* (Paris: Gallimard, 1963 [1935]); Suzanne Toulet, *Le Sentiment religieux chez Flaubert d'après sa correspondance* (Montreal: Editions Cosmos, 1970);

Raymonde Debray-Genette and Jacques Neefs, eds., *L'Œuvre de l'œuvre: études sur la correspondance de Flaubert* (Saint-Denis: Presses Universitaires de Vincennes, 1993); and Thierry Poyet, *Pour une esthétique de Flaubert d'après sa correspondance* (Saint-Pierre-du-Mont: Eurédit, 2000). Charles Carlut's *La Correspondance de Flaubert: étude et répertoire critique* (Columbus: Ohio State University Press, 1968) is a useful compendium.

2 Julian Barnes, *Something to Declare* (London: Picador, 2002), p. 195. This collection includes several of Barnes's reviews of Flaubert's correspondence, as well as reviews of a biography of Louise Colet, and of Chabrol's film version of *Madame Bovary*.

3 See for example, *Correspondance: Gustave Flaubert–Guy de Maupassant*, texte établi, préfacé et annoté par Yvan Leclerc (Paris: Flammarion, 1993) and *Gustave Flaubert, Ivan Tourguéniev: correspondance*, texte édité, préfacé et annoté par Alexandre Zviguilsky (Paris: Flammarion, 1989).

4 See her chapter on Flaubert's letters to Louise Colet in Janet L. Beizer, *Ventriloquized Bodies. Narratives of Hysteria in Nineteenth-Century France* (Ithaca and London: Cornell University Press, 1994), pp. 77–98.

5 Stéphane Mallarmé, *Œuvres poétiques complètes*, ed. Carl Barbier and Gordon Millan (Paris: Flammarion, 1983), p. 77.

6

ANNE GREEN

History and its representation in Flaubert's work

'I love history, madly. I find the dead more agreeable than the living. Where does the seductiveness of the past come from?' ['J'aime l'histoire, follement. Les morts m'agréent plus que les vivants. D'où vient cette séduction du passé?' (Cor. III 95)] The fascination with history that Flaubert evokes in this letter of 1860 lasted throughout his life and colours all his work. Although at first sight his writings may seem to fall neatly into two categories – those set firmly in the France of his own time (*Madame Bovary*, both versions of *L'Education sentimentale*, *Un cœur simple*, *Bouvard et Pécuchet*) and those set in the distant past (most of his juvenilia, *Salammbô*, *La Tentation de saint Antoine*, *La Légende de saint Julien l'Hospitalier*, *Hérodias*) – this chapter will argue that a concern with the past, and how we make sense of it, runs through all of them. If he was seduced by the past, Flaubert also recognised that historians, like novelists, must sift and shape their material and find a perspective through which to view and reconstruct the world. He was acutely aware of the fluid and subjective nature of history, and his gradually evolving views on how to represent the historical past are fundamental to his conception of the creative process.

Flaubert first became interested in historical fiction through the theatre. The letters he wrote between the ages of eleven and fourteen to his friend Ernest Chevalier frequently refer to the plays he was reading, writing, performing, or going to see at the local theatre in Rouen. Many of these were historical dramas, much in vogue in the 1830s – works such as Alexandre Dumas's *Catherine Howard*, Victor Herbin's *Jeanne de Flandre*, Casimir Delavigne's *Les Enfants d'Edouard*, Victor Hugo's *Marion de Lorme* and *Ruy Blas*. This exposure to historical drama coloured Flaubert's first experiments in creative writing. The historical pieces – both drama and prose fiction – which he wrote up to 1838 repeat many of the commonplaces of the Romantic stage: dramatic duels, assassinations, power struggles, intrigue, disguise, mistaken identity, violence and bloodshed. Royalty or members of the nobility play the central roles while the common people – poor, stupid and gullible, scorned by their rulers – are relegated to the background. These early works such as *Dernière Scène de la mort de Marguerite de Bourgogne* (1835), *Un secret de Philippe le Prudent* (1836), or the five-act play *Loys XI* (1838), have little depth or originality and are not based on rigorous historical documentation. They are simply a schoolboy's colourful and lively attempts to emulate the much-admired dramatic style of writers like Hugo and Dumas.

At school Flaubert was fortunate to have the distinguished historian Adolphe Chéruel as history master. Chéruel, a former pupil of the great historian Jules Michelet and later a Professor at the Ecole Normale Supérieure in Paris, not only taught Flaubert at the Collège Royal de Rouen (where he won several prizes in history) but also gave him private lessons every week. The period spent under Chéruel's tuition (1835–9) was probably crucial in stimulating his interest and starting to form his critical faculties. Chéruel was known for inculcating the need for rigour, precision and the fearless pursuit of truth into his students, and undoubtedly Flaubert's own historical training was founded on similar principles. Chéruel showed him the need for a certain critical distance. Yet Flaubert clearly felt a deeply emotional response to the past. As he confided to his private journal in 1841, he sometimes experienced such clear 'historical revelations' that he believed he might have witnessed them himself in a previous life (OJ 738). That sense was acute when he visited Italy in 1845 and was profoundly moved by his contact with classical antiquity; his sense of affinity with certain historical figures made him feel he had once lived in the Rome of Nero or Caesar. But Chéruel's training had insisted that a personal, emotional response to the historical past must be tempered by intellectual rigour, and above all by a recognition of the need for a broad sweep of background information in order to build up a composite picture of a period in all its complexity. Flaubert's writing would constantly return to this tension between scholarship and emotional engagement.

It is a tension that he reflects on in the *Education sentimentale* of 1845 as he describes the gradually evolving ideas of his central character, Jules. Initially, Jules's attraction to the historical past is purely emotional. Dissatisfied with the meanness of the present, he revels in dreams of the excesses of antiquity – extravagant passions and intense conflicts played out against the exotic backgrounds of Egypt, Greece and Rome. Yet he recognises this as an indulgent form of escapism, and moves on from passionate identification with figures from the past to a more analytical perspective. He finds that the more he analyses the past, the more abstract it becomes: ignoring the detail in order to arrive at an overarching view, he is disconcerted by particulars that contradict one another or fail to fit his vision. As time goes on, Jules's approach to history changes once more: what had initially seemed confusing or jarring gradually fades as a pattern emerges from the chaos of the past. He becomes aware that the same ideas and the same crises periodically return in a chain of cause and effect so evident that it seems to have been planned in advance – the historical process resembles, for him, a constantly developing organism that appears to work to a regular pattern.

In Jules's musings one can see Flaubert investigating fundamental theoretical issues of historiography, exploring ideas and rejecting some, adopting others. In particular the view of history as a series of repetitions, inevitable because human nature never changes, was to become an essential and lasting element in Flaubert's view of the historical process. The more history Jules reads, the more he finds his old prejudices and preconceptions about past ages being undermined, and he comes to recognise the infinite complexity of human nature as something that does not change with the passing centuries. He takes delight in discovering weaknesses in great men of the past, or traces of greatness in those remembered for their failings: in this he sees the workings of a levelling justice that moderates both pride and humiliation, and restores man to his natural stature.

The benefits of recognising one's own behaviour in the reassuring perspective of a broad historical context can come, Jules believes, only from the study of 'pure' history. He complains of the inadequacies of historical fiction compared to the work of historians. Historical facts are diminished when selected and manipulated by a novelist who starts off with a preconceived idea and adjusts men and facts to fit, for this will produce a false and lifeless piece of fiction that will pale before the rich complexity of history itself. Here we can see Flaubert engaging with an ongoing contemporary debate about the relative merits of history and historical fiction. Alfred de Vigny, for example, had argued in 'Réflexions sur la vérité dans l'art', first published as a preface to the fourth edition (1829) of *Cinq-Mars*, that the historical novel could show the hidden movements of history and suggest causes and trace their outcome in a way that was closed to the historian. Whereas historians had to rely on already existing material and reproduce 'le vrai' (or what is known to have taken place), novelists with their greater creative freedom could produce 'la vérité', a poetic interpretation of what might have or ought to have happened. In art, said Vigny, probability was far more important than truth. It is, however, indicative of Flaubert's unease about the state of the historical novel at this time that he should present Jules as favouring history rather than historical fiction, and it is a debate to which the characters of his subsequent novels repeatedly return. The ambiguous relationship between history and fiction will later be actively explored – with different emphases and priorities – by Frédéric in *L'Education sentimentale* and by Bouvard and Pécuchet as they try to compose their own historical creations.

Jules comes to acknowledge that although he may have learned to reject received ideas about history, posterity will always select and simplify the events of the past. If history is to be remembered at all, it will inevitably be recalled in a partial and distorted way. Yet perhaps Jules's most crucial insight – one that has great significance for Flaubert's subsequent work – is his recognition that those distortions are significant in themselves, because they tell us something about the people and the period that produced them:

> But those who come after, who see everything in outline and want clear-cut opinions that can be summed up in one word, do not have time to think about everything they have rejected or forgotten or omitted; they have grasped only the outstanding features of events, and then, risking incoherence or absurdity, have combined them into one attribute and melded them into a single expression. Jules narrowly missed going to the opposite extreme, because of seeing every day the faulty judgments, silly enthusiasms and stupid hatred of the masses. He would have admired what they despised and loathed what delighted them, had he not seen that there was generally some basic practical usefulness for the future in all the approximately right ideas they formed about the past. Those ideas do have their own intrinsic importance, since they produce facts in their turn. What does it matter if people misunderstood Sparta in 1793, as long as they believed they were imitating it?

> [Mais la postérité, qui contemple tout de profil et qui veut des opinions bien nettes pour les faire tenir dans un mot, n'a pas le temps de songer à tout ce qu'elle a repoussé, oublié, omis – elle a saisi seulement les traits saillants des choses, puis au risque d'incohérence ou d'absurdité elle les a réunis sous un seul trait et fondus dans une seule expression. Jules faillit tomber dans l'excès contraire; à force de voir chaque jour la fausseté des jugements de la foule, la niaiserie de ses admirations, et la bêtise de ses haines, il aurait admiré ce qu'elle méprise et détesté ce qui la charme s'il n'y avait pas vu, le plus souvent, un fond d'utilité pratique pour l'avenir à toutes les idées plus ou moins justes qu'elle se fait sur le passé. Ces idées ont bien leur importance en elles-mêmes puisqu'à leur tour elles produisent des faits. Qu'importe que 93 ait mal compris Sparte pourvu qu'il ait cru l'imiter? (OJ 1037)]

The realisation not merely that our idea of the past is subjective and constantly changing, but that the erasure and distortion to which the past is subject is of interest in itself, and has its own value, was a radical departure that would shape Flaubert's approach to writing. Willing to see beyond the need for historical accuracy, he recognised that creative 'misunderstandings' of the past could open up new literary possibilities.

In September 1849 Flaubert finished what was to be the first of three versions of *La Tentation de saint Antoine*, and invited his friends Maxime Du Camp and Louis Bouilhet to listen to him read it aloud. Neither knew quite what to expect, but knowing of Flaubert's extensive researches into oriental antiquity and the history of religion, Bouilhet was sure that *La Tentation* would be a detailed reconstruction of the ancient world in the third century. He expected a scholarly examination of the relationship between the rise of the early Christian church and the collapse of the Roman Empire.[1] But as Bouilhet soon discovered, Flaubert's account of the myriad heretics, fantastical beasts and gods which dominate Antoine's visions is far removed from conventional history. What *La Tentation* does, however, is to take the relativism that marked Jules's views on history to an extreme; by transforming his documentation on ancient Oriental heresies and religions into Antoine's hallucinations, Flaubert is exploring new creative possibilities. Instead of posing the historian's questions of when, why and how, he refuses to evaluate the positions he represents, or to offer historical explanations. Instead, everything is presented as the construct of the saint's imagination, and as the Devil points out to him in the final version, apparently fixed reality is not to be trusted:

> . . . things come to you only through the intermediary of your mind. Like a concave mirror, it distorts objects; – and you have no means of verifying them.
>
> You will never know the full extent of the universe; consequently you can have no conception of its cause [. . .]
>
> Form is perhaps a trick of your senses, and Substance a figment of your imagination.
>
> Unless, on the other hand, appearance is the only truth, illusion the only reality, since the world is in a constant state of flux.
>
> [. . . les choses ne t'arrivent que par l'intermédiaire de ton esprit. Tel qu'un miroir concave il déforme les objets; – et tout moyen te manque pour en vérifier l'exactitude.
>
> Jamais tu ne connaîtras l'Univers dans sa pleine étendue; par conséquent tu ne peux te faire une idée de sa cause [. . .]
>
> La Forme est peut-être une erreur de tes sens, la Substance une imagination de ta pensée.
>
> A moins que le monde étant un flux perpétuel des choses, l'apparence au contraire ne soit tout ce qu'il y a de vrai, l'illusion la seule réalité.
>
> (OC I 565)]

In *La Tentation* Flaubert's historical documentation has itself been transformed as if by the Devil's concave mirror. Antoine encounters 'real' figures such as Apollonius, Tertullian and Saint Hilarion who lived centuries apart, and the seething crowds that surround him owe as much to Flaubert's experience of the revolutionary crowds of 1848 as they do to the early Christian period.[2] The research Bouilhet thought would produce a scholarly reconstruction of antiquity instead serves as a springboard that frees Flaubert's own imagination, like Antoine's, to soar far beyond the ancient Egyptian desert. Such was the seductive power of this deeply subjective approach to history that Flaubert returned to *La Tentation* throughout his life.

As if pursuing an ongoing dialogue with himself, Flaubert continued to engage in a critique of his own thoughts about history. Distancing himself from the Romantic stance of his juvenile works and from his eagerness to identify with figures from the past, he projected these aspects of his own recent historical approach into the character of Emma Bovary and showed both their allure and their inadequacy. His account of Emma's fascination with the past – a fascination fed by her reading of Walter Scott – emphasises the superficial, over-emotional and disconnected nature of her historical perception:

> In those days she hero-worshipped Mary Queen of Scots and venerated famous or ill-fated women. Joan of Arc, Heloise, Agnes Sorel, the fair Ferronnière and Clémence Isaure stood out, for her, like comets against the dark vastness of history. Here and there – though more hidden in shadow and with no connection between them – there emerged Saint Louis with his oak tree, the dying Bayard, a few of Louis XI's ferocious acts, a bit about Saint Bartholomew, the white plume of Henri IV, and always the memory of the painted plates celebrating Louis XIV.

> [Elle eut dans ce temps-là le culte de Marie Stuart et des vénérations enthousiastes à l'endroit des femmes illustres ou infortunées. Jeanne d'Arc, Héloïse, Agnès Sorel, la belle Ferronnière et Clémence Isaure, pour elle, se détachaient comme des comètes sur l'immensité ténébreuse de l'histoire, où saillissaient encore ça et là, mais plus perdus dans l'ombre et sans aucun rapport entre eux, saint Louis avec son chêne, Bayard mourant, quelques férocités de Louis XI, un peu de Saint-Barthélemy, le panache du Béarnais, et toujours le souvenir des assiettes peintes où Louis XIV était vanté. (OC 1 587)]

References to the history of France, to past monarchs and vanished regimes, abound in *Madame Bovary*, but these references are always fleeting and partial. Flaubert presents us with a history that has become fragmented and erased; it vanishes into the 'dark vastness' of the past, leaving only isolated, incoherent details which are quickly reduced to platitudes. The disconnected, sentimental jumble of historical figures and facts crowding in on Emma during her craze for things historical at the convent has its counterpart in the flurry of disparate historical allusions dotted throughout the text, ranging from the Empire and the Revolution to Diane de Poitiers, Richard the Lion Heart, Cincinnatus, Diocletian and the Emperors of China, and fading away into a stereotype prehistory when men wore animal skins and lived on a diet of acorns. Elsewhere, history is reduced to a mere mouthful like the Trafalgar puddings served at the ball at La Vaubyessard, or the turban-shaped bread rolls which are said to resemble Saracens' heads and to date back to the Crusades. By the end of the novel Homais is dangerously distorting history for his own ends, evoking the Crusades and the Middle Ages in his campaign against the blind beggar, sycophantically comparing the king to Henri IV, and raising the spectre of the massacre of Saint Bartholomew's Day in support of his protest against a small grant paid to the Church. Flaubert demonstrates that when history is fragmented and reduced, and when all sense of chronology and historical context is ignored, the past dissolves into a jumble of elements as incongruous as the juxtaposed images in one of Emma's keepsake pictures. Such a debased awareness of the past can contribute nothing to an understanding of the present or the future. Emma has no firm points of reference. Past and future, dreams and memories merge and blur, and she can salvage no sense from the past: 'in the brilliant flashes of the present,' we are told, 'her past life, so clear until then, vanished completely, and she almost doubted whether she had ever lived it' ['aux fulgurations de l'heure présente, sa vie passée, si nette jusqu'alors, s'évanouissait tout entière, et elle doutait presque de l'avoir vécue' (OC 1 592)]. Unable to perceive any causal links between past, present and future, Emma is as unable to understand her own history as she is incapable of piecing together the history of France.

Yet while *Madame Bovary* seems to show Flaubert musing on how easy it is for the past to be fragmented and erased in this way, his narrative quietly offers an ironic echo of these pitfalls, and it challenges the reader not to fall into the same trap as Emma. In the famous opening scene describing Charles at school, the narrator draws our attention to the ease with which the past can be forgotten as he tells us that it would now be impossible for those present at the time to remember anything at all about Charles. That warning resonates through the novel. *Madame Bovary* was published in 1856 and is set in the reign of Louis-Philippe (1830–48), but the narrative begins and ends in the present, so there remains a curious gap between the events of the narrative and the 'now' of the narrator – a gap which is implicitly filled by the Revolution of 1848 and its troubled aftermath. Flaubert had of course lived through these momentous events in France's recent history, when widespread discontent with Louis-Philippe's government erupted into an insurrection that resulted in the king's abdication and the proclamation of the short-lived Second Republic, which in turn came to a violent end with Louis-Napoleon's *coup d'état*. Those troubled years had a profound and long-lasting influence on Flaubert and on his work. The conspicuous absence of explicit references to those events in *Madame Bovary* is under-lined by the fact that the significant dates of 22 February 1848 (the start of the Revolution) and 4 December 1851 (the *coup d'état* which ushered in the Second Empire) appear in the novel's early drafts but have been omitted from the final version. The striking omission of any reference to 1848 or the *coup d'état* only emphasises their significance. Flaubert is depending on our awareness of the impending Revolution, for without it we will fail to recognise the fierce irony of Lieuvain's complacent speech at the agricultural fair in praise of France's beloved monarchy and political stability. *Madame Bovary* challenges us not to forget the past but to read from the ironic perspective of historical hindsight – the onus is on the reader to fill in the gap.

Flaubert returned to these issues in *Salammbô* where he finally put his ideas on the historical novel into practice. *Salammbô* took more than five years to write, and it is worth recalling the early stages of its preparation and composition, for they provide a vivid illustration of his approach to historical fiction and of the practical problems he encountered. They show the continuing tension between his passionate, visceral engagement with the past and his scholarly, analytical approach, and in particular they show him confronting the question raised in *Madame Bovary* about the fragmented and forgotten nature of the past. In setting his novel in ancient Carthage, Flaubert was aware that he had chosen a place and period that would be deeply unfamiliar to his readers. By situating his new novel in a distant and forgotten civilisation, he was choosing to grapple not only with the practical problem of how to represent a culture and period of which almost no trace remained, but also with the crucial question – first raised by Jules – of how we make sense of the past.

The first mention of *Salammbô* comes in a letter dated 18 March 1857, in which Flaubert says he intends to write a novel set in the third century BC. By then he had already begun an intensive programme of reading, and by the end of May he was complaining, 'all these volumes have given me indigestion. I'm burping books' ['j'ai une indigestion de bouquins. Je rote l'in-folio' (Cor. II 726)]. Since March, he claimed, he had taken notes from fifty-three different works (including a 400-page memoir on the pyramidal cypress for a detail for his description of the temple courtyard); he was studying the art of war and was satisfied that he could do something new with it; he was working like a Trojan, reading book after book, taking reams of notes. And he continued to devour a vast body of research material until, on 1 September 1857, he began to write. Yet this scholarly research was not enough. Though he had mocked the way Emma Bovary identified with her historical heroines, Flaubert had not shaken off his need for emotional involvement with his subject. His letters from this period describe the agonising process of trying to write, and they show how close he came to abandoning the project because, despite all his reading, he could not fill the conceptual 'void' that terrified him. The psychological element presented particular difficulties, and he despaired of ever portraying his characters convincingly. As he wrote to Mademoiselle Leroyer de Chantepie, his inability to share imaginatively in the experience of his characters was preventing him from giving an accurate account of the period:

> I *feel* that it's false [. . .] and that my characters can't have talked like that. Wanting to enter men's hearts is no mean ambition when those men lived more than two thousand years ago, and in a civilisation that has no similarities with our own. I can glimpse the truth, but I don't have a clear sense of it, the emotional side is lacking. [. . .] If everything I write is flat and empty, it's because I don't throb with my heroes' emotions. It's as simple as that.

> [Je *sens* que je suis dans le faux [. . .] et que mes personnages n'ont pas dû parler comme cela. Ce n'est pas une petite ambition que de vouloir entrer dans le cœur des hommes, quand ces hommes vivaient il y a plus de deux mille ans et dans une civilisation qui n'a rien d'analogue avec la nôtre. J'entrevois la vérité, mais elle ne me pénètre pas, l'émotion me manque. [. . .] Si tout ce que j'écris est vide et plat, c'est que je ne palpite pas du sentiment de mes héros, voilà.
>
> (Cor. II 784–5, 12 December 1857)]

By April 1858 these problems had reached crisis point. Remembering, perhaps, that historians such as Victor Cousin and Edgar Quinet had stressed the importance of visiting historical sites because the spirit of an age left its mark on the physical surroundings,[3] Flaubert set off for Carthage to see for himself the few remaining ruins of the civilisation he was struggling to evoke. The visit had the desired effect. Steeped in the sights and sounds of the Orient, fascinated by the people he met and by the archaeological remains of the area, he felt the emotional engagement he needed. On his return he found he could write about Carthage with truth and conviction. What little he had already written was discarded. '*Carthage* has to be completely redone – or rather, done,' he told Ernest Feydeau on 20 June 1858. '*I'm demolishing it all*. It was ridiculous! impossible! false!' ['*Carthage* est complètement à refaire, ou plutôt à faire. *Je démolis tout*. C'était absurde! impossible! faux!' (Cor. II 817)]

Yet the problem of finding an appropriate language and style persisted. Before visiting Carthage, Flaubert had complained about the difficulty of striking the right note when describing things from a distance of over two thousand years. Evoking images of the gaping void and the translation, both of which have special significance for his view of historical writing, he wrote: 'In order to be understood, one has to produce a kind of constant translation, and what an abyss that creates between the absolute and the work' ['Pour être entendu [. . .] il faut faire une sorte de traduction permanente, et quel abîme cela creuse entre l'absolu et l'œuvre' (Cor. II 783)]. On his return from Tunis there was a brief moment of confidence when he believed that he had found the right tone, but his optimism was short-lived. He soon complained that language was failing him at every turn, and that a dearth of vocabulary very often forced him to alter details.[4] Using circumlocutions would dilute the desired effect; writing in conventional French would produce a banal result; and he was determined not to imitate the '*noble*' style of writers like Fénelon or Chateaubriand.[5] In his adolescent attempts at historical fiction he had used inversion, periphrasis and accumulated epithets, though more in imitation of neo-classical and early Romantic authors than in a serious attempt to reproduce the flavour of medieval French. *Dernière Scène de la mort de Marguerite de Bourgogne*, *Deux Mains sur une couronne* and *Chronique normande du Xe siècle* had all begun by appealing to the reader to imagine a bygone age, and in all of them the narrative was carried by the dialogue – a legacy, perhaps, of his early passion for historical theatre.

But in *Salammbô* Flaubert resorted to none of these devices. He avoids archaisms and fictitious chronicles, and instead uses unfamiliar and esoteric vocabulary to create an exotic sense of a period distanced in space as much as in time. He conveys the strangeness of his characters' language by means of suggestion. By making liberal use of the un-gallic letter K (Kabyres, Kapouras, Khamon, Kinisdo, Melkarth . . .), he subtly communicates the sounds of an outlandish tongue. Direct speech is reduced to a minimum, and when dialogue does occur it is in short, simple sentences. We are told that Salammbô 'used all the Barbarians' idioms simultaneously' ['employait simultanément tous les idiomes des Barbares' (OC I 698)] and are left to imagine what this might mean, just as we are invited to accept that Schahabarim's mysterious words have the power to give meaning to the void without being told what those words are: 'Sometimes he uttered strange words which passed before Salammbô like great flashes of lightning illuminating the abyss' ['Des mots étranges quelquefois lui échappaient, et qui passaient devant Salammbô comme de larges éclairs illuminant des abîmes' (OC I 753)].

The critics' response to *Salammbô* when it first appeared in December 1862 indicates how far Flaubert had diverged from what his contemporaries expected of a historical novel. Confronted with a work that seemed to fit no recognisable category, reviewers were bewildered. 'What is *Salammbô*?'

asked *La Gazette de France*. 'To ask this question is already putting the book on trial' ['Qu'est-ce que *Salammbô*? Poser cette question, c'est déjà faire le procès du livre'].[6] This was indeed the question that contemporary critics were to raise repeatedly as they tried to pigeonhole *Salammbô*. Classifying it variously as an epic, a prose-poem, a drama, an archaeological tour de force, a guide-book to Carthage, they agreed on only one thing: *Salammbô* did not fit the criteria for a historical novel.

Flaubert's most vehement critic was Guillaume Froehner, who published a long and detailed article in the *Revue contemporaine* listing *Salammbô*'s factual errors. Although Flaubert was not in the habit of replying to critics, these accusations of historical inaccuracy stung him into a strenuous letter of defence which he published in *L'Opinion nationale* in January 1863 after compiling an elaborate dossier of his sources to back up his claims of authenticity. But Flaubert's commitment to historical accuracy was less fervent than his reply to Froehner – and his extensive research – might imply. He was willing to acknowledge liberties with historical fact in a letter to Sainte-Beuve (Cor. III 284, 23–4 December 1862), and it is clear from his comments on other historical novelists that the accuracy of individual details was less important to him than the overall impression, the 'colour and tone' of a novel, and above all, its artistic beauty. As he later told George Sand, 'I consider technical details, local information, in short the historical and exact side of things, to be of very secondary importance. Above all I seek *Beauty*' ['Je regarde comme très secondaire le détail technique, le renseignement local, enfin le côté historique et exacte des choses. Je recherche par-dessus tout, *la Beauté*' (Cor. IV 1000)].

According to Maxime Du Camp, Flaubert chose the Carthaginian subject precisely because so little was known about it. But if his readers were ignorant of the 'historical and exact side of things', they would nevertheless have been familiar with a certain *idea* of Carthage, for Carthage and Barbarians featured prominently in the socio-political discourse of mid-nineteenth-century France, where the nation's future was often linked to the collapse of the great civilisations of antiquity, and where Paris was commonly seen as under threat from barbarians who would emerge from within France itself.

Although some critics have seen *Salammbô* as a fictional dead-end where history is used for purely aesthetic purposes, Flaubert has attempted something far more ambitious. Pursuing an idea put forward in the first *Education sentimentale*, he treats the past not as a monolithic block but as a shifting construct, subject to multiple interpretations. *Salammbô*'s repeated emphasis on translation and interpretation draws attention to the process whereby the past is constantly rewritten. The legion of interpreters with parrots tattooed on their chests; the sometimes unreliable translator Spendius; the indecipherable words of Shahabarim; and Salammbô's ability to communicate in many tongues are all perhaps emblematic of Flaubert's own role as creator of 'a kind of constant translation' ['une sorte de traduction permanente']. So we can see that Flaubert was less concerned about complying strictly with his historical sources than about interpreting them in a way that would throw light on his own period as much as on the Carthaginian war. When his research throws up details that happen to coincide with the events surrounding the 1848 Revolution, he seizes on them and integrates them into the novel so that it reflects not only an ancient civilisation but also the state of contemporary France. Modern critics have shown how extensively such analogies are pursued. Social divisions, tensions between Church and State, France's colonial policy in North Africa, reform banquets, political clubs, bourgeois manners, even elements of Haussmann's reconstruction of Paris all find echoes in the Carthaginian novel.[7]

Historical novelists – like historians – generally aim to show the reasons that lie behind certain historical impulses, suggest the causes that determine the course of events, and hint at what might have happened if things had been different, but in *Salammbô* these conventions are undermined. Instead, Flaubert proposes all manner of disparate causes, from the most trivial (Hamilcar enters the war because a stone from one of the mercenary machines lands in his palace grounds) to the most grandiose (Salammbô's love for Mâtho is a fate imposed by the gods). Flaubert's main source, Polybius, blamed the conflict on the Carthaginians' failure to get rid of the mercenaries as soon as they had signed the peace treaty with Rome, and Flaubert uses this explanation, but also attributes the war to individual ambitions, commercial interests and personal animosities. Mystical explanations are equally important: rival deities struggle for supremacy over Carthage and manipulate humans for their own ends. No reason is given more weight than any other. By the time we reach the novel's closing sentence we know that the explanations and motives offered are not to be trusted. 'Thus died Hamilcar's daughter, for having touched the mantle of Tanit' ['Ainsi mourut la fille d'Hamilcar pour avoir touché au manteau de Tanit' (OC I 797)] is so evidently inadequate as an explanation of events that it merely draws attention to the uncertain status of the explanations offered throughout the novel.

As well as challenging a simplistic approach to causality, *Salammbô* also subverts the conventionally linear view of historical chronology by representing time as disrupted or arrested. Repeatedly, time stands still as moments and characters freeze and natural movement is immobilised in a process of petrification that defies any sense of forward progress. The 'black ocean turned to stone' ['océan noir pétrifié'], and the emerald sea which 'seemed frozen' ['semblait comme figée'] (OC I 699) reflect a stasis that threatens this novel where humans are constantly on the point of turning into statues. Hannon is described as looking like a massive idol hewn from a rock (OC I 705), Taanach stands straighter than a stone herm (OC I 708), and by the end of the novel the watching crowds, as motionless as statues of stone, seem to have merged with the architecture of Carthage (OC I 795). Such images challenge the widespread nineteenth-century view of the march of time, of history as progress. Instead, time here seems to stagnate, or else is trapped in a never-ending cycle of repetition that is as inevitable as the movements of the sun and moon or the cycle of the seasons. The irony of the final chapter is that whereas 'everywhere there was a sense of order restored, of a new existence beginning again' ['partout on sentait l'ordre rétabli, une existence nouvelle qui recommençait' (OC I 794)], that sense of triumph and order is clearly illusory. Carthage will be destroyed, and the cycle will continue, still recognisable in Second Empire France.

Flaubert's next major work, *L'Education sentimentale*, seemed to have left the world of the historical novel far behind. Its title focuses our attention on his hero's emotional and sexual development, on that strand of the narrative that follows Frédéric from his timid boyhood encounter with the local prostitute, through his unsatisfactory entanglements with four different women, to the wry reminiscences of maturity. Yet it is clear from Flaubert's correspondence that he conceived of this 'novel of modern manners' ['roman de mœurs modernes'] as a kind of historical novel: 'I want to write the moral history of the men of my generation; "sentimental" would be more accurate' ['Je veux faire l'histoire morale des hommes de ma génération; "sentimentale" serait plus vrai' (Cor. III 409)]. In describing Frédéric's sentimental education Flaubert not only narrates the story of one individual, but charts the mentality of his contemporaries as they live through a recent and climactic period of French history that would have been as familiar to his early readers as the mercenary wars of *Salammbô* were foreign.

But if representing the vanished civilisation of Carthage had posed problems, Flaubert found that writing about his own period had its own difficulties. In *Salammbô* historical figures such as Hamilcar and Hannon were so distant in time that Flaubert knew his readers would have few preconceptions about them, but this was not the case with *L'Education sentimentale*, and he knew how easily the weighty presence of historical figures could unbalance the novel. As he wrote to his old friend Jules Duplan:

> I'm having a lot of trouble fitting my characters into the political events of 48! I'm afraid that the background will overwhelm the foreground. That's the problem with historical novels. Characters from history are more interesting

than fictional ones, especially when the latter's passions are not very intense. Will people be less interested in Frédéric than in Lamartine? And also, what should I select from real Facts? I am perplexed. *It's hard!*

[J'ai bien du mal à emboîter mes personnages dans les événements politiques de 48! J'ai peur que les fonds ne dévorent les premiers plans. C'est là le défaut du genre historique. Les personnages de l'histoire sont plus intéressants que ceux de la fiction, surtout quand ceux-là ont des passions modérées. On s'intéressera moins à Frédéric qu'à Lamartine? – Et puis, quoi choisir parmi les Faits réels? Je suis perplexe. *C'est dur!* (Cor. III 734)]

He easily solved the problem of historical figures by keeping them firmly in the background. The question of what to include was less simple, however, and it lies at the heart of Flaubert's conception of history. In *L'Education sentimentale* he explores the way in which the undifferentiated flux of events gradually, through a process of selecting, excluding and forgetting, takes shape as history. The novel lays bare the problematic nature of this process throughout, and regularly draws attention to the parallels with literary creation. In laying bare the making of history Flaubert is also examining the making of literature.

The novel's opening sentence – 'On the fifteenth of September 1840, at about six o'clock in the morning, the *Ville-de-Montereau*, on the point of departure, was sending up great swirling plumes of smoke by Quai Saint-Bernard' ['Le 15 septembre 1840, vers six heures du matin, *la Ville-de-Montereau*, près de partir, fumait à gros tourbillons devant le quai Saint-Bernard' (OC II 8)] – appears to root the narrative firmly in time and place. The confident display of facts is soon undermined, however, as Flaubert gradually unfolds a view of history that is grounded much less in solid data and 'real events' than in the subtle, shifting connections and confusions of everyday existence. Densely packed with information, the opening promises a reassuringly recognisable narrative, but the text will never again offer the kind of solidity of time and place that is condensed into that first sentence.

Although he was dealing with his own period and had witnessed some of the events of the Revolution at first hand, Flaubert worked to gather a mass of documentation for this novel as he had done for *Salammbô*. He took notes on areas as diverse as fashion, the movements of the Stock Exchange, socialist ideas, the symptoms of croup, troop movements in June 1848 and race-courses. Yet, as in *Salammbô*, documentary accuracy was not his chief criterion. He drew extensively on *Les Clubs et les Clubistes* by Alphonse Lucas for his account of the Club de l'Intelligence, for example, gathering tiny details and expressions but often slightly altering them. Tellingly, he borrowed an authentic revolutionary speech quoted by Lucas, and had no compunction about translating it into Spanish and putting it in the mouth of a revolutionary from Barcelona. In 'translating' the past into fiction Flaubert is less concerned with authentic detail than with conveying a sense of the experience of living history. That experience is primarily one of confusion and incomprehension; the Spaniard's speech (which no one understands) is its perfect representation.

Almost all the recognisably 'historical' section of the novel – the account of the 1848 Revolution – is confined to a single chapter, the first chapter of Part III, and even there Flaubert presents it obliquely, for the most part. The Revolution's flashpoint, when troops fired on demonstrators in the Boulevard des Capucines, is described from Frédéric's distracted viewpoint. He and Rosanette, wandering through the streets of Paris, hear a sound like the ripping of an immense piece of silk: '– Oh! they're wiping out a few bourgeois, said Frédéric calmly, for there are times when the least cruel of men is so detached from other people that he could watch the whole human race perish without batting an eyelid' ['– Ah! on casse quelques bourgeois, dit Frédéric tranquillement, car il y a des situations où l'homme le moins cruel est si détaché des autres, qu'il verrait périr le genre humain sans un battement de cœur' (OC ii 111)]. Frédéric remains detached the following morning when he is caught up in the revolutionary crowds, and instead of working to convey the reality of events, Flaubert presents them through Frédéric's eyes and highlights their entertaining, fictional quality, showing how the dividing line between life and art is blurred: 'Frédéric, caught between two dense crowds, did not move; besides, he was fascinated and enjoying himself hugely. The falling wounded and the dead lying stretched out did not look really wounded, really dead. He felt as if he were watching a show' ['Frédéric, pris entre deux masses profondes, ne bougeait pas, fasciné d'ailleurs et s'amusant extrêmement. Les blessés qui tombaient, les morts étendus n'avaient pas l'air de vrais blessés, de vrais morts. Il lui semblait assister à un spectacle' (OC ii 112)].

As Frédéric's private preoccupations constantly distract him from public affairs, we appear to glimpse the events of the Revolution only sporadically. Yet one of the remarkable aspects of this novel is the way Flaubert conveys the Revolution not so much by focusing on the detail of famous events as by suggesting that they are an integral part of the fabric of the period. A horse-race, a traffic jam, a crowded pavement all express violent disorder as the revolution is echoed and refracted in many forms in the text. In describing Frédéric's visit to the fancy-dress ball, for example, Flaubert stages an oblique dramatisation of the Revolution as guests dressed as royalty, aristocrats, soldiers and workers come together in a swirling, confused mass amidst cries of 'Let's attack!' ['Attaquons!' (OC ii 53)]. Their heated and fragmented discussions prefigure the exchanges at the political clubs, and the evening disintegrates into images of violence, bloodshed and death. The clash of forces is even inscribed in the ancient forest of Fontainebleau: 'There were enormous rugged oaks that rose convulsively from the ground to seize one another, and, firmly established on their torso-like trunks, hurled despairing appeals or furious threats at one other with their bare arms, like a group of Titans frozen in their rage' ['Il y avait des chênes rugueux, énormes, qui se convulsaient, s'étiraient du sol, s'étreignaient les uns les autres, et, fermes sur leurs troncs, pareils à des torses, se lançaient avec leurs bras nus des appels de désespoir, des menaces furibondes, comme un groupe de Titans immobilisés dans leur colère' (OC II 126)]. Stones from the forest's quarry conjure images of fury, violence, urban chaos and 'great unknown cataclysms' ['grands cataclysmes ignorés' (OC II 127)], which Frédéric says have existed since the world began and will remain until the end of time. Flaubert had visited Carthage because he believed that its ruins and surroundings still preserved some of the spirit of a distant age; here, too, physical surroundings catch and magnify the mood of the period. The Revolution is dramatised repeatedly and indirectly, as part of a much broader, natural and eternal process.

If Flaubert does not place the crisis points of 1848 at the centre of his narrative, it is because these events are less important to his characters than their own personal crises. Instead, he shows how the missed opportunities, disappointed ambitions and compromised ideals of the political crisis resonate through personal lives, too. The one is a reflection of the other, and neither can be reduced to a clear-cut resolution. In *L'Education sentimentale* Flaubert presents us with history in the making – history that has yet to solidify into a meaningful shape. So, for example, when Rosanette pours out her life-story to Frédéric, his reaction is the same as his response to the flux of events in Paris: 'it all came out with no transitions, and he was unable to reconstruct the whole picture' ['tout cela sans transitions, et il ne pouvait reconstruire un ensemble' (OC II 127)]. Like Flaubert, uncertain what to select from real events in composing his novel, Frédéric is unable to reconstruct Rosanette's history from the mass of information that confronts him. Repeatedly, Frédéric is portrayed as not understanding what is happening around him, and the fragmented narrative with its gaps and unexplained references mimics his – and our – incomprehension. Yet detailed explanations do not necessarily clarify the meaning of events. Frédéric (like the reader) is baffled by a reference to 'the Calf's Head' ['la Tête de Veau'] but when the allusion is explained to him years later (when the reader has almost certainly forgotten about it), it turns out to refer to an episode in English history that has little relevance either to the situation in France or to the plot of the novel. It merely serves to draw our attention, once again, to the haphazard processes of selection, distortion, ignorance or omission involved in any representation of history.

The Fontainebleau episode is perhaps Flaubert's most sustained dramatisation of this issue. The château is full of associations with great figures from French history, but neither Frédéric nor Rosanette – the one informed, the other ignorant – can make sense of what they see. Rosanette has never heard of Diane de Poitiers:

> 'Which woman?'
> 'Diane de Poitiers!'
> He repeated:
> 'Diane de Poitiers, the mistress of Henri II.'
> She gave a little 'Ah!' That was all.
> Her silence clearly proved that she knew nothing, did not understand [. . .].
> She found the carp pond more entertaining.

> [– Quelle femme?
> – Diane de Poitiers!
> Il répéta:
> – Diane de Poitiers, la maîtresse d'Henri II.
> Elle fit un petit: 'Ah!' Ce fut tout.
> Son mutisme prouvait clairement qu'elle ne savait rien, ne comprenait pas [. . .].
> L'étang des carpes la divertit davantage. (OC II 125)]

Frédéric, on the other hand, does know about famous figures from the past and can set them in a chronological sequence, but he is no more able than Rosanette (or Emma Bovary) to do anything with that knowledge:

> He thought of all the people who had frequented these buildings, Charles V, the Valois, Henri IV, Peter the Great, Jean-Jacques Rousseau and the 'beautiful women weeping in the boxes of the grand circle', Voltaire, Napoleon, Pius VII, Louis-Philippe; he felt surrounded and jostled by these turbulent dead; he was dazed by such a confusion of images, though he did find them rather charming nevertheless.

> [Il songeait à tous les personnages qui avaient hanté ces murs, Charles-Quint, les Valois, Henri IV, Pierre le Grand, Jean-Jacques Rousseau et 'les belles pleureuses des premières loges', Voltaire, Napoléon, Pie VII, Louis-Philippe; il se sentait environné, coudoyé par ces morts tumultueux; une telle confusion d'images l'étourdissait, bien qu'il y trouvât du charme pourtant.
> (OC II 125)]

His banal response is clearly inadequate (though does the reader do any better?), and these detached images are soon followed in his mind by visions of a more distant France peopled by ancient kings and mystical stags as history dwindles to a few received ideas and fades away into the timelessness of myth, just as it does in *Madame Bovary*. This is the kind of timeless, mythical past that Flaubert exploits in *La Légende de saint Julien l'Hospitalier*, where dragons and talking stags coexist with authentic details of medieval life. It is a narrative which depends on our acceptance of a stereotyped mystical view of the Middle Ages, and whose final sentence – 'And that is the story of Saint Julian the Hospitaler, more or less as it is to be found on a church window in my area' ['Et voilà l'histoire de saint Julien l'Hospitalier, telle à peu près qu'on la trouve, sur un vitrail d'église, dans mon pays' (OC II 187)] – emphasises its reduction to a single fixed image while at the same time drawing our attention to the resonantly imaginative construct that Flaubert has created from that image.

At the end of *L'Education sentimentale*, Flaubert shows his characters starting to undergo the same reductive process themselves as Frédéric and Deslauriers reduce the messy complexity of their friends' lives to a few neat phrases:

> Martinon was now a senator.
> Hussonnet held an important position, where he had control over all the theatres and all the press.
> Cisy, deeply religious and the father of eight children, was living in his ancestral château.
> [. . .] 'And your dear friend Sénécal?' asked Frédéric.
> 'Vanished! I don't know!'
>
> [Martinon était maintenant sénateur.
> Hussonnet occupait une haute place, où il se trouvait avoir sous sa main tous les théâtres et toute la presse.
> Cisy, enfoncé dans la religion et père de huit enfants, habitait le château de ses aïeux.
> [. . .] – Et ton intime Sénécal? demanda Frédéric.
> – Disparu! Je ne sais!   (OC II 161–2)]

As Frédéric and Deslauriers summarise their own life histories, their disparate analyses of their personal failure echo the equally conflicting interpretations the novel has offered for the failure of the Revolution, and (like the ending of *Salammbô*), undermine any notion of simple causality. The novel ends not with any conclusive explanation of the political crisis, but with an assertion of the aesthetic value of evoking the past. The closing sentence, 'That was the best time we had!' ['C'est là ce que nous avons eu de meilleur!' (OC II 163)] may be read as referring not only to the two friends' youthful visit to the brothel, but also to the pleasure they derive from recalling and retelling that moment of their shared personal history. In a celebration of the artist's pleasure in the imaginative re-creation of the past, they recount it 'wordily, each completing the other's memories' ['prolixement, chacun complétant les souvenirs de l'autre' (OC II 163)].

If *L'Education sentimentale* explores history in the making and emphasises the undifferentiated confusion of the flux of events, *Bouvard et Pécuchet* shows the pitfalls of trying to force that complexity into a coherent pattern. Flaubert gradually unpicks his two clerks' naïve approach to history. They begin with the assumption that a 'true' historical account is a rigorously scientific accumulation of facts, but as they read through an extensive and indiscriminate collection of historical works they are disconcerted by the inconsistencies they find, and come to realise that a truly objective history is impossible. Unable to unravel the everyday events of their own household, they recognise the futility of trying to reconstruct the life of the past by the simple accumulation of facts, and so they abandon their project of writing the history of the Duc d'Angoulême. This failure brings them to realise that the bare facts of history must be filled out by psychology. Following the opposite trajectory to that of Jules in the first *Education* who dismissed historical fiction as inferior to 'pure' history, they decide that history is defective without imagination, cast aside their history books, and send instead for historical novels. Like the young Flaubert, they are initially delighted by the vivid evocations of Scott and Dumas but their enthusiasm wanes as they tire of the stereotyped situations and notice anachronisms and factual errors. So they pass on to other interests, having demonstrated the folly of the widely held view, mocked in the *Dictionnaire des idées reçues*, that 'only historical novels may be tolerated because they teach history' ['seuls les romans historiques peuvent être tolérés parce qu'ils enseignent l'histoire' (OC II 313)].

Flaubert's historical fiction does not pretend to teach history in that sense. Unlike the conventional historical novel, his work challenges our will to understand, and frustrates any desire we might have to reduce the complexity of existence to a simple meaning. His refusal to perpetuate the simplistic view of the past as 'knowable' in some absolute sense is one of the main achievements of his work. His multiple treatments of 1848 – already hinted at in the first *Tentation*, evoked by its absence in *Madame Bovary*, projected into a distanced analogy in *Salammbô*, shown refracted through personal lives and physical surroundings in *L'Education sentimentale*, and finally re-enacted in caricature in Bouvard and Pécuchet's Chavignoles – dramatise the idea of history as a perpetual translation. History is never fixed or finished, Flaubert seems to be saying: the events of the past have a significance for us that constantly changes in relation to the present, and we fit them into patterns of understanding which are inevitably coloured by contemporary preoccupations. As he wrote in 1864, 'everyone is free to look at history in their own way, since history is merely the reflection of the present on the past, and that is why it must always be rewritten' ['chacun est libre de regarder l'histoire à sa façon, puisque l'histoire n'est que la réflexion du présent sur le passé, et voilà pourquoi elle est toujours à refaire' (Cor. III 414–15)].

NOTES

1 Maxime Du Camp, *Souvenirs littéraires*, ed. Daniel Oster (Paris: Aubier, 1994), p. 289.

2 Mary Neiland, '*Les Tentations de saint Antoine*' *and Flaubert's Fiction. A Creative Dynamic* (Amsterdam: Rodopi, 2001), pp. 92–3.

3 See, for example, Victor Cousin, *Cours de l'histoire de la philosophie moderne*, 3 vols. (Paris: Didier, 1847), vol. 1, p. 180.

4 'Language fails me on every line and at every word, and the dearth of vocabulary is such that I am very often obliged to alter details' ['A chaque ligne, à chaque mot, la langue me manque et l'insuffisance du vocabulaire est telle, que je suis forcé à changer les détails très souvent' (Cor. II 845)].

5 He had already tried this in *La Mort du duc de Guise*, where he copied sections from Chateaubriand's *Analyse raisonnée de l'histoire de France*.

6 Armand de Pontmartin, 'M. Gustave Flaubert – *Salammbô*', *La Gazette de France*, 21 December 1862, p. 1.

7 See, e.g., chapters 4 and 5 in Anne Green, *Flaubert and the Historical Novel. 'Salammbô' Reassessed* (Cambridge: Cambridge University Press, 1982); and Volker Durr, *Flaubert's 'Salammbô'. The Ancient Orient as a Political Allegory of Nineteenth-Century France* (New York: Peter Lang, 2002).

7

MARY ORR

Death and the *post mortem* in Flaubert's works

If *Madame Bovary* was brought to trial on account of its perceived indecencies to public and religious morality, particularly on account of the famous, frenetic cab ride around Rouen and the 'sacrilegious' wake at her bedside, the novel's nineteenth-century censors did not detail Emma Bovary's death pangs among their principal objections. Whether considered a 'fitting' punishment for her adulteries or a sacrifice on the altar of Romantic excess or the orders of Patriarchy, her death remains the unquestioned crux of the novel. As the site of its moral, it also highlights Flaubert's implied ethics of art, to show rather than tell. Indeed, Emma's cruelly detailed agony and almost sadistically protracted death have continued to provide grist to Flaubert criticism. Her final death throes have thus stimulated approaches as diverse as sociocritical, psychoanalytic and feminist, and it is this scene too that has fascinated critics who uphold Flaubert the Realist. Frequently cited are the medical accuracy and meticulous ordering of the various stages of death by arsenic poisoning that Emma endures, an attention to medical detail as precise as that of the almost equally famous club-foot operation at the pivotal point in the novel. Conversely, and with equal conviction, critics arguing for the symbolic or mythic import of Flaubert's *Madame Bovary* will cite the appearance of the blind beggar in her final moments, the significance of Emma's triple coffin, or the decidedly ironic or gnomic ending of this Flaubert novel as indicative of his later novels and short stories. Little critical attention has been paid, however, to the no less problematic and seemingly non-violent deaths that accompany the more visible, violent and hideously graphic ones in Flaubert's works, not least in *Madame Bovary*. The peculiarly quiet but very sudden ends of Charles Bovary and of Salammbô, or of Julien, Madame Aubain and Monsieur Bourais when contrasted with the violent deaths of Julien's parents or John the Baptist (Iaokanann) in the *Trois Contes*, demonstrate in a different key the same heady mix of realism and symbolism, the macabre and the sublime, eroticism, agony and death. If Flaubert's aesthetics include descriptive doubling or tripling, layering or puncturing with the 'small detail that suggests the truth' ['petit détail qui fait vrai'], the first port of call in this chapter is to scrutinise such techniques afresh by focusing on the important, silent deaths that are an unnoticed hallmark of his work.

The endings of Flaubert's works have elicited close critical analyses and spawned a host of readings of his novels, as undecidable, ironic, postmodern, the embodiment of art for art's sake, or the epitome of the banal reality that endings are neither happy nor tragic. What has escaped proper notice, and is the second issue to revisit in this chapter, is Flaubert's critical use of the *post mortem* as a model for the endings of his works. An autopsy provides official and public certification of death as well as an explanation of its causes. Whereas death or death-bed scenes in classical texts end the work in question and drive home moral points (not least because characters' words conform to the paradigms of conversion, pragmatic acceptance of circumstance, or some return to a sense of order determined by cause and effect or other powers), final words in Flaubert are at least doubly distinct. Neither oblique or euphemistic nor overtly rhetorical in the vein of an obituary or valedictory speech, his final death sentences are of utmost poignancy, whether dressed in under- or overstatement. They are never the last utterances of the protagonists themselves, whose deaths, moreover, rarely provide the closing moment of the text. Unlike the paradigms of the death-bed utterance, what is reported from the characters' lips is often reduced to an incomplete, hesitant or tangential utterance or to silence. Félicité in *Un cœur simple* is inarticulate throughout her life but most articulately present by her wordless death rattle; Charles cannot speak his love for Emma but enacts it in his imperious funeral arrangements; Iaokanann's booming prophecies in life in *Hérodias* are in his death a mighty *voice off*, and Julien's apotheosis in *La Légende de saint Julien l'Hospitalier* is 'renarrated' by being transfixed as an image in a stained glass window. Moreover, those seen as saintly or unredeemed in their fictional lifetimes remain altogether consistent to their ends. What happens in their life in fact often bears little relation to the quality or timing of their death. Closing statements in Flaubert then are always quite separate from the death-bed and the central protagonists. They belong to a 'living' but unnamed narrator as self-styled *moraliste*. Never a mouthpiece of conventional legal, theological, philosophical or social commentary, this maker of epilogues frames the moral and aesthetic complexities that end all Flaubert's works, but is a figure in search of a definition that the genre of the *post mortem* may help to clarify.

If double deaths and the form of the *post mortem* are two key elements in Flaubert's writing, the third facet of Flaubert's art of death that this chapter will explore is the particular intensity of his death scenes. The moment of the characters' deaths marks a fascinating break with old or new forms of order, whether religious, political, legal or aesthetic. The crucial hiatus marked by Flaubert's final death scenes arguably makes of such moments the vehicle *par excellence* to problematise moral and evaluative judgment itself. Reconsideration of Flaubert's representation of death therefore reopens a number of key debates categorising Flaubert as the realist dissecting the ills of his contemporary society, or Flaubert the master craftsman of self-consuming style. Re-examination of the apotheoses of Emma Bovary and of Félicité in *Un cœur simple* for the commingling of eroticism, horror and moral elevation will lead us to question how far Flaubert's combination of seemingly oppositional artistic perspectives and emotive styles constitutes the shock tactics at the heart of his writing. By returning first to Flaubert's best-known scenes in his most widely read and adapted work, *Madame Bovary*, this chapter will draw out the surprise that non-specialist readers encounter. For those familiar with Flaubert's work, comparison of these scenes with parallel episodes in *Salammbô*, *L'Education sentimentale* and *Trois Contes* will propose that the freshness of Flaubert's art is most manifest in the shocking banality of the known rather than the exoticism of the other.

The death of key female protagonists (Emma Bovary, Salammbô) is frequently remarked on and remembered in both Flaubert's finished eponymous novels, and seems the fitting crown and point of closure in fictions about the end(s) of the individual and the collective. Yet the manner and personification of these deaths also crystallise their banality as double cliché: the topos of death as a maiden and death as cliché of clichés litter cultural representations, especially those in high Romantic or high Tragic mode. As especially sensitive to the power of cliché to unlock its *bêtise* and its humanity, Flaubert signals in his deployment of stereotypical deaths (the failed romantic suicide for Emma, and the failed tragic heroine for Salammbô) the risks of such representation. Pressing convention at its most conventional may backfire if readers fail to notice the unconventional in such re-use. Clearly Emma's awful final hours reframe the (easy) suicide of the 'romantic' heroines of her reading, just as Salammbô's dramatic and very public display of 'little death' (*la petite mort*, or orgasm) in the moment of actual death make intensely explicit the hitherto implicit or deliberately teasing eroticism of earlier scenes such as her congress with Mâtho in his tent. Neither death, however, parodies or makes over the banality of the *Liebestod* ['tragic love'] genre *per se*. *Madame Bovary* and *Salammbô* certainly rework the drama *par excellence* of death and love, *Romeo and Juliet*, not least by quickly moving passive 'Juliets' from their balconies – Emma is literally on one with Rodolphe at the *Comices*, Salammbô is elevated above Mâtho at the opening banquet scene – to more active 'Romeo' roles. Similarly, 'Montague–Capulet' antagonisms and oppositions are reworked in the paradoxical similarities between all factions in Norman or Carthaginian contexts. If Emma fails to see in Charles her unsuspecting Romeo because she prefers instead to fall for cardboard ones, Salammbô knows hers only too well, but fails to acknowledge until too late her own power in her destiny to make Mâtho hers. Nevertheless, the poisoned chalice (literal and figurative) remains the Flaubertian heroine's lot even if she has engaged in a quest to the death of finding love.

Yet it is not over their dead bodies alone that Flaubert negotiates the double cliché of death and the maiden.[1] It is the double death of *Romeo and Juliet* taken to new extremes in Flaubert that holds the key. In *Madame Bovary*, Emma's death is matched by Charles's quietly sudden, but no less unproblematic and dramatic, end. Like Philemon without his Baucis, Charles arguably cannot live a moment longer without Emma, so having buried her he has nothing else left to live, or, more ironically, to die, for. And if Salammbô's final collapse into the arms of death seems to herald the narrator's final gloss of events, a death sentence to which we shall return, hers is but a momentary death by comparison to the long and gory detailing of Mâtho's gruesome ritual slaughter by the High Priest, Schahabarim, preceding it. In both novels, the double death follows the same pattern. Long, slow and agonising death is matched (and arguably eclipsed) by its more terrifying foil: quiet, painless but instantaneous *rigor mortis*. The graphically detailed agonies paradoxically imply the inevitability and presence of death whereas the inexplicable, sudden and silent strike brings death up close and unawares. By doubling death in its most extreme forms – long agony and intolerable swiftness – all kinds are levelled to reveal the fullest horror of all: death is as much a young man as a maiden in Flaubert's representations. As the ends of Julien and Iaokanann in *Trois Contes* or Dussardier in *L'Education sentimentale* would confirm, the gendering of death as feminine therefore does not apply, or only superficially, in Flaubert's aesthetic. Moreover, neither of Flaubert's 'Romeos', Charles and Mâtho, dies as do the 'Juliets' to the letter of the Shakespearean model. Instead of taking their own life by the (manly) sword, each has a highly unusual death by another's blade and one sanctioned by the hands of higher powers. In what is a highly charged and arguably hyper-heroic execution by ritual slaughter, Mâtho's public death by the High Priest Schahabarim's spatula-knife plucking out his heart is the culmination of a long bodily torture from human goads and fingernails. And just as Charles must witness Emma's demise, Salammbô as focaliser of the fictional and readerly audience must watch her lover's (homo)eroticised end which further prefigures the eroticism of her own. If Charles will die in as unexplained, sudden and seemingly painless a manner as Salammbô, his end is equally charged with (auto-)erotic tension: the lock of Emma's hair in his hands aligns the necrophilic and masturbatory climax to Charles's paroxysms to suggest a cause of death unverifiable by medical science but no less a *petite mort*.[2] However, the thrust of the blade of Canivet's scalpel as he performs the autopsy cuts Charles open in exactly the same place as Mâtho, the chest, in order that the heart can be viewed and the subject pronounced (truly) dead. The high priest of science therefore does the same job as Schahabarim (or Sénécal in *L'Education sentimentale*), executioner of the final will and testament of the Fathers.

Regardless of historical context, the power structures in Flaubert's works demonstrably scapegoat the feminine – Emma and Salammbô must die – but also characters embodying alternative masculinities. Beyond such gender interest and distinctions, however, there is one feature that Flaubert makes unambiguous, the instruments of such destruction. These are always the lesser (hench)men as upholders of the system. The grim reaper's scythe takes a typically Flaubertian form of macabre reworking as both ritual and surgical knife in the hands not of the iconic skeleton, but of the living. It is the double deaths within Flaubert's works, therefore, that defy the clichés of death as a maiden or as a horseman.[3] The erotic in female or male form is but the sugar coating on the bitter pill of death behind its clichés. The 'dark continent' that all Flaubert's texts explore is therefore not the power or horror of female sexuality, or even male sexuality, but death itself. It is perhaps this that is the famous 'nothing' that Canivet discovers in his *post mortem* verdict on Charles. However, whether supremely inexplicable (Charles, Salammbô or Julien) or in its full gory agony (Emma, Mâtho or Félicité), ostensible 'dying by Death' is the climax that Flaubert permits all his most virile creations, male and female, to enjoy. Their deaths in the fullness of life, youth, love, calling, service always take precedence (literally in the text as well as evaluatively) over those living on as textual nonentities in that space beyond the deaths of the main protagonists. The living death of a life of clichés is therefore the worst and last end to occur in Flaubert's works, meted out to all his most unlikeable heroes, Homais and his double Lheureux in *Madame Bovary*, Hamilcar and his double Schahabarim in *Salammbô*, Hérode and his double Hérodias in *Trois Contes*. Madame Bovary *mère* is among Flaubert's very few women characters to be allowed such a dubious honour.

It is indeed dubious honour epitomised on which *Madame Bovary* actually ends, the *croix d'honneur* that Homais receives as the last word on the novel. Alan Raitt is surely right to point out the uncertain chronology of the last line of *Madame Bovary* (Flaubert's use of the construction 'venir de' ['to have just done something'] ties the action of Homais receiving his medal to the narrative present), as well as the importance of this scene in Flaubert's scenarios.[4] Neither consideration pinpoints the *coup* of such an ending which surpasses even the double deaths of the two main protagonists. If these have weighed up the clichés of death, they do not constitute the final death sentence reserved for the textual *post mortem* which seals all Flaubert's works. While the final utterance here sends up and problematises the literary convention of good rewarded and evil punished, and is couched as a seemingly flat and factual statement, the spotlight is on the moral gap between Homais's *modus vivendi* and the intense speculation on the 'justice' of the double deaths. The pattern that Flaubert establishes in *Madame Bovary* will be refined in the ensuing *œuvre* but is most overt here. There is a fictional *post mortem* from an internal perspective – in this case Canivet's inquest on Charles ('he found nothing' ['Il ne trouva rien' (OC I 692)]) – followed by the final, unattributable line of the text as metaphorical *post mortem* on the society in which such outrageous miscarriages of judgment and reward could occur. Homais had already appeared before a court on charges of duplicity and been acquitted. This time, for the same acts trumpeted more overtly, society decorates him.

As a seemingly impersonal statement and diagnosis of the body politic, the final line of *Madame Bovary* therefore reattaches itself to the inclusive 'we' who open the novel, and sweeps up the sentiments of collective complicity which gather throughout the text. Chief among these is the universal failure to distinguish between surfaces and depths (which critics have mostly attributed to Emma in her confusion of reality and dream, actuality and novelette cliché) whereby charlatans and pretenders are applauded and rewarded while the victims of deception of every sort are punished. The recent past viewpoint of the final sentence of *Madame Bovary* shares such an acceptance of this reward system, but also challenges it by analogy with the delimited time-scale of *post mortem* examination where the causes of death are satisfactorily established prior to the interment of the corpse. It is the unsatisfactory report of the final sentence that makes it a direct indictment of the value systems of the fictional and readerly living, and how they contributed to and judged the deaths of the central protagonists. Homais's final prize can thus be read as the award *post hoc, ergo propter hoc* handed out considerably *after* the paltry reward for long and faithful service given to Catherine Leroux at the agricultural show (and not even mentioned in Homais's report and self-congratulatory puff for the *Fanal de Rouen*). What the final line implicitly encourages is the same moral indignation in the astute reader as elicited by the 'reward' of the peasant woman and the mismatched and larger prizes given to the less worthy. The tone and tenor of the final line is not only reminiscent of Lieuvain's speech: it is also a neatly turned (double) pastiche of the pseudo-Rousseauesque world Homais promoted in the *Fanal* article, of idyll, harmony, and reward notably for men (OC I 625–6). If Homais's charlatanism from start to finish is rewarded, whereas Charles's bungling but sincere actions are doomed to fail, the ultimate hollowness (*rien*) of Homais's victory, like his person and acts, is also the more reprehensible. For those whose agonies are invisible and within, the ultimate textual irony is that they are in fact justly 'rewarded': they die before having to witness the cruelty of the unjust receiving society's highest accolades.

The inevitability of the unjust end for Homais, leaving the reader of *Madame Bovary* with a bitter taste in the mouth akin to the arsenic in Emma's, is replicated in *Salammbô*. The ending invites similar moral repugnance, but instead of exploiting understatement akin to the factuality of medical autopsy, the *post mortem* conclusion captures the overriding shock of events by means of its overstatement. While the horrific and quick succession of the main protagonists' double deaths directly contributes to the shock effect, and endorses the Barbarians' judgment earlier in the novel of the truly barbaric practices of the Carthaginians as an allegedly civilised nation, it is the aftershock of the final line that is the novel's most cold-blooded definitive statement and statement of the definitive. Although critics frequently cite this line for its ambiguity and irony – 'Thus died the daughter of Hamilcar because she had touched the cloak of Tanit' ['Ainsi mourut la fille d'Hamilcar pour avoir touché au manteau de Tanit' (OC I 797)] – or as emblematic of Flaubert's refusal to conclude, it is in itself completely unambiguous as a moral judgment. Given the parallel and counterpoint readings of double death in *Madame Bovary* and *Salammbô*, the moral double move of the final words in *Madame Bovary* sheds light on the ending of *Salammbô*. The *post mortem* on Charles as figurative judgment of the hollowness of the values of a society represented by Homais finds its collective face in *Salammbô*. In spite of the apparent seamlessness between the narrative viewpoint of the novel as a whole and the report of the two preceding deaths in particular, the impersonal *post mortem* cannot be taken as final certification of the cause of the preceding events. To place full blame and Tanit's divine retribution for a single instance of sexual 'misconduct' on Salammbô, when there is overt lack of censure for any of the many acts – massacre, scorched earth, torture, wanton bloodshed, rape, cannibalism, sodomy, the ritual sacrifice or vivisection of Mâtho – instigated by the Empire and its patriarchs in the name of Moloch, constitutes an ostensible miscarriage of justice by any lights. The supercilious, highly partisan and judgmental concluding (over)statement as some final writ served on Salammbô (the symbol of *Carthage* as acme of civilisation) has to be preposterous. Is not the reader rather to judge as a 'Barbarian', revolted by the civilised (Carthaginian) practices and value systems epitomised in the last line? As is the case in *Madame Bovary*, surely the right-thinking reader is to take the *contrary* moral stance to the one upheld?

The novel as a whole undoubtedly points in such a direction, but by careful juxtaposition of deliberately polarised viewpoints, so that their similarities (and hypocrisies) are the more apparent. As the almost symmetrical battle lines have previously illustrated, Carthaginian and Barbarian are almost interchangeable. Indeed, various characters in the novel such as Spendius and Schahabarim change sides, or change the rules by double-dealing behind the scenes. Hamilcar exchanges Hannibal for a slave boy to sacrifice to Moloch, while Narr'Havas significantly enters a pact of allegiance with Hamilcar entailing marriage to his daughter immediately after the famous scene in the tent between Mâtho and Salammbô. Thus, while like Homais both appear to be rewarded as the novel closes, the message is the same. The victory Carthage enjoys is momentary and hollow, for the Empire will soon fall to the might of Rome. This is, however, heralded by similar 'fulfilment' of Narr'havas's plan to become Hamilcar's successor in this very final scene which spectacularly and publicly backfires. If he has at last 'got the girl' (rather than a *croix d'honneur*) by subterfuge and self-promotion rather than merit, his physical possession of the prize is doubly empty in spite of his protective arm around her and his raised cup to the genius of Carthage (and by implication his own). The dramatic irony is that even before Hamilcar's and Narr'Havas's ingenius plot was hatched, Mâtho has already 'got the girl'. Worse still, the prize herself slips from Narr'Havas's grasp when her mimicry of his actions undoes their particular intentions and directly turns his short-lived triumph into a public downfall. The posturing of Narr'havas, Homais's cousin germain in leopard skin, is as ridiculous as his reward (like Homais's *croix*) is empty. Both are fool figures, however, whose *bêtise* censures the censorious, including the self-congratulatory reader until recently on their side. The inversion of the 'moral of the story' and wrong moral thinking are then completed in the final lines as *post mortems* in both novels: society is condemned for its under- and overstatements of injustice.

It is precisely the laws that govern fictional endings as moral judgments that Flaubert makes manifest, especially in his reworking of the model of grand tragedy in *Salammbô*. The unbelievably moralistic judgment 'by the power of the gods' of the final words concludes a concatenation of all the key elements of high classical tragedy in condensed form. By catching such clichés together in a supreme moment of melodrama, shock, and tingling eroticism channelled through Salammbô's histrionic fall over the back of the throne on her wedding day, her undone hair cascading to the ground, Flaubert wittily puts *dénouement(s)* on graphic display in erotic form. At the same time, she has of course undone Narr'Havas for all to see, by mimicking his cup-raising gestures and thus undercutting his duplicitous role-playing as tragic hero. Salammbô's raised cup can then be read as a mocking toast, not to Moloch, but to the victory of Tanit in aesthetic eternity where 'the good, the true and the beautiful' may indeed be plucked out in their prime and for exemplary death by the gods, whereas those remaining will grow old and die ingloriously in obscurity. Moreover, as a completely fictional creation in a cast otherwise historically based, Flaubert reinvents Salammbô as more than a Phèdre or an Athalie with suitably political or religious *dénouement*. Hers is the final climax and star death role of the novel on which the impersonal narrator's censorious tying up of the loose ends hinges. The extraordinarily well-timed intervention of the goddess, causing her to slip from Narr'Havas's possessive grasp, in fact saves her from a fate worse than death, not merely marriage to Narr'Havas, but textual mediocrity and false blame. If the epilogue is a bid at a final word, it smacks of the same assumptions and accusations as Giscon's after the night in Mâtho's tent. Salammbô cannot be returned to any neatly explicable order of things reliant on over-simplified binary suppositions and subordinations, such as Tanit to Moloch, female to male, sun to moon (which the text has in effect undone in any case). The last line then operates as did the *zaïmph* in its literal covering to tease and unmask reader censoriousness in the earlier tent scene of the novel. Salammbô and *Salammbô* thus artfully converge like their counterpart trope, the *zaïmph*, as the mysterious and mundane veil of Tanit. As figures that undo, especially clichéd endings and *dénouements*, the fictional cloak and the heroine veil and unveil the final verb of the novel, the past historic form of the most definitive verb of all, *mourir*.

As in *Madame Bovary*, the very time frame of the final sentence underpins the sense of suspension of (dis)belief but not the moral import of the novel. Preceding this most definitive of verbs is the equally definitive 'Thus' ['Ainsi'], used to clinch logical argument, and connect cause with effect. The 'logic' and astonishing death sentence relying on 'the gods' in the epigraph in *Salammbô* turns out to be as unsupported and contentious as Canivet's *post mortem* by medical pathology. Both endings therefore epitomise the double standard – whether in sexual, moral or empirical codes of judgment – yet in their false logic contain the call for greater moral realism. Any comfortable distance and safe moral position the reader may have constructed are ultimately confounded. Both final lines as textual *post mortems* then provide both an epigraph and an epitaph to the protagonist in question, and an inquest on the barbarous practices that trade under the name of civilisation.

This pattern of moral dissection and *post mortem* of double deaths of central protagonists might not initially appear to fit the double ending of

L'Education sentimentale. In the penultimate chapter and first 'ending', Frédéric and Madame Arnoux meet for the last time to counterpoint the final chapter and second ending where Frédéric and his friend Deslauriers are reunited once more. All three, however, live on into old age (and obscurity) beyond the novel's hero-shaping events such as grand passion and revolution. Although an alternative love story may finally be uncovered in the second ending thanks to the intensity and ironic deflation of heterosexual consummation in the penultimate chapter,[5] this double *dénouement* seems principally to mock the endings of high Romance and high Tragedy or the genre of sentimental education itself, the *Bildungsroman*. Flaubert's art of death is no less apparent, however, in terms of the particular obsessive intensity of both endings, and more important, the fascinating hiatus between them. If there is no literal death-bed moment here (reserved for the earlier death and elaborate funeral of Dambreuse, or the momentary shock of Dussardier's shooting), there is a break with old and new forms of order. This is felt almost viscerally in the penultimate chapter by the reader who is made to share all Frédéric's emotional reactions in a life-and-death scene for the future of his relationship with Madame Arnoux. From initial surprise when she comes to visit and 'give herself' (as Salammbô in Mâtho's tent), to the seeming unity of their shared reminiscences, Frédéric's attitude suddenly changes when they return after a stroll to his rooms. In a *dénouement* of similar significance to Salammbô's, Marie Arnoux's removal of her hat allows her head of white hair to be strikingly visible in the lamplight. It is this moment of supreme shock and horror that begins to undo the remaining scene. As happened to Charles and Mâtho, for Frédéric 'it was like a blow full on the chest' ['[c]e fut comme un heurt en pleine poitrine' (OC II 161)]. It is therefore not Marie Arnoux's moral 'looseness', her 'seduction' of Frédéric, that is the turning point of events, but her unmistakable and fully embodied presence as an older woman that is life-changing. The shock of her hair breaks for ever the obsession and idealisation Frédéric has cherished since his first glimpse of her, 'like an apparition' ['comme une apparition'], with her 'wide straw hat with pink ribbons blowing in the wind behind her' ['large chapeau de paille, avec des rubans roses qui palpitaient au vent derrière elle'] in the first chapter (OC II 9–10). Instead of passion (which has fuelled all his inaction throughout the novel) Marie Arnoux's physical reality triggers Frédéric's inner repulsion which is almost nameless in its horror: incest. Her clichéd adieu are then embodied definitively in her final act, the cutting off of a lock of her hair as a memento (mori). The violence of this moment, its silent and intense shock, renders Frédéric typically inert, but also transfixed. The pronouncement by the anonymous narrator which closes the chapter, 'And that was all' ['Et ce fut tout' (OC II 161)], provides a one-line (death) sentence on Frédéric's relationship and a narrative jolt for the reader to understand empty yet potentially fatal attractions. The penultimate chapter leaves Marie Arnoux as the older woman and mother she has always been rather than the unattainable lover of his fantasies, so that this scene and sentence exorcise fantasy itself as a living death stultifying all ambitions, personal and political.

The peremptory judgment of 'And that was all' is, however, doubly undone. Perspicacious readers will note that it is an almost verbatim repetition of a statement used during the famous episode and mock idyll at Fontainebleau. Here, while looking at the paintings in the Salle des Fêtes, Frédéric asks Rosanette whether she would have wanted to be Diane de Poitiers, but has then to gloss the historical and cultural significance of this figure as the mistress of Henri II to elicit her response. 'She gave a little "Oh!" That was all. Her silence clearly proved that she knew nothing and did not understand' ['Elle fit un petit "Ah!" Ce fut tout. Son mutisme prouvait clairement qu'elle ne savait rien, ne comprenait pas' (OC II 125)]. Frédéric's interpretation and judgment of Rosanette's exclamation as a lack of (formal) education rebounds on both him and the reader. The 'all' covers the full horror of Rosanette's *sentimental* education which she reveals shortly afterwards (OC II 128). Unprecedented in *L'Education sentimentale* in terms of what the female protagonists are allowed to say of themselves, her full, graphic and harrowing tale sets the record straight. Sold as a child by her mother to a much older man for his physical (ab)use of her, she therefore knows only too well what it is to be a mistress, but not a royal courtesan or by her own will. Final words are thus challenged by retelling from another's viewpoint. The 'all' of the penultimate chapter in like manner generates the stuff of the final chapter which culminates in a similar verbalisation of initiation into sexual experience, or its failure. The last chapter is then an acceptance and final testimony shared by Frédéric and Deslauriers of both characters' undoing throughout the novel when set against the values of success in their society. Their wonderful stereophonic agreement on which the novel closes (that the best of all possible worlds was an abortive youthful visit to a brothel prior to the action of most of the novel) then seems to offer an accord of the living similar to the order of a *post mortem*. If definitive statements clearly fail in *L'Education sentimentale* to tie up emotions and motives dead or alive, does the ending of *L'Education sentimentale* convey any moral or educative purpose?

It is the banal and unsentimental tone of the final chapter that recasts both over-sentimental nostalgia trips and retrospection as modes of guaranteeing the past. The reminiscences indulged in by both protagonists are not a place to learn moral lessons but a comfort zone almost to blanket out familial, political or other public responsibility. Such cosy amorality of the couple's winter idyll sits very uneasily with the ugly events which the narrator throughout has reported, even if at arm's length. Where the deaths of Emma and Mâtho and their consequences on others are brought fully to the reader's attention, the distance both Frédéric and Deslauriers and the novel's narrator maintain to the end questions depth of engagement and responsibility in the lives of others as the moral problem of their times. While Flaubert cleverly models this final chapter on fictions which tie up the loose ends of the plot for major and minor characters, the list of unheroic ends pertaining to all the remaining characters and the seemingly harmonious accord of the novel's key protagonists offer an open but no less critical evaluation of a generation and its uncertain future. Authorial voices or narrators as *moralistes* in *L'Education sentimentale* are therefore dead. The shock for the reader is to take responsibility for, and work out the lessons of, history and story left open in the text.

Understanding as if through a glass darkly is the moral perspective which similarly but more literally ends and resets *La Légende de saint Julien l'Hospitalier* in a stained glass window. Such double takes on events are also apparent in *Un cœur simple*. Final descriptions of Félicité's agony-cum-apotheosis rely upon partial, bifocal viewpoints. La Simonne, as the sole witness of Félicité's death throes, reports on the potentially analogical Corpus Christi celebrations through the small circular 'bull's-eye' ['œil de bœuf'] window in Félicité's upstairs room while Félicité herself, now both blind and deaf, 'sees' the fantastical parrot as Paraclete as if from the mind's eye. The much discussed final main verb of the story, 'she believed she saw' ['elle crut voir' (OC II 177)] offers a similarly varifocal narrative stance combining the proximity of the fantastical with the distance of reasoned reality. What is most obvious and most covered up, however, is that the ending of *Un cœur simple* (as also *La Légende de saint Julien l'Hospitalier*) captures in freeze-frame the strike of death itself, whether arriving at a deeply symbolic or a physiologically inevitable moment. How such horror is to be interpreted, pictured or borne (like the unusually dead weight of Iaokanann's severed head at the ending of *Hérodias*) lies with the reader, not the text.

The bleak message of Flaubert's endings is that reward is not linked to merit, and is not certain either in this or the next world, but is this the ultimate moral of his art? Although undecidability has recently been the favoured critical stance and testifies to the ambivalence of Flaubert's conclusions, the doubling of deaths and their textual *post mortems* make it impossible to retain evaluative neutrality as a critical option. If the endings do nothing else, their under- and overstatements promote re-evaluation by hindsight of the key scenes which led directly to them, such as the gruesome deaths of the central protagonists and the more important hiatus (the tense and time frame designated by a *post mortem*) immediately thereafter. It is this period of reflection that Flaubert targets at the end of all his works, but in *Madame Bovary* most overtly. Here the reader is set alongside the remaining fictional bystanders to deaths protracted or sudden. Thus, the Homais who is completely powerless to save Emma, because he knows only the formula but not how to make an antidote, is the same self-satisfied nonentity who pontificates at her wake and continues to trumpet his way to the *croix d'honneur*. His crass and empty replication of all the acts and rites of the Church he lambasts has been well documented by critics in the scene that elicited the full wrath of the censors, the sacrilegious eucharistic meal he and the priest Bournisien share at the end of the long wake over Emma's dead body (OC 1 687). More morally reprehensible than his acts is the mask of words Homais uses to avoid disclosure of the truth, and not only his failure of duty as 'pharmacist' concerning the dispensing of poisons to Larivière. Most striking is the tenacity of his verbal defences, his 'not me' reaction in the aftermath of Emma's death. The carefully juxtaposed narrative viewpoints of him as father (bringing his sons to watch Emma's last moments for *their* edification), his ushering of Charles from the death-bed on the pretext of rational 'moderation' of the latter's full emotional outburst, clearly demonstrate his panic reaction against his own self-disclosures: Emma's suicide and death bring him the closest yet to discovery of his *own* mortality and non-existence. The long wake scene is, then, the reconstitution in wordy order of the world in its right anti-clerical shape to redraw the defences of the living against death itself, visibly and rationally contained and adjacent to him in another's body, one *very different* from his own. In stark contrast are the sincere, practical and mundane reactions of minor or secondary characters such as Bournisien, Madame Lefrançois and the tearful Félicité (as later Justin) in the laying out and rituals of death, and the more accentuated and extreme reactions of Charles. Having contemplated death in the face of love, his own emotional attacks and imperious commands for Emma's funeral bespeak his wordless and powerless responses and mute acceptance of death itself in his ultimate seizure. Charles, the long lock of Emma's black hair in his hand, presents a complete moral counterpoint to Homais but also Rodolphe whose tin of locks of hair is demonstrably part of the same trophy culture as a *croix d'honneur*, a culture which leaves its perpetrators free and intact, but emotionally dead.

If Homais is the negative, selfish and immoral focaliser of the emotive hiatus between Emma's death and burial, and Charles is its truly stricken and authentic witness, this crucial hiatus involves all the protagonists with death in *Madame Bovary*. Their convergence (as the final ritual celebrations in Carthage where all echelons of society and the priesthood are present) represents the full spectrum of public responses to death itself. While the novel encapsulates in Emma and Charles man *and woman* in the face of death, to refigure the title of Philippe Ariès's study of the history and customs of dying,[6] the public view represented for the reader is at the same time made the reader's. We are a party to the intensely intimate and private last moments in Emma's bedroom, her wake and funeral *via* Charles, but then to his death in a mocking, Norman garden of Gethsemane. Exploitation of the *post mortem* hiatus and its aftermath is similarly employed in *Salammbô* to reiterate the same unavoidable spectacle but in utterly public guise. The gruesome or magnetic fascination of another's death cannot on reflection occlude knowledge of one's own mortality. Working with the distancing effects of the high melodrama – the 'unreal' because another world's rites, rituals and sense of public proprieties – *Salammbô* pulls no punches in its inclusion of representatives of all echelons and parts of society. Children and high priest are all parties in this collective orgy of victory in the destruction of another, defying personal demise by exemplification of such an end in a chosen victim's ritual sacrifice. Yet the reader, while first seated in the collective distance of the Carthaginian amphitheatre, must suddenly share in Mâtho's final thoughts, memories and consciously recorded thoughts as in Emma's. The veil is stripped back like Mâtho's very skin so that proximity and horror replace impersonal observation. It is only once this has been achieved that the reader is also made aware of an alter ego experiencing the same mixed reaction and overtly emotional engagement, Salammbô. Her exchange of glances with Mâtho is powerfully also the reader's before the intensity is fixed and broken by the return from Salammbô's reported thoughts to a more 'objective' comment on her highly subjective physiological and emotional reactions. The time lapse of what are the moments of hiatus signifying her own totally dead faint provide an aftershock for the reader caught up with narrative attention deflected to Narr'havas. Unless the reader has also undergone moral flaying and vivisection through experience of the horror of the text, the final summations will only be endorsed, not challenged. Reader complacency or, worse, complicity with the logic and dogma of Schahabarim's religious sacrifice have too readily also offered up Salammbô's heart and person as scapegoat so as to tidy up the 'civilised' orders of the living.

The 'moral' of both novels is therefore more than 'it is better to have loved and lost, than not to have loved at all', or 'die well while young'. Félicité's long agony in *Un cœur simple* at the end of a similarly agonising and long life of service (as long and thanklessly unrewarded as Catherine

Leroux's in *Madame Bovary*) points up the moral imperative inherent in all Flaubert's works, but one which is perhaps most neatly encapsulated in his *Trois Contes*. Regardless of worldly or religious value systems, the characters who are true to themselves and to values of faith and love encapsulate altogether human capacity and dignity even if misguided. Being or dying in full humanity breaks the character free from the *bêtise* to which they are also prey. Emma and Charles, Salammbô and Mâtho, Félicité and Julien are all captured by Flaubert in their capitulations to being human in shockingly public display. His depictions *in flagrante delicto* are then not the erotic titillation of sexual congress (the cab ride, the tent scene, Julien's bodily covering to warm his mysterious guest), but the embrace of *death*. It is this, in fact, which is manifest in the clearest and most literal of terms in the *Trois Contes*, especially its middle story. If Julien embraces a life of destruction and, like Saul-Paul, a life of service with equal single-mindedness, it is the embrace of death itself as an act of love that seals the story. The radiance and immanence of the endings of each of the tales is less religious 'reward' than a heartfelt and altogether human welcome of death itself. Thus, the reader is left to gaze with horror at the severed head of Iaokanann, the decaying relics of the Corpus Christi procession, Félicité's final 'stroke', and the leprous body of Julien's final visitor as the artefacts which are the stuff of *post mortems* but not of the understanding of the meaning of death.

Flaubert's endings therefore everywhere counter neat resolution or the logic of social or aesthetic conventions. Félicité's famously enigmatic, humorous, mocking or sacrilegious apotheosis is paradigmatic of Flaubert's undoing of tidy (rational) certainty to highlight life's real fragilities, whether the mortal coil itself, or human interpretation of 'last things'. The real shock of finitude is not lessened by being bathed in religious, utterly secular or unreligious settings as *Salammbô*, *L'Education sentimentale* or *Hérodias* respectively demonstrate. Equally, extreme deaths (violent or non-violent) and the shock in their aftermath serve in Flaubert's hands only to highlight the pain of the lives that led to them. Emma's final hours of psychological, physiological and emotional trauma within the privacy of the bedroom and on the marital bed are as nothing compared to the slow undoing which led her there, the suffocation and confusions of her desires and the possibilities for enacting them. Salammbô's final moments allow similar flashbacks, but on the social orders which have brought all the preceding events to such a pass. If *Madame Bovary* and *Salammbô* remain among Flaubert's most concerted dissections of sexuality, violence, and sacrifice to some higher set of values than those of the surrounding world, this chapter has demonstrated that Emma and Salammbô are not the dead bodies over which art and society crow, but the unusually proactive agents by which we get under the skin of their respective societies. On moral and aesthetic grounds, then, the neat tie that critics have discerned between death and the feminine (including biographical influences) in Flaubert's works is concertedly undone in the *dénouements* of both his eponymous novels, as in the *œuvre* as a whole. The double deaths and the *post mortems* in all Flaubert's works depend richly on the puncturing of the double standard of 'right' final judgments. Unlike the overweening commentator moralist at the end of *Salammbô*, the nameless maker of epilogues who fronts Flaubert's moral position is much more akin to la Simonne in *Un cœur simple*. Accompanying Félicité's final moments between life and death, and onlooker on the religious festival of death in the world outside and below, she is supremely the critical vivisector of the living who remain humanly uninvolved because of their own blinkered views. Epilogues *à la Simonne* then also eschew the medical or scientific discourses and logic of the pathologist diagnosing and validating causes of death. Rather, by dealing with those supremely human rites of passage captured and attended to by midwives and women laying out dead bodies, Flaubert's most telling final lines pronounce the morality of the mortician. It is profoundly human interest that grounds the ethics of Flaubert's art in a life's work, particularly in his female creations, that censures the pillars of society for their lack of humanity.

Death has always been the great mystery which draws together religion, law, science and art. In a century obsessed by the death of the Enlightenment's revolutionary optimism at its beginning and by the death of God at its end, Flaubert's unerring ear to his generation hears the cacophony of theories about ends and means of overcoming (as *inter alia* positivism, socialism, art for art's sake) as a chorus in different keys. If Zola is credited later in the nineteenth century for his depiction of crowds, Flaubert's spectrum of representations of responses to death is a comparable achievement. These are most visible not in the battle scenes, however horrific and lurid, but in the banquets and public feasts that are the collective masks of Eros and Thanatos. As Mario Vargas Llosa maintains, what happens upon rereading 'those scenes that are volcanic craters' in Flaubert is the discovery of 'secret facets, unpublished details'.[7] If Vargas Llosa has identified them in the erotic and the 'perpetual orgy' as also the site of Flaubert's aesthetic mastery, this chapter has pointed further to their shockingly doubled voices of death. In Flaubert's evaluation of his society, what is superficially or morally visible or verifiable counts for very little. Most at stake through the scalpel of his pen is the unseen but altogether real evidence of a beating and human heart. It is, then, primarily in the deaths of his life-affirming yet non-conforming characters that the moral work of mortality is revealed in all Flaubert's novels and short stories.

NOTES

1 As Elizabeth Bronfen contends in *Over Her Dead Body: Death, Femininity and the Aesthetic* (Manchester: Manchester University Press, 1992).

2 A comparison of the death of Salammbô and the death of Charles is striking: 'His head was thrown back against the wall, his eyes were shut, his mouth open and he was holding a long lock of black hair' ['Il avait la tête renversée contre le mur, les yeux clos, la bouche ouverte, et tenait dans les mains une longue mèche de cheveux noirs' (OC I 692)].

3 See Sarah Webster Goodwin, 'Emma Bovary's Dance of Death', *Novel*, 19:3 (1986), 197–215, p. 207. For the fullest study to date of death, the *danse macabre* and its medieval heritage in *Madame Bovary*, see Yvonne Bargues-Rollins, *Le Pas de Flaubert: une danse macabre* (Paris: Champion, 1998).

4 Alan Raitt, *The Originality of 'Madame Bovary'* (Bern: Peter Lang, 2002), pp. 105 and 118–20 respectively.

5 For an account of this alternative love story, see Mary Orr, 'Reading the Other: Flaubert's *L'Education sentimentale* revisited', *French Studies*, 46 (1992), 412–23.

6 Philippe Ariès, *L'Homme devant la mort*, vol. II, *La Mort ensauvagée* (Paris: Seuil, 1977).

7 Mario Vargas Llosa, *The Perpetual Orgy* (London and Boston: Faber and Faber, 1987), p. 10. Quoted as examples are the agricultural fair, the ride in the cab, Emma's death.

8

LAURENCE M. PORTER

The art of characterisation in Flaubert's fiction

Of what does a fictional character consist? What choices does Flaubert make in devising his imaginary beings? And how do his styles in character creation compare with those of other authors? Flaubert's two greatest achievements are the creation of richly varied dramatic characters and the depiction of ludicrous grotesques. The inner life of the former transcends simple dichotomies: their psychopathology generates delusional projections that blur the boundaries between fantasy and reality; their vague wishes and abortive projects problematise the relationships between thought and action; their dysfunctionality is florid. The inherent mediocrity of the grotesques, displayed as they blindly conform to, unthinkingly cite, or skilfully manipulate cultural clichés, provides the major vehicle of satire. At times, as with Emma Bovary, these two character types overlap.

We shall examine six dimensions of characterisation: (1) denotation (the strings of naming, recalling and characterisation that allow readers to distinguish among individual characters, and to trace each throughout the work); (2) description, including physical appearance, analyses of feelings, attributions of character traits, and reporting of thoughts; (3) function (characters' roles in moving or delaying the plot, and serving as thematic vehicles: the personified narrator, author or reader may at times play such a role); (4) connotation (triggering unstated associations in the reader's mind, especially those potentiating subjective, episodic, thematic, allegorical or anagogic (i.e., relating to spiritual maturation) meanings); (5) character types; and (6) the patterns of personal relationships, which constitute the essence of Flaubert's fictional worlds.

These elements vary according to Flaubert's choice of genre. The major prose genres of his maturity are fourfold: realist novels, a historical novel, legends, and an 'anatomy' (an encyclopaedic compendium of one or more broad domains of human knowledge, often loosely connected by a rudimentary plot). The realist novels, *Madame Bovary* and *L'Education sentimentale*, assemble obscure, invented bourgeois protagonists short on

money, opportunity and resolve, and characterised by self-defeating or rou-
tinised behaviours. They appear on the stage of the reader's here and now:
recent times and imaginary composite settings in northern France.

The historical novel *Salammbô* presents invented protagonists and some
historically prominent secondary characters limited by fate, motivated by
passion, and living far away and long ago. Legends (*Trois Contes* and the
three versions of *La Tentation de saint Antoine*) evoke prominent protagonists attested by Jewish and Christian religious texts, impelled by supernatural forces, and once again set in remote times and places. (*Un cœur simple*
is a modern, 'unknown' legend.) The anatomy, *Bouvard et Pécuchet*, depicts
modern Saint Anthonies to whom grace is lacking; their ordeal is temptation
not by the Seven Deadly Sins co-ordinated by the Devil, but by the pretensions of the branches of human knowledge. Saint Antoine's adventure ends
when he can recognise the Devil's proffered delights as delusions, and return
to his prayers. Bouvard and Pécuchet conclude by resuming their copying.
But as the drafts and plans of Flaubert's projected volume two – preserved
in the 'Sottisier' (his lifelong collection of conversational banalities and ludicrous opinions) – reveal, instead of passively retranscribing human absurdity
as they had done before, they will expose it by juxtaposing damning, self-
cancelling, mutually contradictory claims to know the truth.

As colour-coded wiring allows us to trace electrical circuits, *denotation*
(the ways in which a text refers to fictional characters) allows us to distinguish among them. Once extended beyond a single mention, denotation
becomes anaphoric, threading a single identity through the story along referentially synonymous strings of proper nouns, pronouns, common nouns
and attributive phrases. The default choice for first mentions, in third-
person narration, promptly names and identifies the character. Flaubert's
juvenilia often foreground the heterodiegetic ('outside the story') dimension through romantic, self-conscious references to the author's concept
and composition: 'Let those memories of sleepless nights revisit me!' 'Why
write these pages?' 'The hero of this book . . .' ['A moi donc ces souvenirs
d'insomnie!' 'Pourquoi écrire ces pages?' 'Le héros de ce livre . . .' (OJ
243, 367, 835)]. In Flaubert's maturity, he prefers the impressionistic alternative, which initially presents the character as unknown (Charles Bovary and
Emma Rouault, Frédéric Moreau, Jacques and Marie Arnoux, Bouvard and
Pécuchet).

Denotation sets the stage for *appellation* (the way one fictional character
addresses another). In *Madame Bovary*, appellation becomes a powerful
vehicle for satire. Characters who try to control how they are named ('Call
me Ishmael') illustrate the vanity of false claims to distinction: Charles's
first and second wives both insist on being addressed as 'Madame' by their

servants; as a further affectation, Emma hires an untutored girl as maid-of-all-work, and trains her to address her mistress in the third person; 'Madame' used in Félicité's thoughts to refer to her harsh employer in *Un cœur simple* reveals how habitual the honorific was between them, reflecting Madame Aubain's imperious demand for absolute superiority in their relationship. Félicité uncritically submits to this claim.

In *Madame Bovary*, the insincerely flattering appellation 'docteur' helps Homais and Rodolphe ingratiate themselves with Charles (a paramedic). Homais hopes that Charles will overlook his illegal medical consultations; Rodolphe's feigned respect masks his arrogance in usurping Charles's role as Emma's sexual partner. Charles is charmed (OC 1 627). The prime example of manipulative appellation in *Madame Bovary* is Rodolphe's show of despair at being able to address Emma only with a name (Madame Bovary) that belongs to another, a name Emma herself resents having. Rodolphe's tactical use of 'Emma' creates decisive breakthroughs in his campaign of seduction (OC 1 627, 628), while contrasting starkly with his private denotations of the health officer's wife: 'She', 'that doctor's wife', 'she', 'one', 'Poor little woman!', 'It', 'it', 'how to get rid of it afterwards?' ['Elle', 'cette femme de médecin', 'elle', 'on', 'Pauvre petite femme!', 'Ça', 'cela', 'comment s'en débarrasser ensuite?' (OC 1 618)] Emma at times calls Charles 'my friend' ['mon ami'] to create the semblance of a loyalty and appreciation that she rarely feels.

Unvarying denotation naming the speakers throughout Flaubert's *Tentation de saint Antoine* gives the characters a hieratic, symbolic rigidity. (Many are in fact allegorical figures, especially in the 1849 and 1856 versions.) Simultaneously, the device of using a single name-tag to introduce all instances of a character's speech highlights by contrast the varieties of appellation used by that character to express shifting feeling tones in an interaction. For example, note the alternation between flattery, insult, and condescension in Hilarion's speeches to Antoine: 'a saint like you', 'Hypocrite', 'good hermit' ['un saint tel que toi', 'Hypocrite', 'bon ermite' (OC 1 533–4)]. In the realist novel, however, when Flaubert inserts a patch of unvarying theatrical denotation to signal clichéd speech in the latter part of chapter twenty-three in *L'Education sentimentale* of 1845 (OJ 988–98), such denotation becomes equivalent to an ironic punctuation mark, like the italics Flaubert uses to signal trite popular or jargon expressions, or like the hyphens linking the words of the unvarying, unreflective racist slogans satirised by Léon-Gontran Damas or Aimé Césaire.

The chosen denotation in Flaubert's realistic novels often suggests that the protagonists do not 'fit in'. Repeatedly in the first scene where Charles Bovary appears in *Madame Bovary*, both classmates and teacher refer to him slightingly as 'le *nouveau*' – the 'new boy'. Taller than any of his classmates, he appears obviously too old for the class; his heavy shoes are inappropriate for school; he has outgrown his clothes. In every detail, here as later, he is *de trop*.[1] 'Flavoured' denotation or appellation, suggesting an emotional link to the character, may shift from voice to voice in Flaubert. At the end of Charles's humiliation in the classroom scene, the teacher tells the 'poor devil' ['pauvre diable' (OC I 575)] to go and sit on the dunce's bench. We cannot be certain whether it is the teacher or the narrator who feels a glimmering of sympathy for Charles. But later, after Rodolphe abandons Emma and she falls gravely ill, while Charles struggles with financial problems, it is surely the omniscient narrator who denotes him as 'the poor lad' ['le pauvre garçon' (OC I 645)].

Aside from the shifting, coruscating emotional climate that denotation creates or reinforces, the device serves two major, contrasting structural functions – as an *embrayeur* (a way of 'shifting gears' among our ways of looking at the self-same character) that fosters relativity, or as a structural support. Often, Flaubert as narrator moves from the subject pronoun to the proper name to signal that he is entering the individual subjectivity of the character – provided that the latter is on stage at the present time of narration.

Scrutinising expressions used for denotation may seem pedantic, but this exercise highlights an essential feature of Flaubert's style in character portrayal. Denotation represents the default choice for narrative. It seems essential for preserving coherence. Flaubert, however, often makes the marked choice of removing denotation. Free direct or indirect discourse – the verbal representation of a person's thoughts or words, without attribution – results. Free *direct* discourse (unattributed dialogue) accelerates the narrative by removing regular, alternating designation through naming or pronoun reference (e.g., Diderot's *Lui* and *Moi* in *Le Neveu de Rameau*). It heightens the dramatic impact of the passage affected, while inviting the reader to pass over it quickly. Free *indirect* discourse (FID, alias *style indirect libre*) in contrast slows our reading. The device is actually not 'free' but rather, ambiguous: it intrudes a phantom presence of the implied author or narrator beside the character. We do not know which words to ascribe to whom; some may belong to both. FID forces readers to pay closer attention to a passage, to examine it for signs of naïveté, prejudice, self-deception, or bad faith. Context provides clear clues to which character's discourse may be presented in 'unbound' form, through focalisation: the character most recently denoted – provided that the denotation is accompanied with a verb of perceiving, thinking, writing, or saying – is the one whose discourse appears in the nearest following passage of FID. For added clarity, Flaubert often refocalises on the same character at the conclusion of the FID. Here is a compound example from *L'Education sentimentale*, depicting the anti-hero Frédéric Moreau's best friend, Deslauriers, feeling and reacting to his resentment against Frédéric for having broken his promise to lend fifteen thousand francs:

> [*Focalisation with pronoun and verb designating thought processes*] Then he pondered how to go about getting back the fifteen thousand francs. [*Free indirect discourse*] A sum like that meant nothing to Frédéric! But if *he* had had it, what leverage! [*Focalisation designating mood*] And the former clerk felt indignant that the other's fortune was so great.
>
> [*The mood becomes so strong that it erupts as a soliloquy*] 'He makes a wretched use of it. He's an egoist. Well! I don't give a damn about his fifteen thousand francs!'
>
> [*Free indirect discourse*] Why had he lent them? For Mme Arnoux's pretty face. She was his mistress! [*Refocalisation with the proper name of the character, and a verb designating thought processes*] Deslauriers was sure of it. [*Another burst of indignation erupts as a soliloquy*] 'That's one more thing money is good for!' [*Summarisation of Deslaurier's mood*] Hateful thoughts flooded him.

> [Alors, il chercha comment s'y prendre pour recouvrer les quinze mille francs. Une pareille somme n'était rien pour Frédéric! Mais, s'il l'avait eue, lui, quel levier! Et l'ancien clerc s'indigna que la fortune de l'autre fût grande.
>
> 'Il en fait un usage pitoyable. C'est un égoïste. Eh! je me moque bien de ses quinze mille francs!'
>
> Pourquoi les avait-il prêtés [à Jacques Arnoux]? Pour les beaux yeux de Mme Arnoux. Elle était sa maîtresse! Deslauriers n'en doutait pas. 'Voilà une chose de plus à quoi sert l'argent!' Des pensées haineuses l'envahirent.
>
> (OC II 97)]

This example suggests that soliloquy is a form of free *direct* discourse: the imperfect tense and the third-person subjects of FID yield to present-tense, first-person speech. At such moments, the phantom of the impersonal narrator dissipates, giving the character an ostensibly unmediated presence, more apparent energy, and greater potential for translating thoughts into action. The quotation marks surrounding the soliloquies are redundant, not strictly necessary; but they reinforce the frontier between the homodiegetic (the story proper) and the heterodiegetic (the domain of the author communicating the story to the readers), the quotation marks introduce a territory of pure 'thereness' inhabited by 'them', the characters, as opposed to the 'hereness' of narrative transmission, involving 'us'.[2]

The passage continues with another focalisation; analysis of Deslauriers's inmost feelings by the omniscient narrator; FID; soliloquy; omniscient psychoanalysis; soliloquy; omniscient psychoanalysis; soliloquy; omniscient psychoanalysis; and narration blended with omniscient analysis, leading to Deslauriers's angry attempt to avenge himself on Frédéric, and his infatuated attempt to merge himself with Frédéric's identity, both by seducing Madame Arnoux. In other words, in the continuation, the identities of narrator and character, at first partially blurred by the single instance of FID, separate once again into the character's vivid presence (soliloquy) on the one hand, and, on the other, the detached, godlike insight of the privileged author. This separation ostensibly 'frees' the character for action, while quietly accumulating in the analysis the factors that determine that action: *consciously*, Deslauriers's mounting indignation against his unfaithful friend liberates him from reservations about seducing Frédéric's 'mistress'; *unknowingly*, Deslauriers is compelled to try to seduce Madame Arnoux because he loves Frédéric. He will later consummate this love in another triangulated relationship by marrying Louise Roque, whom Frédéric had intermittently planned to marry.

Description functions epistemologically to reveal details of fictional beings to us readers – and, occasionally, to observer-characters – at moments of slowed or zero narrative speed. Description may involve the virtual reader, whose viewpoint may provisionally fuse with that of a character (Frédéric Moreau on first seeing Madame Arnoux, Charles Bovary first seeing Emma Rouault) through impressionistic observation: limited knowledge, distance, obscured vision, or muffled sounds blur perception. A human object of description may reveal itself through forms of self-characterisation such as free indirect discourse, soliloquy, or stream of consciousness. These form a subset of description, 'independent' of the controlling narrator. Other characters, singly or collectively, may reveal facets of the target character through their implied or specified observations and discourse. The implied author reveals through omniscient commentary.

Despite its implicit dependency on facts, the historical novel needs to initiate the reader into circumstances that are by definition unfamiliar. Whereas our familiar traditions, based on our shared cultural competence, are *our story* – our legends, what in our culture is known to and venerated by us – 'history' *per se* is someone else's story. Its characters come without a built-in identity. Therefore, in historical fictions, denotation often inseparably intertwines with and depends on description. As if to illustrate Flaubert's self-criticism that the base of *Salammbô* (the history of Carthage) is too large for its statue (the title character), Flaubert devotes the first eight pages to a tableau of the mercenaries' banquet outside the city before introducing Salammbô herself.

Upon the heroine's dramatic appearance, the mercenaries feasting around the base of a palace realise her identity after a moment whose duration is represented by only three words: 'Suddenly the highest terrace of the palace blazed with light, the middle door swung open, and *a woman, Hamilcar's daughter herself,* draped in black robes [*noun + emphatic designation of parentage + descriptive, synecdochal phrase*], appeared on the threshold' ['Le palais s'éclaira d'un seul coup à sa plus haute terrasse, la porte du milieu s'ouvrit, et une femme, la fille d'Hamilcar elle-même, couverte de vêtements noirs, apparut sur le seuil' (OC 1 697)]. After that, Flaubert denotes her as 'she' four times in present-tense narration and description, then as 'Salammbô' in a relative clause describing habitual past action, plus two more 'she's' describing her continued approach, before launching into a descriptive paragraph constructed – typically for descriptions – as a series of synecdoches, a selection of her body parts and of items that she wears or carries, each representing the person: 'her hair', 'braids of pearls', 'her temples', 'her mouth', 'her breasts', 'an array of glowing gems', 'her arms', 'her ankles', 'a slender golden chain', 'her wide cloak', 'her steps' ['sa chevelure', 'des tresses de perles', 'ses tempes', 'sa bouche', 'sa poitrine', 'un assemblage de pierres lumineuses', 'ses bras', 'les chevilles', 'une chaînette d'or', 'son grand manteau', 'ses pas' (OC 1 697)]: six body parts, one item of clothing, three items of jewellery, and one form of movement, organised in a sequence that descends her body from hair to feet, thus imitating her own actual descent from the top level of her palace to the gardens below. Typical of hypotyposis (vivid description, often functioning to imbue a character with a supernatural aura), the fourteen lines of this paragraph include at least six specific notations of colour, and eight mentions of the excess of adornment with which Salammbô is loaded, and which literally expands her in space – her powdered hair dressed in the form of a tower, the long train of her dress dragging along the ground, and so on.

After briefly describing the party of priests who accompany her, Flaubert links her directly to the perceptions of the Barbarian soldiers through a mitigated form of impressionism: they know who she is, but none of them is acquainted with her. She embodies a world of luxury and female beauty that they have never known; they have been deprived of any semblance of that world during months of combat. They are dazzled. They have seen her praying on the roof of her palace at night, blurred by the candles that surround her, by the moonlight that makes her seem ethereally pale, and by the mystifying power of her status: 'something divine enveloped her like a fine mist' ['quelque chose des Dieux l'enveloppait comme une vapeur subtile' (OC 1 697)]. As if to underscore the lack of communication between her culture and theirs, she intones a mysterious lament, and then begins singing the epic of Melkarth, god and forefather of her family, in 'an ancient Canaanite tongue that the Barbarians could not understand' ['un vieil idiome chananéen que n'entendaient pas les Barbares' (OC I 698)]. Contrived by the omniscient author, this moment of hypercommunicability (without Flaubert's gloss, we readers would not understand that ancient language either) further distances us from the soldiers' unawareness, whereas in the realistic novel, we regularly if not always would share only the limited knowledge of a character or characters through whom the scene was viewed.

The 'hard-edged' perceptual world of the epic recurs in the historical novel, which focuses sharply on at least its main characters. The modernist novel, in contrast to the historical novel and the epic, presents a 'soft-focus', impressionistic world, grounded in subjectivity, the landscape of thought. An impressionistic style blurs denotation of the object of perception itself: we do not know, at least at first, to whom certain words in the text refer. But with Flaubert, such a style forms part of a steadily sharpening focus that dispels uncertainty. As the forty guests arrive in their wagons and carriages for Emma and Charles's wedding in *Madame Bovary*, one first hears a vehicle approach; then it is revealed as one of six types of carriage; it stops and a mass of people exit, but they gradually resolve into men, women, and children, and then into five clear social levels marked by their clothing. This zoom-in perspective allows Flaubert to create an effect of true-to-lifeness, which he then promptly undermines by displaying his knowledge through pedantic enumeration. When he has completed the passage, all is known.

In contrast, the more authentically realistic modernist novel, such as Virginia Woolf's *Mrs Dalloway*, does not always resolve the first vague impressions into clarity (see the street scene where passers-by try to guess the identity of passengers in a momentarily stalled luxury car, or to decipher a sky-writing advertisement). Flaubert's *Madame Bovary* at times reflects an awkward, self-contradictory evolution towards such a modernist style. His anonymous first-person plural narrator first lists more than twenty sharply observed details of Charles's appearance, but then mentions that because the new boy was half-hidden behind the classroom door, it was difficult to get a good look at him. He concludes his account of Charles's schooldays by saying that it would be difficult for anyone in the class to remember much about him 'today' – a statement belied by the preceding descriptions, and further belied when he drifts into the role of omniscient author, going on to relate the origins, character, and intimate feelings of each of Charles's parents. *L'Education sentimentale* of 1869 avoids most such clumsiness in treating point of view.

Recurring descriptive motifs, considered as intertextual phenomena, imply overarching narrative conventions rooted in beliefs about 'human nature' that simultaneously characterise and prepare the plot. For example, *L'Education sentimentale* (1869) opens with the same deep structures as *Salammbô*. First, a twofold literal correlative of chance: a tableau (a steamboat journey brings many strangers together) and wandering through a crowd (which brings two particular people together); second, internal reduplication, not Salammbô's epic chant this time, but a debased modern equivalent, in the *genre troubadour*, an old harpist's 'oriental romance, all about daggers, flowers, and stars' ['romance orientale, où il était question de poignards, de fleurs et d'étoiles' (OC II 10)]. An epic proper recalls family and ethnic traditions, and the obligation to maintain them through heroic action; in contrast, the 'oriental romance' releases the nineteenth-century audience from their current obligations (such as Frédéric's duty to support his family by returning to his widowed mother, whereas he would rather disrupt somebody else's family) into escapism. The suppressed restlessness of both characters, dissatisfied with the routine assigned them by life, brews their *disponibilité*. The motif of wandering suggests that neither Salammbô's nor Frédéric's will is going to shape events.

The 'historical novel' achieves its reality effect through the ample use of exotic proper names, which remain vague to the modern reader (gods, rulers, characters, places), whereas the 'realistic novel' achieves its own reality effect by means of the concrete: precise notations of date, time of day, and nested images, each of which becomes the ground for the next (in *L'Education sentimentale*, these are Paris, the quai Saint-Bernard, the departing steamboat *la Ville-de-Montereau*). But impressionistic elements persist: initially, Salammbô could be seen only imperfectly, blurred by a nimbus of moonlight; similarly, in *L'Education sentimentale*, clouds of escaping steam blur the steamboat's crowded, cluttered deck. The first people mentioned form anonymous, undifferentiated groups: 'people', 'the sailors' ['des gens', 'les matelots']. Then the focus zooms in on 'a long-haired youth of eighteen, holding a sketchbook underneath his arm' (OC II 8). Obviously trying to resemble a Romantic artist, he contemplates the church towers, and sighs as if to express his lofty, unquenchable aspirations. In the next paragraph, Flaubert enhances our steadily growing awareness by revealing his name, status as a recent secondary-school graduate, home town, and his mother's conventional plans for him: she hopes he will become a lawyer, and inherit money from the surly uncle in Le Havre whom she has sent him to visit and cajole.

Frédéric then strolls among the passengers on deck. Suddenly, as he enters the first-class lounge, a one-line paragraph announces 'It was like an apparition' ['Ce fut comme une apparition' (OC II 9)]. 'Like', implying 'from *his* point of view', promptly undercuts the presumed objectivity of the presentation formula 'It was'. A pretty young woman's eyes dazzle Frédéric. As in *Salammbô*, the description descends, from her hat to her dress, but first it has been focalised in Frédéric's viewpoint – 'he looked at her' ['il la regarda' (OC II 10)] – followed by a paragraph break. In the next paragraph, the synecdochal elements of the woman include: her hat (its ribbons), hair, eyebrows, oval face, dress (light-coloured muslin, polka dots, many folds), nose, and chin. Eleven elements compared to ten for Salammbô; here, five refer to facial features, and six to clothing, organised in terms of two master synecdoches (face, dress) and eight second-order synecdoches – parts of parts (facial features, details of the clothing).

In brief, the representation of clothing has become both more important and more complex in the 'realistic' novel, as opposed to *Salammbô*. Here, a stronger sublimation of the body and sexuality has been displaced to the folds of the dress, and to clothing that hides the body instead of – like Salammbô's jewellery – accentuating it. Frédéric continues to hover around the unknown person, and in a second cycle of observation, his gaze returns to her face and then to her body. This prolonged 'double take', unspecified in *Salammbô* (though we assume that Mâtho along with the other mercenaries was staring at Hamilcar's daughter before she approached to offer him wine), provides an advance mention (a disconnected notation without an explicit causal connection to its immediate context) of Frédéric's enduring erotic obsession, and sets the stage for future plot movement, deferred because the sexual attraction is not yet mutual. All Frédéric's ensuing erotic adventures will be second-rate substitutes.

Flaubert's satiric evaluation of Frédéric's love appears in juxtaposed, clashing tones as he reports the young man's reactions:

[*Effusive exaggeration*] Never had he seen such splendid tanned skin as hers, such a seductive figure, fingers so delicate that the light shone through them. [*One of Flaubert's favourite ironic words; ludicrous anticlimax*] Stupefied, he gazed at her sewing basket as if it had been something extraordinary. [*Neutral reporting of what could be a normal curiosity*] What was her name? Where did she live? What was her life like? What had been her past? [*Comic, fetishistic triviality*] He hoped to become familiar with the furniture in her bedroom, with all the dresses she had ever worn, the people she spent time with; [*Flaubert's characteristic, dynamic use of 'and'/'et' to mark the start of a new, more intense phase of a process*] *and* the very desire for physical possession disappeared [*effusive exaggeration*] beneath an even deeper longing, in a painful curiosity without limits.

[Jamais il n'avait vu cette splendeur de sa peau brune, la séduction de sa taille, ni cette finesse des doigts que la lumière traversait. Il considérait son panier à ouvrage avec *ébahissement*, comme une chose extraordinaire. Quels étaient son nom, sa demeure, sa vie, son passé? Il souhaitait connaître les meubles de sa chambre, toutes les robes qu'elle avait portées, les gens qu'elle fréquentait;

et le désir de la possession physique même disparaissait sous une envie plus profonde, dans une curiosité douloureuse qui n'avait pas de limites.

(OC II 10, my emphases)]

Through a bitter irony, years later, Frédéric will indeed come to know many pieces of Madame Arnoux's clothing and bedroom furniture during what he experiences as a public profanation: her husband goes bankrupt and much of the couple's property is sold at auction. Later still, at the end, when she finally comes to offer her body to him, she has aged so much that he no longer desires her.

Descriptions of individuals among the characters of a novel can serve as mainly decorative – providing a gallery of handsome or of grotesque background types; as predictive – the body is the mirror of the soul; or as *leurres* (misleading clues) that prepare surprises when the ugly person proves noble and idealistic, the austere scholar proves lustful, and the handsome person proves selfish and narcissistic (these three reversals are illustrated, in Hugo's *Notre-Dame de Paris*, by Quasimodo, Claude Frollo, and Gaston Phœbus respectively). Flaubert reverses such conventions in his last novel, *Bouvard et Pécuchet*: no longer is the mirror of the novelistic text unfaithful; it is so faithful that its reflection abolishes meaning. A double description of the two eponymous copy clerks applies Bergson's definition of the comic as 'mechanical repetition imposed on a [single] living being' to the dyad. Flaubert makes the behaviour of one character reduplicate the behaviour of the other:

> Two men appeared.
> One came from the direction of the Bastille, and the other from the Botanical Garden. [. . .]
> When they had reached the middle of the boulevard, they sat down, at the same moment, on the same bench.
> To mop their foreheads, they took off their hats, which each of them set on the ground; and the smaller man saw, written inside his neighbour's hat, 'Bouvard', while the latter could easily make out, inside the cap of the individual wearing a frock coat, 'Pécuchet'.
> 'How about that,' he said. 'We both had the idea of writing our name inside our headgear.'
> 'Of course; somebody in my office could make off with my hat.'
> 'That's like me; I'm an office worker too.'
> Then they studied each other.
>
> [Deux hommes parurent.
> L'un venait de la Bastille, l'autre du Jardin des Plantes. [. . .]
> Quand ils furent arrivés au milieu du boulevard, ils s'assirent, à la même minute, sur le même banc.

Pour s'essuyer le front, ils retirèrent leurs coiffures, que chacun posa près du sol; et le petit homme aperçut, écrit dans le chapeau de son voisin: Bouvard; pendant que celui-ci distinguait aisément dans la casquette du particulier en redingote le mot: Pécuchet.

– Tiens, dit-il, nous avons eu la même idée, celle d'inscrire notre nom dans nos couvre-chefs.

– Mon Dieu, oui, on pourrait prendre le mien à mon bureau!

– C'est comme moi, je suis employé.

Alors ils se considérèrent.   (OC ii 202)]

Flaubert creates the narrative semblance of a stage-set, onto which the two men come from opposite directions. At first only their height and weight differentiate them; their actions and gestures create a perfect bilateral symmetry like the paired images on playing cards, followed by narcissistic recognition.

Two paragraphs of contrasting physical description follow; but the differences in their outward appearance only accentuate the sameness of their views. Most of their ensuing conversation is reported using the pronoun denotation 'they' (a device we may call choral voice) to suggest that they echo commonplaces: mutuality erases communication. From Pécuchet's remark 'How nice it would be in the country!' ['Comme on serait bien à la campagne!'] flows the action of the entire novel – a retreat to the country together. So will rather than chance directs the clerks' course; but the remark, which might seem to initiate a breakaway, actually echoes the Ancient Roman poet Horace's topos (conventional subject) *beatus ille* ('fortunate is he [who can live in the country]') in the *Epistles*. It also refers intertextually to Charles Bovary's longing remark when he looks out over the distant countryside from his garret window in Rouen, while pursuing his studies to become a country Health Officer. All these characters' acts will be re-enactments.

The narrative *function* of fictional characters, as explored by A. J. Greimas's influential study of *actants*, has promoted the view that characters are essentially variants and adjuncts of the dramatic mover, the person whose initiatives make things happen.[3] Greimas allows that his concepts of actantial functions (subject, object, sender, receiver, helper, opponent) need not always be confined to human beings, that one character may fulfil more than one role, and that the set of actantial functions may be redistributed among the characters at one or more moments in the plot. Despite such flexibility, Greimas's model can become less clear-cut and less helpful when the major subject of a text is communication. For his model does not intend to differentiate among three sets of personified entities: those that appear only in the homodiegetic dimensions of a text (e.g., the protagonist and secondary characters in third-person narration), or only in the heterodiegetic dimensions (e.g., the frame narrator or personified audience), or in both (e.g., the personified author or the first-person narrator). Moreover, function involves characters' roles not only as creators, protagonists, assistants, opponents or objects (motivations) of the plot, but also as bystanders, observers and commentators. In Flaubert's youthful story *Les Funérailles du docteur Mathurin*, for example (as in Plato's *Phaedo*), the protagonist must die, and can do nothing to prevent it (OJ 617–37). Death is his opponent; his friends are both helpers and receivers; and the doctor is subject, object, sender and receiver all at once. Facing death, he rediscovers, reaffirms and shares the wisdom that is his legacy to his friends. All the human characters who appear on stage in the *Funérailles*, a symposium, are solidary. Elsewhere, Flaubert's human creations are mainly marginal, ignorant, passive or ineffectual in relation to the progressions of greatest interest in his stories.

In *Salammbô*, for instance, function follows form. Immediately after the opening description cited above, the priest's daughter reaches the level of the garden filled with the feasting mercenaries, and thus symbolically enters the plot. Concomitantly, she begins to communicate with the soldiers. Wandering through the crowd, speaking to individuals in their various languages, Salammbô encounters the officer Narr'Havas, who will become her official fiancé, and the giant Libyan Mâtho. Instead of rendering the three characters' emotional reactions in terms of their subjectivity, Flaubert translates them into the language of action: unconsciously drawn to Mâtho, Salammbô pours him wine. Their mutual attraction will become an effective dramatic motor. Jealous, Salammbô's suitor Narr'Havas promptly wounds him in the arm; Mâtho pursues Narr'Havas, who vanishes, and instead meets the freed slave Spendius, who binds his arm and offers service. From the initial sexual spark, much of the future action will ignite. Mâtho will lead the mercenaries in attacking Carthage in order to claim their rightful pay; he will be captured, tortured, and led beneath the eminence from which Salammbô and her suite watch. As she and Mâtho stare at each other with burning eyes, and she longingly remembers being possessed by him, both collapse and die in turn. The novel and the life of Salammbô conclude together with the ritualistic phrase 'Thus perished the daughter of Hamilcar, for she had touched the veil of Tanit' ['Ainsi mourut la fille d'Hamilcar pour avoir touché au manteau de Tanit' (OC I 797)]. The official sacred history of the priests supersedes and obliterates the personal history of the lovers' illegitimate, blind passion.

Finally, Greimas's model takes account neither of ambiguity nor velleity – dubious knowledge and wavering will. The predominant plot motor in

Flaubert's novels, as opposed to the short narratives, is temptation. Emma Bovary believes that resisting temptation once entitles her to yield to it the next time. Waves of 'self-sacrifice' alternate in her behaviour with troughs of self-indulgence. The same psychic rhythm obtains in saint Antoine, with the difference that Emma descends to what Catholic theology defines as the third and final stage of sin, *consensus voluntatis* ('acting out', sins of intention), whereas Antoine nearly always stops at the second, *delectatio morbosa* (sins of thought).[4]

In the three versions of *La Tentation de saint Antoine* (1849, 1856, 1874), Flaubert deliberately ensures that we do not know whether the Greimasian 'sender' (whoever provides the temptations) might be the Devil, God, or Antoine himself. If the Devil, we have examples of *tentatio subversionis*, temptation used to seduce and destroy. If God, we have *tentatio probationis*, an ordeal that can generate merit when the protagonist – like the Biblical Job – succeeds in a test of his faith. In Antoine, we have examples of psychic projection of his own impulses, ascribed to a supernatural being, and unrecognised owing to repression. In a prolonged state of morbid delectation, Antoine nevertheless resists the temptations of sloth, gluttony, lust, anger, avarice, envy and pride. But through a mere technicality: he greedily throws himself on a heap of coins and jewels, only to find that they were an illusion created by the Devil. Why could they not have been real? Even his self-flagellation in punishment for having imagined himself as the heathen king Nebuchadnezzar modulates into voluptuous fantasies of the Queen of Sheba. In any event, as Antoine's former disciple Hilarion (the Devil in disguise) later argues, the saint is consistently guilty of bad faith and thought-crime: 'You hypocrite! You bury yourself in solitude the better to give in to your overflowing lusts! You deprive yourself of meat, wine, warm baths, slaves and honours; but how you let your imagination offer you banquets, perfumes, naked women, applauding crowds! Your chastity is just a more refined corruption, and that scorn for the world comes from your powerless hatred of it!' ['Hypocrite qui s'enfonce dans la solitude pour se livrer mieux au débordement de ses convoitises! Tu te prives de viandes, de vin, d'étuves, d'esclaves et d'honneurs; mais comme tu laisses ton imagination t'offrir des banquets, des parfums, des femmes nues et des foules applaudissantes! Ta chasteté n'est qu'une corruption plus subtile, et ce mépris du monde l'impuissance de ta haine contre lui!' (OC I 534)] All Antoine can do in reply is to break down into sobs.

When he recognises the steadily growing Hilarion, who now calls himself 'La Science', as the Devil, Antoine realises he can become free only by confronting him directly. So he accepts a ride into space on the Devil's back.

His virtuous resistance and his sinful lust for knowledge become inextricably entangled. As he ascends, the comforting illusions of the Ancients' cosmologies – the harmony of the spheres, the crystalline roof of the heavens, the spirits of the dead inhabiting the moon, angels holding up the stars – all disappear. At first he feels joyously enlightened. But then the Devil preaches a quasi-Spinozistic doctrine that the universe has no purpose; God is no person, but an indivisible substance found in all things. The transcendent cannot be apprehended; hope for union with a personal God is vain. Antoine despairs, but as the Devil is about to devour him, the saint's hand accidentally brushes against his rosary (1849, 1856) or he lifts his eyes one last time to seek divine help (1874), and the Devil departs. The saint then recognises the Devil's insidious words as restatements of the pagan doctrines he had once studied with a sage. At length, he recovers his ability to pray, and thus returns full circle to his starting point, after having experienced each of the Seven Deadly Sins. Flaubert's manuscript notes prove that he had always intended to have the saint triumph at last, exhausting all the Devil's stratagems with his resistance.[5]

Taking Flaubert's five great novels in the order that their definitive versions were completed, one sees that it is the protagonists' epistemological function that differentiates two main phases of the author's career. First, there is blindness (until 1862, with a new episode in 1875–7): a passionate, self-destructive protagonist in a tragic narrative functions as an expendable object in several youthful works, *Madame Bovary*, *Salammbô*, and, later, the three saints' lives told in the *Trois Contes*. Emblematic of this phase would be Flaubert's observation that Charles Bovary 'did not seek to ask himself why he took pleasure in returning to Les Bertaux' ['ne chercha point à se demander pourquoi il venait aux Bertaux avec plaisir' (OC I 580)]. Second, there is insight (1863–81): the protagonist functions as a filter of consciousness in a work whose scattered episodes cohere thematically rather than narratively, revealing the vanity of ambition (*L'Education sentimentale* of 1869), desire (*La Tentation de saint Antoine*, 1874 version), or knowledge (*Bouvard et Pécuchet*). The paradigmatic sentence here would be Flaubert's summation of the intellectual evolution of the two clerks in the last of these works: 'Then a pitiful faculty developed in their minds, that of being able to recognise stupidity and to tolerate it no longer' ['Alors une faculté pitoyable se développa dans leur esprit, celle de voir la bêtise et de ne plus la tolérer' (OC II 275)].

Should one seek a conceptual model to compare the functions of Flaubert's characters, an epistemological grid based on relative blindness and insight seems most accurate. Using examples from *Madame Bovary*, with no pretence of completeness, one could characterise major groups of his realistic character types in terms of blindness, illusion or perceptiveness, thus:

1. Pragmatism, insight, competence, and altruism (Larivière)
2. Pragmatism, insight, and competence without altruism (Rodolphe, Lheureux)
3. Pragmatism and competence without insight or altruism (Homais, Emma before Charles's bankruptcy)
4. Altruism without pragmatism, competence or insight (Charles from Berthe's birth to Emma's death)
5. Delusion giving way to the acceptance of mediocrity (Léon, Justin, Charles's mother)
6. Delusion leading to self-destruction (Emma after Charles's bankruptcy; Charles after Emma's death)
7. Blind, nearly subhuman repetition without redeeming features (Charles, before Berthe's birth; Charles's father, Bournisien, Binet, the blind beggar)

By basing his hierarchies of characters on insight rather than on moral criteria, Flaubert distinguishes himself from the many nineteenth-century authors such as Jane Austen, George Eliot, Henry James, and the normative criticism prevalent at the time, which sought to impose moral principles as a universal standard.[6]

Connotation refers to at least four sets of implications that may arise from the characters' thoughts and actions: *the interpretative* (elements of present situations or traces from past ones – clues – invite the decoding of hidden behaviours and meanings); *the predictive* (elements of present situations provide advance mentions or foreshadowing of future situations or events); *the axiological* (moral evaluation of situations in the narrative present and past); *the deontological* (ethical imperatives that readers are invited to hold in mind as guidance for the future). The interpretative and predictive connotations help us read the plot; the axiological and deontological connotations help us discern the themes ('messages') of a work.

Description, which in Flaubert is often strikingly original and richly detailed, generates connotations that tie character portrayal to both plot and theme. Charles Bovary's awkward earnestness in the first scene where he appears reveals his moderate intelligence, his lack of self-confidence, and his inability to penetrate others' biases and intentions. The title implies he will have a wife; in connection with the first scene, it hints that his marriage(s) will fail. When he goes to treat Emma's father for a broken leg, and sees her for the first time, her description conveys Charles's idealised view of her, the first pretty young woman he has seen.

From a distance, he notices her blue wool dress with three flounces. The material (wool rather than linen or silk) suits the farm, but the flounces suggest conspicuous consumption and narcissistic ornament inappropriate for a farm girl. The blue is associated by Flaubert throughout *Madame Bovary* with the mystified vision of deluded overvaluation.[7] Shortly afterwards, at closer range indoors, Charles is struck by the whiteness of Emma's nails, which he apparently reads as daintiness and elegance, but which to us suggests her selfish personality and her unwillingness to get her hands dirty with farm work. Emma's father confirms our impression that she is narcissistic when he decides he would be willing to give her to Charles in marriage because she is not much help on the farm. That she takes a long time to find her sewing kit to make a pad for her father's splint reveals that she uses it seldom, although 'work' (and the French synonym *ouvrage*) in the nineteenth century often served as synonyms for 'sewing'.

The mediocrity of Flaubert's characters transcends satire and becomes plot when two of them – Emma and Léon, for example – inspire each other through narcissistic mirroring. They then acquire the confidence to embark on limited but disastrous adventures that they would never have thought of alone. Even muddy waters can overflow. When imitation remains mere unreflective conformity, it levels humans into an undifferentiated mass; but when imitation is lived as emulation, and springs from a (deluded) resolve to transform oneself for the better, it becomes inventive insofar as a (willed) repetition produces a result always distinct – in both motivation and outcome – from the original. It generates a story.

Bouvard and Pécuchet, like Emma and Léon, stimulate each other to action – but their imitative projects encompass many domains of human knowledge. Like scientists, they test others' hypotheses by seeking to reproduce reported experimental results. When they at last abandon these efforts, mutually proposing to 'copy as before' ['copier comme autrefois' (OC II 301)], their new hobby will differ fundamentally from the passive reproduction with which they earned their living as copy clerks, as well as from the active reduplications of the experimental method – for they will choose their own passages from the rubbish heap of human thought, and juxtapose them with others that contradict them, to expose the general absurdity of pretensions to knowledge. The clerks' deconstructive criticism literally dissolves the comforting delusions of the cultural code (as it dissolves the novel form), making them intolerable to everyone they know, and undermining prior to its inception any project that they might undertake.

Thus Flaubert's characters come to signify only as part of a social nexus – in their interrelationships with other human entities within both the homodiegetic (accounts of the characters' relationships to their world) and the heterodiegetic (the implied author as creator rather than reporter, the implied and the personified readers, the historical author and public) dimensions. They are seen and judged by themselves, by other characters, or by the implied author. In other words, they may be presented from inside the self, from inside their society, or from outside their society when the implied author presents that society as exotic, or when s/he seems in it but not of it.

The ontological status of a character may remain steady, evolve, or remain undetermined. In *Madame Bovary*, for example, Binet and Bournisien stay fixed in their repetitive roles as grotesques; Homais and Lheureux change in function as they increasingly succeed and as their success emboldens them, but do not change in terms of the values connoted by their characters; Charles undergoes a conversion from stolid petit bourgeois to impractical romantic – from inadequate to self-destructive – while Léon evolves in just the opposite direction. Most of the situations of Flaubert's characters remain base or grotesque, and few of us readers would wish to emulate anything that they do. Flaubert's realistic tales are above all cautionary.

Flaubert's *character types* are limited mainly to dupes, persecutors and grotesques. The two main foundations of Flaubert's concept of character are unreflective conformity and temptation. Naïve, belated imitations of the romantic hero by Emma Bovary and Léon Dupuis, Henry Gosselin and Jules (in *L'Education sentimentale* of 1845), or Frédéric Moreau provide a broad basis for Flaubert's bourgeois critique, and a vehicle for the young bourgeois's aspirations ('every notary bears within himself the ruins of a poet', Flaubert remarked in *Madame Bovary* ['chaque notaire porte en soi les débris d'un poète' (OC I 672)]). Throughout life, as Flaubert understands it, the herd instinct makes people drift towards superficial agreement for the sake of companionship and comfort. He repeatedly exposes the jarring dissonance that underlies such agreement.

When the Bovarys have just arrived at Yonville, and take supper at the inn with Léon and Homais, Léon and Emma 'entered into one of those vague conversations where the drift of the sentences always leads you back to a fixed centre of mutual sympathy' ['entrèrent dans une de ces vagues conversations où le hasard des phrases vous ramène toujours au centre fixe d'une sympathie commune' (OC I 602–3)]. To a perceptive observer, however, Emma's strong, restless character contrasts sharply with Léon's irresolute, dreamy personality.

Flaubert underscores this difference through the very defects of Léon's imitation. Emma contradicts Homais, who expresses sympathy for her, thinking she must be tired from having been bounced around in the local stagecoach: 'moving always entertains me; I like to go to different places' ['le dérangement m'amuse toujours: j'aime à changer de place']. Even as the object of the verb in the first clause, she imagines herself as free; in the second, as subject, she takes the initiative. Léon's overstated agreement is telling: 'It's so dreary, sighed the clerk, to have to live nailed down to the same few places!' ['C'est une chose si maussade, soupira le clerc, que de vivre cloué aux mêmes endroits!' (OC I 601)] Unlike Emma at this juncture, he imagines himself as helpless and imprisoned. Nevertheless, he ranks above Charles in the power hierarchy of the conversation; for when the health officer observes that Léon wouldn't care for changes of scene so much if he too were obliged continually to journey on horseback, Léon contradicts him, turning to Emma to say that he finds nothing more agreeable than riding – when one has a chance to do it, he adds. The irony of this advance mention emerges, and emphasises Léon's weakness, later, when Rodolphe uses the pretext of a horseback ride to seduce Emma, a seduction that Léon has not even begun owing to his timidity and indecision. Somewhat later in their first conversation (OC I 602), speaking of literature, Léon claims, 'I like poetry especially. I think verse is more tender than prose, and much better at making you cry' ['j'aime surtout les poètes. Je trouve les vers plus tendres que la prose, et qu'ils font bien mieux pleurer']. Emma, who prefers strong sensations, has little interest in tenderness or tears, and contradicts him: 'But poetry gets tiresome after a while, and now, on the contrary, I love stories that sweep you away, and scare you. I can't stand ordinary heroes and moderate feelings, as one finds in real life' ['Cependant ils [les vers] fatiguent à la longue, et maintenant, au contraire, j'adore les histoires qui se suivent tout d'une haleine, où l'on a peur. Je déteste les héros communs et les sentiments tempérés, comme il y en a dans la nature'].

Léon's hasty, inept agreement glaringly exposes the incompatibility of the two young people's characters: 'Indeed, the clerk remarked, because they don't touch your heart, those works miss the real goal of Art. It is pleasant, amid the disillusionments of life, to be able to fall back, in your imagination, onto noble characters, pure affections, and portrayals of happiness' ['En effet, observa le clerc, ces ouvrages, ne touchant pas le cœur, s'écartent, il me semble, du vrai but de l'Art. Il est *doux*, parmi les *désenchantements* de la vie, de pouvoir se reporter en idée sur de *nobles* caractères, des affections *pures* et des tableaux de *bonheur*' (my emphasis)]. Léon's tastes are closer to the Romantics under Napoleon I, to Chateaubriand or Senancour; Emma's are closer to the frenetic and Gothic literature of the following generation. One finds similar discrepancies in the mutually admiring first conversation between Bouvard and Pécuchet. All unawares, Flaubert's characters agree more on social than intellectual grounds – which helps explain the conservative priest Bournisien's surprising remark to the militantly Voltairean, deistic pharmacist Homais after Emma's wake: 'One of these days we'll reach an understanding!' ['Nous finirons par nous entendre!' (OC I 687)]

Alongside such silly, innocuous scenes, Flaubert keenly depicts virulent emulation, in the form of collective persecution, as a key principle of social cohesion. It betrays an animal instinct, close to that which leads a flock of hens or a school of sharks to attack and rend a bleeding member from their group. So, in the first scene of *Madame Bovary*, Charles's new schoolmates – significantly denoted as *nous,* as the horde – mentally mark him as different (*le nouveau*), and then promptly unite in persecuting him because he is awkward; later, nearly everyone sadistically blames Hippolyte for the disastrous outcome of Charles's and Homais's ignorant, illegal surgical experiment on him; similarly, at the conclusion of the novel years later, 'everyone set about to *take advantage*' ['chacun se mit à *profiter*' (OC I 689)] by billing the distraught Charles for invented lending library fees, music lessons, or other services and items allegedly purchased by his late wife.

In later works, Flaubert acutely depicts the interdependence of violence and the sacred in theocratic societies, and of violence and legitimation in the secular state. In theocracies, our animal blood lust, repressed into the personal and political unconscious, emerges in disguise when it becomes projected onto the idea of the will of a fantasised deity. Sacrificing victims, be they innocents or rebels, then contributes to serve a purportedly transcendent ideal. Thus, in *Salammbô*, children are burned alive in the furnaces of the sun god Moloch, and the Barbarian prisoners of war are tortured and executed as the centrepiece of a public entertainment that reaffirms the solidarity of members of the State. In *L'Education sentimentale* of 1869, le père Roque's and Sénécal's separate, gratuitous murders of unarmed Republican demonstrators presciently characterise the freelance, state-sanctioned atrocities that reaffirm the legitimacy of the modern secular state, two years before Thiers's troops slaughtered more Parisians – including women and children – than were executed during the Reign of Terror. Frédéric Moreau, an exception, floats untouched on the surface of society, does not truly participate. The brutal mechanism churns away beside him while he remains intact, as we realise during his retreat to the Forest of Fontainebleau at the height of the 1848 Revolution.

Artistic self-consciousness provides an escape hatch from society in Flaubert's last novel. Defeated and ostracised, Bouvard and Pécuchet, in their return to copying at the end of their story, retreat from society to text. Postmodernist before the fact, the two clerks and their story achieve resolution by shifting from the homodiegetic (the action of the story) to the heterodiegetic (the production of the text).

Our concluding question is whether Flaubert has an identifiable authorial signature when creating characters, and how his techniques of characterisation situate him in relationship to other authors. Not universally in his works, but overall, it would appear that he depicts either negation or failure. Pernicious temptation drives most of his realistic plots: there, temptation never functions as a refining ordeal (*tentatio probationis*), but only as a closed loop or a prelude to disappointment, disillusionment or self-destruction (*tentatio subversionis*). Characters' velleities of resistance serve only to dramatise their self-deception and bad faith. Emma Bovary, having concealed her lust for Léon, feels entitled to an affair with Rodolphe – and, later, with Léon – by way of compensation for her provisional virtue. When characters succumb, they are destroyed: if they resist, the plot goes nowhere, for they have few other inner resources. The heaven into which Saint Julien (wrapped in Christ's arms), Félicité (seeing her parrot in gigantic form hovering over her death-bed as the Holy Spirit), or Emma Bovary (at the moment when, dying, she gives the Crucifix the most passionate kiss of her life) imagine they are borne away is the non-artist's equivalent of the 'skies' (in theatre), of the author's heterodiegetic trapdoor through which s/he exits at the end. But once you exit, your story is done.

In the 1869 *Education sentimentale* Flaubert sardonically de-dramatises temptation, by showing a character resisting it in one form either through inertia, or because another temptation seems more attractive. Characters repeatedly yield to it in a way that is itself unfulfilling and pointless. In a corrupt society full of dupes and persecutors, Flaubert implies, no successful love relationship, loyal friendship, or dignified occupation is possible. The apparent attainment of goals represents only a higher sarcasm by the implied author, who grants his characters something worthless. Frédéric finally starts an affair with the long-coveted courtesan Rosanette Bron, but finds her stupid and uneducated; he 'seduces' the pretty, fashionable socialite Madame Dambreuse (who wants revenge on her husband, and is on the rebound from another affair) to discover that she is domineering and physically unexciting; his childhood companion Louise Roque desperately wants to marry him, but remains emotionally immature and unpolished as she becomes chronologically an adult; when Frédéric's obsession, the unattainable Madame Arnoux, finally offers herself to him, she has lost her physical attractiveness – exposing Frédéric's sentiments as lustful rather than ethereal. The one viable social option Flaubert imagines is chaste male bonding, at times homoerotically tinged through the inadvertent or deliberate sharing of women.

Curiously, Flaubert's concept of character in the 'realistic' novels is essentialist. No change is possible, except for one that would exclude the heroes from society. This contrast of successful but vile integration versus noble isolation already appears sharply, self-mockingly drawn in the *dénouement* of the 1845 *Education sentimentale*, where the fate of the worldly Henry and the writer Jules are described:

> Jules has become a serious, great artist whose patience never tires, and whose commitment to the ideal never lapses. [. . .]
>
> Do you know that Henry is about to make a rich, powerful, splendid marriage? [. . .] Within four or five years he will be in parliament, and once he's there, the sky is the limit.
>
> Jules left for the Middle East yesterday, taking two pairs of shoes that he intends to wear out trekking through Lebanon, and a volume of Homer that he will read on the banks of the Hellespont.

> [Il [Jules] est devenu un grave et grand artiste dont la patience ne se lasse pas, et dont la conviction à l'idéal n'a pas d'intermittences. [. . .]
>
> Savez-vous qu'Henry va faire un riche, un puissant, un superbe mariage? [. . .] Avant quatre ou cinq ans il sera député, et une fois député où s'arrêtera-t-il?
>
> Jules est parti hier pour l'Orient, emportant avec lui deux paires de souliers qu'il veut user sur le Liban, et un Homère qu'il lira au bord de l'Hellespont.
>
> (OJ 1075, 1079)]

The superlatives and the prideful negations quietly ridicule Flaubert's own ambitions as a writer – who has just completed his first major work. The direct address to the readers, and the excited rhetorical questions, suggest that Henry's success enthrals them much more than Jules's isolation. The clichéd romantic pose of the last sentence recalls Flaubert's own life to date (he spent an hour every morning reading Homer instead of studying law), while implying that Jules's projects for extensive travelling (*'veut* user') may not eventuate, but that we may be sure that he will *read* ('lira'), adventuring vicariously in the twofold cocoon of his retreat from France, far both in virtual time and physical space.

Contrast the fundamental existentialism of Hugo's *Les Misérables*. Despite Hugo's overarching, mystical, redemptive cosmology, in its details his work allows for different individual outcomes – in this life – depending on altered circumstances. These possibilities do not belong to parallel worlds, as do the parastories in Stendhal's *Le Rouge et le Noir* (*if* Julien and Madame de Rênal had lived in a warmer climate, they would have been more scantily dressed, and their mutual attraction would have become apparent to them sooner), which self-consciously express the author's hypercreativity, but to a domain of the characters' choices, which ultimately entail their moral responsibility.

Flaubert seldom flaunts his total control of his novelistic world by evoking hypothetical alternative outcomes for his stories, but his characters rarely have free choice. The question is seldom whether his characters will succeed in resisting temptation, but only for how long. In Flaubert's view, love is the illusion of freedom. And politics, a temptation Flaubert tried hard to suppress in *L'Education sentimentale* of 1869 but which revives in *Le Candidat* (1874), was too corrupted to be possible. Blindness, hypocrisy or callousness poison all Flaubertian relationships. Art at its best is a vain attempt to exorcise our emotional need for others, through pitiless exposure of their defects. But Flaubert's grotesques are his self-indulgence, irresistible to the satirist in him. Excrescences, they provide him with a holiday from the plot, with its constant, unwelcome reminder of life's failures.

NOTES

1 For a detailed analysis of the initial draft's hypotyposis (vivid description) and its eventual minimisation in the first description of Charles, see Laurence M. Porter and Eugene F. Gray, eds., *Gustave Flaubert's 'Madame Bovary': A Reference Guide* (Westport, CT: Greenwood, 2002), pp. 33–5.

2 In philosophic parlance, an 'indexical' (known as a 'deictic' in linguistics) is a word designating or referring back to a particular person, time or place: *she*, *they*, *here*, *then*, and so forth.

3 A. J. Greimas, *Sémantique structurale* (Paris: Larousse, 1966).

4 According to Catholic theology, the first stage of sin is 'the surprise of the senses', the involuntary perception of an attractive but forbidden object. Even Christ fell subject to this stage, when thrice tempted by the Devil. Saints experience the second stage as well, and the rest of us, all three.

5 Bibliothèque nationale de France, Paris: NAF (Nouvelles Acquisitions Françaises) 23669, fol. 290/432; NAF 23671, fol. 107. For a more detailed examination of the *Tentation*'s evolution, see Laurence M. Porter, *The Literary Dream in French Romanticism: A Psychoanalytic Interpretation* (Detroit, MI: Wayne State University Press, 1979), pp. 47–67. These pages are to be republished in a forthcoming volume of the *Dictionary of Literary Biography* devoted to Flaubert, edited by Eric Le Calvez.

6 In *The Trouble with Principle* (Cambridge, MA: Harvard University Press, 1999), Stanley Fish reveals himself as a perhaps unwitting heir to Flaubert's scepticism.

7 See Stirling Haig, *The Madame Bovary Blues: The Pursuit of Illusion in Nineteenth-Century French Fiction* (Baton Rouge, LA: Louisiana State University Press, 1987), pp. 79–93.

9

ALISON FINCH

The stylistic achievements of Flaubert's fiction

Flaubert is the foremost nineteenth-century French innovator in prose style. But he had pioneering predecessors and like-minded contemporaries: the century was one in which the best writers treated prose as an experimental medium. Its relationship to poetry was both manipulated in practice and discussed in debates that became ideological as well as aesthetic. There is no sharp chronological dividing line. In the first decade or so of the nineteenth century, prose works such as Constant's *Adolphe* (1816) were still using a spare, maxim-studded style that owes much to the deft economy and bareness of the best seventeenth- and eighteenth-century writers. However, a new kind of prose had been emerging as from the end of the eighteenth century: Rousseau's *Rêveries du promeneur solitaire* (1782) has been hailed as the work that began to move towards the Romanticism of the early nineteenth century, not only because of its often wistful introspection but also because of the fluid, rhythmic style in which it celebrated both thought and 'nature'. And in the same period that *Adolphe* was being composed, Chateaubriand was writing lush narratives like *René* (1802), reliant on a vocabulary designed to evoke an undefined awe ('immense', 'confused', 'majestic'), on sighing cadences, on self-pitying exclamations and on extended similes. Whilst some of these similes are successful, others strike us now, at least, as clumsily over-elaborate (such as one in which Chateaubriand compares the setting sun to the pendulum of the clock of the centuries slowly oscillating in a golden fluid). However that may be, Chateaubriand did have a 'poetic' conception of prose, and his stress on the imprecision of feelings (*le vague des passions*) bore fruit. In his writing, this imprecision often indeed remains vague, but he opened the way for later attempts to convey multilayered and contradictory emotions – not only in the verse of drama, not only in the brilliantly lapidary style of the *moralistes* and other earlier prose writers, but also, now, in a lexically rich and figurative prose. In many areas, he set the tone for that insistence on the suggestive which was to be crucial for later poets like Baudelaire and Mallarmé, and for novelists such as Stendhal and Flaubert himself.

Stendhal, writing some twenty-five years before Flaubert, gave the burgeoning debate some key emphases. He detested Chateaubriand's bombast, and criticised what he saw as unnecessary 'ornament' in all forms of art: in prose, such ornament being fanciful metaphor rather than 'natural' writing. But he did stress that the writer should evoke, rather than explain, heightened states of mind; and in the 1820s, he and Victor Hugo (from different vantage points) championed change and modernity in literature, and brought out the politics underlying an aesthetic hierarchy that had hitherto promoted verse over prose and 'noble' words over 'humble' ones. Prose is the vehicle of the ordinary man; therefore prose must now move into the foreground. This is not to say that all those subsequent writers who blur the dividing line between prose and poetry are champions of the proletariat: far from it. And it is not to overlook the market forces that promoted fiction rather than verse simply because, with a newly literate public, this was where publishers could make their money (a development that shapes the plot of Balzac's *Illusions perdues*, 1837–43). But running through the century, and every now and then surfacing unmistakably, is the sense that prose has the right to claim for itself the prestige hitherto accorded to verse, and that experimentation is essential if prose is to usurp some of the functions of poetry and to reflect the tensions of modernity. Thus Baudelaire, in the famous dedicatory letter that heads his prose poems, claims to be seeking, in order to describe modern life, 'the miracle of a poetic prose, musical without rhythm or rhyme, supple and abrupt ['heurtée'] enough to adapt to the lyrical movements of the soul, the undulations of reverie, the jolts ['soubresauts'] of consciousness'.[1] But this letter, for all its boldness, was not published until 1862. Nerval had already, nine years previously, published his exquisite and densely written novella *Sylvie* (1853); six years previously, in 1856, the extraordinary *Madame Bovary* had appeared; and in a still earlier private letter of 1852 to his lover Louise Colet, Flaubert had already claimed that prose was born 'just yesterday', that verse was the essential genre of *ancient* literatures, and that, whilst 'all combinations' of poetic form had been achieved, those of prose remained to be tried (Cor. II 79; my italics).

Flaubert does nevertheless owe a number of techniques to predecessors. To take only two of the most distinguished of these authors: his use of plurals and abstract nouns probably derives from the seventeenth-century dramatist Racine, even if they had served rather different ends in the earlier writer. In Racine, they give dignity and an illusion of an inner force that – often threateningly – has become a player in its own right; in Flaubert, they tend more to create a sense of the emotion overflowing the carrier of that emotion – sometimes comically so. In Racine's *Britannicus* the eyes of the abducted Junie are said to have 'timides douceurs' (Act I sc. ii) ['shy sweetnesses'], and, in his *Phèdre*, Hippolyte, temporarily persuaded that he has misinterpreted his stepmother's confession of love, says: 'Ma honte ne peut plus soutenir votre vue' (Act II sc. v): literally, 'My shame can no longer bear your sight' rather than, for instance, 'I am too ashamed for you to look upon me any more'. In Flaubert, we find honeymoons with 'suaver indolences' ('de plus suaves paresses': I discuss this a little later), and a double abstract to convey Frédéric's fatuity at an early stage of *L'Education sentimentale*: 'Il trouvait que le *bonheur* mérité par l'*excellence* de son âme tardait à venir' (OC II 9, my italics) [literally: 'He felt that the *happiness* deserved by the *excellence* of his soul was taking a long time to come']. Lest Racine's influence be doubted, Flaubert, as if in homage, copies verbatim at a key moment one of his most famous phrases, 'un long étonnement' ['a long astonishment']. (The phrase occurs in the same speech from *Britannicus* and in *Salammbô* (OC I 702).) It has also been pointed out that Jane Austen uses free indirect style, the technique for which Flaubert is perhaps most famous, a half-century before him. This is the indirect reporting of speech, or more often thought, without the indicators 'She thought that', 'he supposed that'. Here is Austen's *Emma*, in the wake of learning that Mr Elton is in love not with Harriet, as she had supposed and wished, but with herself:

> How could she have been so deceived! [. . .] Perhaps it was not fair to expect him to feel how very much he was her inferior in talent, and all the elegancies of mind. The very want of such equality might prevent his perception of it; but he must know that in fortune and consequence she was greatly his superior.[2]

Austen was well known in nineteenth-century France. No doubt Flaubert's choice of the name Emma for his own heroine is in part a tribute to her, as is – for example – the recasting of this very sequence of thoughts in Emma Bovary's famous 'So how could she (she who was so intelligent!) have misjudged yet again?' (See below, p. 159.) Throughout the novel, Flaubert makes the tribute to Austen ironic with his own more circumscribed Emma; and here, in the context of the disastrous club-foot operation, the rewriting is harsh, designed perhaps to make Austen seem over-indulgent by comparison. But the inspiration is unmistakable; and indeed, recent commentators have started to move away from the stress on 'Flaubert and sons' (the title of a book written in the 1980s) and towards that of 'Flaubert and fathers' (or mothers), bringing out Flaubert's thematic and stylistic debts not only to Racine and Jane Austen but also to Molière, Voltaire and Stendhal, as well as to Greek and Roman writers. However, when we feel (justifiably) tempted to move back to Flaubert's predecessors rather than forward to his literary progeny, we should perhaps turn to Proust's late essay 'On Flaubert's

"style"' ['A propos du "style" de Flaubert'], written in 1920, when much of
A la recherche du temps perdu had already been published and Proust was
at the height of his powers.[3] Proust does not pause to mention influences
on Flaubert; what he highlights is the ground-breaking nature of his stylistic
achievements.

Proust had written a droll pastiche of Flaubert in 1908, capturing his
habits of writing observantly and benignly (*Contre Sainte-Beuve*, pp. 12–15).
But in the 1920 piece, possibly because he now wishes to dispose of a rival,
he can be condescending or plain outrageous – so outrageous that even
critics who cite his comments often pass over them in silence, as if rendered
speechless by this degree of rudeness. Proust had described Balzac's images
as 'striking, right' ['frappantes, justes'] (*Contre Sainte-Beuve*, p. 270). By
contrast, he says of Flaubert that 'there is perhaps no fine metaphor in the
whole of Flaubert'. Flaubert's pages are a great *'Trottoir roulant'* (a *'rolling
Pavement'* – the emphatic and dismissive punctuation is Proust's; he may well
intend readers to remember Flaubert's own comparison between Charles
Bovary's flat conversation and a street pavement (OC 1 588)). His remark
that the blank near the end of *L'Education sentimentale* is the finest thing
in it is surely malicious.[4] And in another commentary, written in the same
year, Proust casually observes that Flaubert was not endowed with great
intelligence, has only average intelligence: 'chez Flaubert [. . .], l'intelligence,
qui n'était peut-être pas des plus grandes [. . .] l'intelligence moyenne de
Flaubert' (*Contre Sainte-Beuve*, p. 612). All of which suggests that when
France's greatest prose stylist does praise Flaubert, we should take the focus
of the praise seriously. Even when Proust is being complimentary, of course,
it may be that (like many creative writers-turned-critics) he is promoting via
the other author aspects of his own enterprise. Nevertheless, what he returns
to again and again is Flaubert's innovativeness.

He singles out in particular Flaubert's grammatical suppleness and mastery
of syntax: Flaubert is 'a man who, through the entirely new and personal use
he made of the definite and indefinite past tenses, of the present participle, of
certain pronouns and prepositions, has renewed our vision of things almost
as much as Kant, with his Categories, renewed theories of Knowledge and
of the Reality of the external world'. This statement alone covers central
aspects of Flaubert's writing. Flaubert does radicalise the imperfect tense –
Proust owes to him his own use of what could be called 'the imperfect of
action'. In their hands, this tense suggests that the definite event has been
swallowed up into a flowing process. The French imperfect is often translated
into English by a simple past: '[Emma] s'irritait d'un plat mal servi ou d'une
porte entrebâillée, gémissait du velours qu'elle n'avait pas, du bonheur qui
lui manquait, de ses rêves trop hauts, de sa maison trop étroite' (OC 1 611)

['[Emma] grew irritated at a badly served dish or a door left ajar, groaned over the velvet she did not have, over the happiness she was missing, over her too-lofty dreams and her too-narrow house']. The English simple past ('she grew irritated/she groaned') can encompass both action and continuous description; however, French makes a distinction, to convey which fully translators of the imperfect would have to resort constantly to the awkward 'used to do', 'would do', 'was doing'. Flaubert writes long passages in which almost every verb is in the imperfect, thus suggesting at its mildest a pleasurable repetition (as when Emma and Léon peruse Emma's fashion magazines: 'Léon se mettait près d'elle; ils regardaient ensemble les gravures et s'attendaient au bas des pages' (OC 1 607) ['Léon would sit beside her; they would look at the prints together and wait for each other at the bottom of the page']); at its most unbearable, boredom and inescapability. Flaubert even puts speech indicators into the imperfect, having characters supposedly say many times what must have been a specific utterance. Emma's and Rodolphe's rendez-vous 'se terminaient toujours' ['always used to end'] with the 'eternal' question (from Emma): 'Do you love me?' But then we read: '– Tu n'en as pas aimé d'autres, hein? – Crois-tu m'avoir pris vierge? exclamait-il en riant' (OC 1 639) ['"You haven't loved anyone else, have you?" "Did you think I was a virgin, then?" he would exclaim, laughing']. Rodolphe would hardly have made the macho joke every time. This use of the imperfect has several functions, among them the advantage that fictional time becomes more easily manipulable, because less dependent on a succession of events; and, with this, the novel takes a step closer to being written in that other continuous tense: the present. We are as yet a century away from the *nouveau roman* of the 1950s and 1960s, one of whose distinguishing features will be that its dominant narrative tense will be the present. But, equally important, the present is the main tense of lyric verse in the nineteenth century and earlier; by bringing the imperfect into prominence in prose fiction, Flaubert is creating the novel's equivalent of this poetic present.

The novel is also generally thought to be dependent on firm distinctions between characters themselves, and between characters and things. It would be anachronistic to claim that Flaubert does not make such distinctions: a number of critics from the 1980s on have argued against overemphasising unreliability in his works. Nevertheless, when Proust talks of Flaubert's 'new' use of pronouns, he has in mind a certain blurring, created by what he calls Flaubert's 'grammatical rigour': having quoted an example from the second page of *L'Education sentimentale*, he claims that in that novel, 'the revolution has taken place ['la révolution est accomplie']; that which before Flaubert was action has now become impression'. Again, this revolutionariness is not always translatable. There is a clear distinction in

English between 'he/she' on the one hand and 'it' on the other. But because all French nouns have a gender, the personal pronouns 'il' and 'elle' may refer to things and emotions as well as to people; and there are moments, particularly in *Trois Contes*, when (if only momentarily) we may be unsure who or what is being designated. In *Hérodias*, the Samaritan Mannaëi has entered the temple of Jerusalem in order to defile the altar with human bones. The narrative now goes on:

> Ses compagnons, moins rapides, avaient été décapités.
> Il l'aperçut dans l'écartement de deux collines.
>
> (OC II 188)

This has to be translated thus: 'His companions, less speedy than he, had been decapitated. [New paragraph] He first saw it in the gap between two hills.' In the French, however, 'it' ('l') could here mean him or her; it is also so far away from the noun to which it refers ('temple') that there are hesitations on that score too, since the altar is the nearest preceding singular noun. So Mannaëi might be seeing a man, a woman or some unspecified thing. It is only when we read on that we realise what exactly lies in that gap, at which point – but not before – the 'it' retrospectively takes on grandeur, becomes, as it were, an 'It'. In this foregrounding of the pronoun we see again not simply a trait characteristic of Flaubert, but a change being as it were imposed upon French narrative prose, which had always been more dependent than English on demonstratives (and still to some extent is): in Stendhal, for example, we may find 'Ce prince' rather than 'Le prince', and certainly 'Ce prince' rather than just 'Il'. Thus the defined gives way to something more doubtful, something that overspills margins.

Proust also praises what he calls 'the continuous, monotonous, bleak ['morne'], indefinite movement ['défilement']' of Flaubert's pages, saying once more that it is impossible not to recognise that they are 'without precedent in literature'. Indeed, another function of Flaubert's imperfects is to contribute to this sense of enveloping 'continuous movement'. Proust is paying tribute to a prose style that creates an illusion of governing every word and shaping every aspect of syntax within what Romantics thought of as an 'organic' individuality – a type of 'uniformity', but one that can encompass discrepancy and incongruity without taming them. (Adrianne Tooke cites Flaubert's own view of art as a 'discordant harmony', a 'harmony of disparate things'.[5])

The other major fellow-practitioner to have commented on Flaubert's enterprise is Henry James, who famously attacked Flaubert for his creation of mediocre characters, arguing that the action of a fine novel had to be reflected through a fine sensibility; thus it followed that *Madame Bovary* and especially *L'Education sentimentale* were fundamentally flawed.[6] Many subsequent commentators have taken issue with James, but since the core of the rebuttal must reside in an appreciation of Flaubert's style, and particularly in his development of free indirect style, some discussion of James's criticisms has a place in this essay. First of all, we might return to the historical significance of Flaubert's choice of subjects – subjects here meaning both characters and social or intellectual traits of the period. To foreground the set ideas and clichés of mediocre figures, and the popular images that have shaped their modes of communication, is to make a statement about the changing habits of thought and speech of the nineteenth century; amongst other things, it suggests the growing power of mediated fantasies and language in a period when advertising and journalism were taking an ever firmer hold. Nineteenth-century Don Quixotes are no longer simply reading and acting upon tales of chivalry. They pose for pictures like contemporary actresses (as does Emma, with sidelong look, in the miniature that even Rodolphe judges tasteless (OC I 642)); they mouth slogans: 'France wishes to be ruled by an iron hand' ['un bras de fer'] – not entirely meaningless, since, as one critic has shown, such slogans are self-serving too.[7]

James's concerns were also unlikely to have encompassed the recommendations of Stendhal and Hugo, and Flaubert's development of these. Flaubert's choice of a 'debased' form of inner or vocalised speech, for protagonists who are foolish or plain stupid, moves modern literature even further away from the grand, the powerful or the consensually beautiful, and endows the vision of the artist with crucial importance. The content, or the 'quoted' discourse, may be ugly, but the treatment is what renders the work beautiful: a beauty that is disturbing because it retains the grotesqueness of the scene or utterance – does not synthesise or wish it away – yet simultaneously creates aesthetic pleasure. Earlier artists had also triumphantly achieved such incongruities, of course. The point is that the nineteenth century theorises them and, with Flaubert, makes whole works depend on a discomfort whose ostentation and pervasiveness is new, and which is tantamount to a declaration that if beauty is to be found, it will be not in the subject but in the presentation. Flaubert is therefore a central contributor to a Europe-wide movement away from the image of art as a mirror towards that of art as a lamp.[8] That is to say, if art is a mirror, to be beautiful it must depict 'objectively' beautiful objects; whereas if it is a lamp, illuminating and doubtless transfiguring whatever it sheds its beam on, then its object is less important – need not even be grounded in what we deem 'truth'. 'There is no "true"!' said Flaubert; 'there are only ways of seeing' (CHH XVI 308).

Thus one way to refute James's charge is to agree that Flaubert's heroes and heroines are mediocre – that, after all, is part of the intention – but to argue that the manner of telling the mediocrity is both exquisite and invested with irony. Let us take Emma's dreams about the honeymoon days she would like to have had.

> Pour en goûter la douceur, il eût fallu, sans doute, s'en aller vers ces pays à noms sonores où les lendemains de mariage ont de plus suaves paresses! Dans des chaises de poste, sous des stores de soie bleue, on monte au pas des routes escarpées, écoutant la chanson du postillon, qui se répète dans la montagne avec les clochettes des chèvres et le bruit sourd de la cascade. Quand le soleil se couche, on respire au bord des golfes le parfum des citronniers [. . .]. Que ne pouvait-elle s'accouder sur le balcon des chalets suisses ou enfermer sa tristesse dans un cottage écossais, avec un mari vêtu d'un habit de velours noir à longues basques, et qui porte des bottes molles, un chapeau pointu et des manchettes!
>
> (OC I 588)

> [To savour their sweetness you would probably have to set off for those places with marvellous names where wedding-nights beget a more delicious lethargy. In a post-chaise, with blue silk blinds, slowly you climb the steep roads, and the postilion's song is echoing across the mountains with the sound of the goat-bells and the murmuring waterfall. As the sun is going down, on the shore of the bay you breathe the scent of lemon-trees [. . .]. Why could she not be leaning out on the balcony of a Swiss chalet, or hiding her sadness in a cottage in Scotland, with a husband wearing a long-tailed black velvet coat, and soft boots, a pointed hat and frills on his shirt!][9]

This hand-me-down dream becomes more and more ineffably foolish as it goes on. Yet it is aesthetically pleasing, and the beauty, while conveying the second-handness, is clearly not itself second-hand. Neither Emma nor the authors she admires would have been able to find a phrase like 'de plus suaves paresses' (literally, 'suaver indolences': the plurals are virtually impossible to render gracefully in English). Nor would she or they have carried onwards the alliterations in *p* and *s* that, as well as marking this particular phrase, run through the whole passage. The impact of the daydream is also created by the assonances (for example, those in *ou* and nasal *an* or *on*): thus, 'goûter la douceur'; 'sans, noms, ont, Dans, monte, écoutant, chanson, postillon'); and by the successive phrases that have equal numbers of syllables. Here are only two examples: 'Que ne pouvait-elle s'accouder [8]/ sur le balcon des chalets suisses [8]/ ou enfermer sa tristesse [7]/ dans un cottage écossais [7]'. These phonetic networks revivify the sense impressions (blue silk, echoing songs, the smell of lemons) even while we are aware that to conjure them up in this combination is absurd. The ludicrous final image of the fancily togged-up spouse – ludicrous yet heralded with that sensuously symmetrical rhythm – completes our discomfiture: through his style, Flaubert is creating a new and modern literary beauty, one that is inseparable from unease and a forced recognition that it is the writing and the writing alone that is creating the pleasure.

Disjunctions between subject and treatment occur throughout Flaubert to make us squirm – in different ways depending on the context, of course: for example, the fine rhythms of *La Légende de saint Julien l'Hospitalier* increase, yet sit strangely with, the horror of the protagonist's butchery of animals. *L'Education sentimentale* is a stylistic tour de force, in its slippery movement between monotony and a taut, often witty, evocation of that monotony – creating a slippage also between what we suppose to be narrator's constructions and what then turn out to be a character's hackneyed thoughts. (It is more difficult to pinpoint the moments of transition here than in *Madame Bovary*.) Perhaps the most uncomfortable moment in Flaubert – perhaps the most embarrassing in European literature – is the end of *Un cœur simple*. The servant Félicité, the 'simple heart' of the title, is dying in her tawdry room. Her half-rotten stuffed parrot, which she has increasingly endowed with the qualities of the Holy Ghost, is outside 'participating' in a religious procession. The incense burners, 'allant à pleine volée' ['going full tilt'], send a blue vapour into Félicité's room.

> Elle avança les narines, en la humant avec une sensualité mystique; puis ferma les paupières. Ses lèvres souriaient. Les mouvements de son cœur se ralentirent un à un, plus vagues chaque fois, plus doux, comme une fontaine s'épuise, comme un echo disparaît; et, quand elle exhala son dernier souffle, elle crut voir, dans les cieux entr'ouverts, un perroquet gigantesque, planant au-dessus de sa tête.
>
> (OC II 177)

> [She moved her nostrils, smelling it with a mystic sensuality; then closed her eyelids. Her lips were smiling. The movements of her heart slowed one by one, each time vaguer, gentler, like a fountain running dry, like a fading echo; and, when she breathed her last, she thought she saw, in the half-parted heavens, a gigantic parrot, hovering high above her head.]

Again, alliterations (this time mainly in *p* and hard *c*), the range of senses evoked, the perfect octosyllable of the final phrase ('planant au-dessus de sa tête'), combine to give this death a pleasingly touching pathos; they allow us to respond even to the rather hackneyed fountain and echo similes. But at the same time, we wince at Loulou's apotheosis and at the final demonstration, *in excelsis* and in technicolour, that Félicité's good-heartedness is inseparable from simple-mindedness. Flaubert had remarked many years previously, apropos of Emma, that irony does not detract from pathos, but, rather, 'excessively increases' it, 'l'outre'; 'outre' also implies 'outrageously' (letter to Louise Colet, 9 October 1852, Cor. II 172). This excess or outrageousness permeates the indigestible end of *Un cœur simple*.

All in all, then, it would appear that Henry James either wilfully overlooked, or did not fully recognise, the significance and skill of Flaubert's aesthetic enterprise, and the key role that irony plays, principally in free indirect style but also at other levels of the writing. Many more recent commentators have discussed, with great subtlety, these and other aspects of Flaubert's stylistic achievements; even those who do not focus directly on the style usually pay tribute to it. One outstanding essay remains the short work on *Madame Bovary* by Alison Fairlie, written in the early 1960s; this critic took up Baudelaire's characterisation of *Madame Bovary* as 'ce livre essentiellement suggestif' ['that fundamentally suggestive book'] and developed it with such acute analyses of Flaubert's style and structure that her interpretations have influenced all subsequent Flaubert criticism.[10]

Some scholars have, for example, shed new light on Flaubert's search for the *mot juste* by way of an examination of drafts and variants. Thus, one critic recounts Flaubert's annoyance when the newspaper serialising *Madame Bovary* suggested that the (real) newspaper title in the novel, *Le Journal de Rouen*, be changed to the fictitious *Le Progressif de Rouen* ['The Rouen Progress']; but he then invented the still more satisfactory *Le Fanal de Rouen* ['The Rouen Beacon'], a title which not only preserves the political neutrality and rhythm of the original (even rhyming with it), but is still more 'right' in its new pretentiousness.[11] Other reworkings show Flaubert suppressing unnecessary explanation and leaving concise comments to speak for themselves: in *L'Education sentimentale*, he had originally written of Frédéric and Madame Arnoux: 'Il était bien entendu qu'ils ne devaient pas s'appartenir. *Mais* cette convention, qui les garantissait du péril, *en leur donnant sur tout le reste plus de liberté*, facilitait leurs épanchements'[12] ['It was entirely understood that they were not to belong to each other. *But* this agreement, which protected them against peril, *for it gave them increased freedom in every other respect*, made their effusions easier']. Flaubert removed the italicised words between one edition and another, thus allowing all its force to 'facilitait' and letting the reader guess how and why the facilitation is possible. Some critics have justifiably argued that Flaubert slyly traps the reader into feeling stupid; no doubt this is so when, say, we find ourselves identifying with Emma, only to be bumped out of the identification as an overt crassness on her part makes us suddenly recoil. But revisions like this one show that Flaubert also assumes intelligent and morally aware readers – readers who will be able to respond to the suggestiveness working on every page. When these readers learn that Rodolphe keeps letters from former mistresses in an old biscuit tin, they will understand that he regards the mistresses, then, as mere snacks. And such readers will appreciate the placing of even quite ordinary words. In *La Légende de saint Julien l'Hospitalier*, the first manifestation of the hero's cruelty comes when, as a child, he locates the hole of a mouse that has been irritating him in chapel and waits for it to emerge so that he can kill it. Flaubert writes not 'Au bout de longtemps un museau rose parut' ['After a long time a pink snout appeared'] but 'Au bout de très longtemps' (OC II 179) ['After a very long time']. The simple 'very' shows unusual tenacity in the budding sadist, implying that most children would already have given up and left.

Other critics, exploring those areas where style becomes inseparable from structure, emphasise the symbolism of certain of Flaubert's images, and the lexical networks created both within and across individual works. Things catching at Emma's clothes suggest both her sensuality and her entrapment: on walks with Léon, honeysuckle and clematis catch the fringe of her silk dress (OC I 606); later, at the moment of sexual consummation, her dress catches on the velvet of Rodolphe's jacket (OC I 629). The numerous words in *L'Education sentimentale* conveying grubbiness, muddiness, create a pattern linking the dirt of Paris to the moral grubbiness of the characters, and also symbolically reflect the deliberate 'greyness' of much of the narrative tone. As for networks running across works, one such is formed by 'good', 'goodness'. Flaubert's characters praise each other with the word 'bon': 'Oui, [. . .] tu es bon . . . , toi', says the dying Emma to Charles (OC I 681); Madame Arnoux says to Frédéric: 'Oh! comme vous êtes bon!' (OC II 108).[13] 'Goodness' is, however, a problematic label, and Flaubert demonstrates some of its inherent difficulties in *Trois Contes*, which, apparently disparate, are united – it has been argued – by their depiction of three 'saints'.[14] But the first, Félicité, is perhaps 'good' only because she is too stupid to understand that she is being exploited. The second, Julien, comes to sainthood by way of an extreme personal brutality and the fulfilment of a curiously unchristian augury; while the third, that most famous saint John the Baptist, would appear to be somewhat mad. Thus the embodiments of 'goodness' undermine the ideal of 'goodness', or at least suggest its vagueness. However, the word 'tender' has its own network in Flaubert, and this, with its combination of moral and physical connotations, is less treacherous. Félicité looks on her young charge Virginie making her First Communion, 'et, avec l'imagination que donnent les vraies tendresses, il lui sembla qu'elle était elle-même cette enfant' (OC II 170) ['and, with the imagination that true tenderness bestows, she thought she was herself that child']. We shall encounter another 'tender' in a moment, with 'attendrir' ['to move someone to tenderness, to pity']. Through a cumulative use of 'tendresse' Flaubert promotes it as the most yearned-for and valuable emotion – more valuable than an ill-defined 'goodness' or than the infatuation that believes itself to be love.

Before moving on to what might be thought of as more 'tangible' aspects of Flaubert's style, let us look at a last example of his suggestiveness, that to be found in the famous lamentation over the inadequacies of language in *Madame Bovary*. Emma has just been telling Rodolphe that he is 'good, handsome, intelligent' (here again is 'good' as a cliché). Rodolphe, having heard such things many times, cannot see that feelings may differ underneath the sameness of expression:

> Parce que des lèvres libertines ou vénales lui avaient murmuré des phrases pareilles, il ne croyait que faiblement à la candeur de celles-là; on en devait rabattre, pensait-il, les discours exagérés cachant les affections médiocres; comme si la plénitude de l'âme ne débordait pas quelquefois par les métaphores les plus vides, puisque personne, jamais, ne peut donner l'exacte mesure de ses besoins, ni de ses conceptions, ni de ses douleurs, et que la parole humaine est comme un chaudron fêlé où nous battons des mélodies à faire danser les ours, quand on voudrait attendrir les étoiles. (OC II 639)

> [Because libertine or venal lips had murmured similar phrases to him, his belief in the frankness of these ones was rather weak; you had to knock something off their value, he thought, since exaggeration is a disguise for mediocre feelings; as if the soul's fullness did not sometimes overflow through the emptiest metaphors, for no one, ever, can give the exact measure of their needs, their ideas, their pains, and human language is like a cracked cauldron on which we beat out tunes for bears to dance to, when we should like to move the stars to tenderness.]

This has been cited as a breach of Flaubert's own rule of authorial 'impersonality' – he steps out of the narrative in order to impose on us a maxim. Such generalisations are commoner in his works than is sometimes supposed; Stirling Haig calls them 'theolocutives' – the delivery of a statement by that invisible god whom Flaubert said the author should resemble (*Flaubert and the Gift of Speech*, p. 16). In this passage, indeed, the narrator is also speaking to one of his own characters – the 'as if' being an implicit reproach to Rodolphe. But, as is the case with the maxims of other French *moralistes*, and those of Flaubert's immediate predecessor Constant, the effect is more intricate than might at first be supposed. The generalisations may appear to be setting forth 'laws' of human behaviour, but, rather than reducing complexity and contradiction, what they often draw attention to is the strangeness and paradoxicality of man; and they can be couched in language that is itself multilayered, playful and metaphorical. We may sometimes agree with Proust that Flaubert's similes lack the force of the rest of his writing: they can appear contrived. Here, however, the figures of speech work powerfully with the syntax. This latter is carefully provocative, as in the word-order of 'personne, jamais, ne peut donner l'exacte mesure de ses besoins, ni de ses conceptions, ni de ses douleurs'. The sequence implies: needs present themselves first; it is needs that dictate ideas; these ideas may precipitate pain; and pain (physical and emotional) is finally the victor. The figurative itself plays a crucial role. The statement of the impossible relationship between consciousness and imperfect language has influenced countless later writers; it no doubt owes its impact not only to its conceptual sophistication but also to the hint of overflowing tears in the physical 'débordait', and to the visual and tactile sensations conjured up by the clumsily dancing bears. Nor is the cracked cauldron simile an isolated monolith. A depth of cultural tradition is appealed to in the comparison of language to a cauldron or an old piano ('chaudron' can mean both in French). Here Flaubert suggests (as does Baudelaire) that something unites all artefacts, whether language; or music both great and tinny; or – cooking. Artefacts take what is raw, 'natural', and transform it into something that bears the stamp of human ingenuity, however faulty. The generalisation is thus expanded through a double meaning that is sensory on many different levels.

Flaubert also creates the dynamism of this climactic 'theolocutive' through linguistic play. Phonetic links are numerous, one obvious example being the alliteration of *p* throughout ('parce que', 'pareilles', 'pensait-il', 'plénitude', 'par', 'puisque personne', 'peut', 'parole'). A ludic as well as a serious purpose dictates the reappearance of Rodolphe's 'rabattre' – to knock something off the price – in the 'battre' of 'beating out the tunes', these tunes being a 'cheap, reduced' version of what ought to be finer. At the end, any French reader would be expecting to read: 'quand on voudrait *atteindre* les étoiles' – when we should like to *reach* the stars. But Flaubert alters a few letters and turns the verb into 'attendrir'. Without losing the idea of ambition, he transforms it into what we really want from those cold distant stars – tenderness. Finally, there is perhaps, too, a hidden word-play in the bear image, one that would have a special import in Flaubert's lexicon of stupidity. These are animals, *bêtes*, and the French word *bête* also means 'stupid'. Humans are *bêtes* in both senses – if not the actual bears, then as their dancing masters not far removed. Darwinism was not the only blow inflicted on man's status in the nineteenth century; Philippe Dufour (*Flaubert et le pignouf*, p. 12) remarks that Flaubert contributes to the humiliation by demonstrating our lack of control over that prized possession, language.

Flaubert's stylistic suggestiveness operates, then, at profound as well as visible levels. 'Style', he wrote in a letter of 1859, 'is as much *under* as *in* words' (Cor. III 22; his emphasis). But there is, too, the other Flaubert, the one we may think of as the 'realist' writer, in so far as it is possible to make a distinction – for often particular perspectives complement or overlap each other; sometimes, however, there is a tension between the 'suggestive' and the 'realist'. Flaubert pays more attention to sensory detail – colour, smell, differing tactile pressures – than slightly earlier novelists such as Stendhal, and even than Chateaubriand, whose scene-setting can dissolve into a convenient exclamation over its indescribability. Furthermore, in Flaubert as in Balzac, sensory detail is central to what is presumably a historiographical purpose. In some of Flaubert's comments, critics have detected a belief that nothing changes over the centuries; but other remarks (such as those on the conception of *L'Education sentimentale*) do reveal the curiosity of the chronicler, albeit a sometimes idiosyncratic one, and the works themselves show a keen awareness of differences between cultures. Many tableaux in *Madame Bovary* and *L'Education sentimentale* simultaneously highlight and ironise the 'commodity fetishism' of a powerful capitalism that – according to numerous commentators – contributed to the development of the realist novel. At its most banal, this realist novel simply reflects the fetishism, but at its finest it offers a critique of it too. As for other societies altogether, in *Salammbô* and *Hérodias* the décor, the sartorial information, and, not least, the stage-props supporting nightmarish incidents induce not at all a recognition that 'here are the brothers and sisters of nineteenth-century Frenchmen', but rather provoke a sense of irreducible strangeness – an unsettling acknowledgment that there is something we moderns cannot understand or appropriate in alien and long-dead cultures.

Thus 'distinctness' (always stylised, of course) plays an important part in Flaubert's local stylistic effects and in his wider intentions. And in purely structural and aesthetic terms the ambiguous and the emphatically delineated enhance, serve as foils for, each other. Thus, to return to our cracked cauldron/piano: we start with modifiers, temperate wording: the phrases Rodolphe hears from Emma are not – say – identical to those he has heard from others, but 'similar'; he does not utterly disbelieve Emma – his belief is 'rather weak' ('il ne croyait que faiblement'); the soul's fullness only *sometimes* overflows into trite wording. But then – more telling after this series of apparently qualified statements – comes the superlative of 'les métaphores les plus vides' ['the emptiest metaphors']; the absolutes 'personne, jamais' ['no one, ever']; and the firm assimilation of language to the fissured object – no 'sometimes' creeping in here: the climax is achieved in part through rhetorical surprise.

There are many more obviously sensuous examples of this use of contrast. At Homais's soirées Léon stands behind Emma as she plays cards, seeing an 'Impressionist' picture: 'De ses cheveux retroussés, il descendait une couleur brune sur son dos, et qui, s'apâlissant graduellement, peu à peu se perdait dans l'ombre' (OC I 607) ['From the coiled mass of her hair, shades of brown flowed down her back, until, fading away gradually, little by little, they ended in shadow' (Wall, p. 78)]. And (the indistinctness here creating comedy) Léon reads verse to Emma in a *trailing* voice that he carefully ('soigneusement') allows to *die away* during the love passages. But Homais is now playing a noisy game of dominoes with Charles, and since he is good at it ('il y était fort') he beats Charles 'à plein double-six' ['with a full double-six']: no room for ambiguity there. The images of visual and aural dying-away are thrown into relief by the clatter, and arithmetical character, of this prosaic game. Similar sensory contrasts shape the auctioning-off of Madame Arnoux's effects: 'des blancheurs' (literally, 'whitenesses') fly through the air as undergarments, lace pieces, blouses are thrown from one hand to another; but then the focus moves to the pathetic detail of a hat's drooping broken feather – suggestive, of course (of lost jauntiness), but whose concreteness is enhanced by the deliberately imprecise ghostliness of those preceding 'blancheurs' (OC II 158). Tooke, throughout her *Flaubert and the Pictorial Arts*, shows how often Flaubert's writing hovers between an illusion of the visual and a sense that the visual is being undermined or dissolved; what is pleasing – and disturbing – is the tension thus created between 'image' and text.

So Flaubert plays on disjunction and incongruity at physical as well as moral levels, and this play is dependent on the reader's responding, if only temporarily, to the bodily or psychological 'definite'. Even the famously ambiguous free indirect style is less equivocal at certain moments than at others – when, for example, it plainly shows Emma getting things wrong. Can there really be any argument about the interpretation of those thoughts of Emma's as she hears Hippolyte's screams during the amputation for which she is in part responsible? 'Comment donc avait-elle fait (elle qui était si intelligente!) pour se méprendre encore une fois?' ['So how could she (she who was so intelligent!) have misjudged yet again?'] Charles, listening too, is suffering guilt and agitation, but to Emma he is 'cet homme qui ne comprenait rien, qui ne sentait rien!' ['that man who understood nothing, felt nothing!'] (OC I 637). Irony is not always unresolvable: it is sometimes designed to be easily penetrable – to be closer to the sardonic than to the irreducibly double meanings of a Mallarmé; to be in the nature less of a poem than of a joke.

For, as well as the open ending, Flaubert enjoys the punch-line. *Hérodias* closes with John the Baptist's severed head being carried away by three of Christ's followers: 'Comme elle était très lourde, ils la portaient alternativement' (OC II 199) ['As it was very heavy, they took turns to carry it']. These last nine words have an emphatic paragraph to themselves. Their physicality serves many functions. They are a critique of a founding Western myth, and of all those paintings, from the Renaissance on, that depict Salome gracefully carrying the head on a platter (for how could a frail girl hold up this heavy object?); medical knowledge steps in to correct a fantasy. The words are also suggestive, reminding us that death transforms the most inspired minds into merely clunky things, and symbolic in that this particular head is *heavy* with significance for Western culture. But in its grotesque concreteness, in the suddenness with which the statement is advanced and then dropped, this last paragraph resembles also a *détail cocasse* – the quirky detail beloved by comic raconteurs – and more specifically, since it comes at the end, it resembles the climax of a joke (a grim one, to be sure). The finale of *Un cœur simple* can be read similarly; and those other deflations that are to be found throughout Flaubert also often have a joke-like structure. Certainly, there is a kind of smooth seamlessness in Flaubert's writing, but that should not blind us to its equal reliance on a pattern of build-up followed by bathos – a bathos that is comic as well as ironic. So, after Julien is taken up to heaven, the narrator ends his beautifully written tale with the information that he has recounted the story '*roughly*' as it appears in a local stained glass window ('à peu près', OC II 187): narrative self-consciousness here combines with a tongue-in-cheek let-down. The clearest proof of Félicité's utter incapacity for abstract thought comes when she is looking at the dot that represents Havana in Bourais's atlas. Flaubert builds up to the clinching moment, saves the best for the end: 'Elle se pencha sur la carte; ce réseau de lignes coloriées fatiguait sa vue, sans lui rien apprendre; et, Bourais l'invitant à dire ce qui l'embarrassait, elle le pria de lui montrer la maison où demeurait Victor' (OC II 171) ['She bent over the map; the mesh of coloured lines tired her eyes without showing her anything; and, when Bourais invited her to say what was puzzling her, she asked him to show her the house where Victor was living'].

Flaubert is in other respects a comic as well as an ironic writer. The comedy often crystallises an insight that had hitherto remained implicit. Thus Deslauriers quickly grasps a central truth about Frédéric's love for Madame Arnoux (one which still escapes some readers), namely that this love is inextricably bound up with a powerful feeling for Arnoux himself:

> et Deslauriers commença une intolérable *scie* [Flaubert's italics], consistant à répéter son nom cent fois par jour, à la fin de chaque phrase, comme un tic d'idiot. Quand on frappait à sa porte, il répondait: 'Entrez, Arnoux!' Au restaurant, il demandait un fromage de Brie 'à l'instar d'Arnoux'; et, la nuit, feignant d'avoir un cauchemar, il réveillait son compagnon en hurlant: 'Arnoux! Arnoux!' (OC II 30)

[and Deslauriers started up an insufferable gag, which consisted of repeating Arnoux's name a hundred times a day, at the end of each phrase, like some idiot's mannerism. If you knocked on his door, he replied: 'Come in, Arnoux!' In the restaurant, he would ask for Brie 'Arnoux-type'; and at night, faking a nightmare, he would wake his companion up with yells of: 'Arnoux! Arnoux!']

Repetitiveness is one of Flaubert's sources of comedy, here exploited by a character as well as by the narrator: this is, incidentally, one of the rare occasions in Flaubert when we are laughing *with* one character as well as *at* another. (There are interesting differences here from Molière, who often makes us laugh with, say, witty maidservants or such characters as Alceste's cool inamorata Célimène in *Le Misanthrope*.)

Flaubert also conveys the lack of dignity of *homo sapiens* in quietly farcical vignettes. These have an earthiness, sometimes a vulgarity found in earlier French authors such as Rabelais and Molière, and which reappear in nineteenth-century writers as a deliberate rejection of *goût*, the 'good taste' that had been a criterion for most seventeenth- and eighteenth-century writers. In *L'Education sentimentale*, characters are splashed with mud; Frédéric is a 'sucker', parting with money too readily and left to pay the restaurant bill. In *Madame Bovary*, Emma's baby is sick on her elegant dress. And Charles's morning-time appearance is, to be sure, dictated by Flaubert's technique of 'focalisation' (showing only what a given character would pick out: thus we here see Charles through Emma's growing repugnance, which governs the details selected); but there is also a more general comedy at work, reminding the reader how absurd sleepers can look: 'Comme il avait eu longtemps l'habitude du bonnet de coton, son foulard ne lui tenait pas aux oreilles; aussi ses cheveux, le matin, étaient rabattus pêle-mêle sur sa figure et blanchis par le duvet de son oreiller, dont les cordons se dénouaient pendant la nuit' (OC I 588) ['Having long been used to a cotton nightcap, he found his silk handkerchief was always slipping off; and so his hair, in the morning, would be hanging down over his face, white with feathers from the pillow, which used to come undone in the course of the night' (Wall, p. 33)]. Other characters too are caught off guard – ruffled physically, metaphorically or both. When Frédéric (seemingly unawares) interrupts Arnoux in the middle of adulterous lovemaking, the joke is not just on the young man who has been furiously ringing the bell, then gives a final timid tap at the door; it is also on the rumpled Arnoux: 'La porte s'ouvrit; et, sur le seuil, les cheveux ébouriffés, la face cramoisi et l'air maussade, Arnoux lui-même parut' (OC II 31) ['The door opened; and there on the threshold, hair tousled, purple in the face and looking disgruntled, was Arnoux himself'].

As these examples show, along with his 'Impressionist's eye' Flaubert has the eye of a cartoonist: it is sometimes difficult to distinguish between the two, as when the guests arrive at Charles's and Emma's wedding:

> Tout le monde était tondu à neuf, les oreilles s'écartaient des têtes, on était rasé de près; quelques-uns même qui s'étaient levés dès avant l'aube, n'ayant pas vu clair à se faire la barbe, avaient des balafres en diagonale sous le nez, ou, le long des mâchoires, des pelures d'épiderme larges comme des écus de trois francs, et qu'avaient enflammées le grand air pendant la route, ce qui marbrait un peu de plaques roses toutes ces grosses faces blanches épanouies.
>
> (OC I 583)

> [Every head of hair was freshly clipped, ears were sticking out, cheeks were close-shaven; some there were who had left their beds before dawn, when there was scarcely enough light to be using a razor, and now had great diagonal gashes across their upper lip, or, along the jaw, flaps of detached skin as big as a three-franc piece, inflamed by the fresh air along the way, so that all those great white beaming faces were blotched with bits of pink. (Wall, p. 21)]

Flaubert creates, too – it scarcely needs saying – a comedy of language, of speech: some critics have pointed out that, as well as on free indirect style, his fiction relies on a theatrical sense of dialogue and on what might almost be termed sociolects. Thus clerics have their own 'jargon' in Flaubert; Homais is not merely unique, but also represents a particular popularising way of massacring what should be the pellucid language of science.[15] Flaubert's drafts show him honing and exaggerating direct speech – cutting overly colloquial phrases, making conversations often preposterous: excessively literary, or entertainingly cacophonous.[16] And in his targeting of current political clichés, Flaubert has sometimes been hailed not only as a chronicler, or as the parodist he transcendentally is, but also as a fully fledged satirist. This would depend on one's definition of satire: if, as has been said, satire aims to rouse indignation and stimulate a wish to reform, perhaps Flaubert is less the satirist and more the *moraliste* casting a now compassionate, now wry, gaze on the foibles of mankind. But if he is at moments approaching satire, then again this must depend on something we believe (and Flaubert's contemporaries believed) to be recognisable and even definable.

In both his practice and his theory, Flaubert is incontestably one of those writers who have shaped the modern view of 'good prose writing'. His stylistic sensitivity and adventurousness have had an enormous influence on literature both inside and outside France. Without him, it is inconceivable that Zola would have incorporated argot into free indirect style in his own narratives or that Maupassant would have achieved such mastery of the telling detail, left without further elaboration. Virginia Woolf and James Joyce model their delicate and multilayered writing to some degree on Flaubert's. It is probable that the late nineteenth-century development of free verse – which was to become the dominant twentieth-century verse form – owes as much to Flaubert as to those contemporaries of his who wrote prose poems. And it is unlikely that Proust – for all his ungraciousness – would have composed a work so dense in simile, and so dependent on the contrast between fine writing and joyously flawed speech, if he had never read *Madame Bovary* and *L'Education sentimentale*.

NOTES

1 Charles Baudelaire, *Petits Poèmes en prose: Le Spleen de Paris*, ed. Henri Lemaitre (Paris: Garnier, 1962), p. 7.
2 Jane Austen, *Emma*, ed. R. W. Chapman (London: Oxford University Press, 1966), pp. 134, 136.
3 Marcel Proust, *Contre Sainte-Beuve, précédé de Pastiches et mélanges et suivi de Essais et articles*, ed. Pierre Clarac and Yves Sandre (Paris: Gallimard, 1971), pp. 586–600.
4 This is the 'space' implying the passage of years just before the chapter starting 'Il voyagea' (OC II 160) ['He travelled']. Some critics have however taken Proust's comment seriously, while others, following such twentieth-century writers as Beckett and Blanchot, have validly argued that in many circumstances Flaubert would appear to promote silence over speech (for example, implicitly contrasting 'genuine' but inarticulate characters like Hippolyte with speciously fluent ones like Homais). See, for example, Diana Knight, *Flaubert's Characters: The Language of Illusion* (Cambridge: Cambridge University Press, 1985), especially chapters 2, 3 ('The merits of inarticulacy', 'By-passing speech').
5 Adrianne Tooke, *Flaubert and the Pictorial Arts: From Image to Text* (Oxford: Oxford University Press, 2000), p. 29.
6 Henry James, 'Gustave Flaubert', in *Literary Criticism. French Writers, Other European Writers* (Cambridge: Cambridge University Press, 1984), pp. 314–46.
7 Françoise Gaillard, 'A little story about the *bras de fer*, or, how history is made', in Naomi Schor and Henry F. Majewski, eds., *Flaubert and Postmodernism* (Lincoln, NE: University of Nebraska Press, 1984), pp. 84–99.
8 M. H. Abrams, *The Mirror and the Lamp: Romantic Theory and the Critical Tradition* (Oxford: Oxford University Press, 1953).
9 Gustave Flaubert, *Madame Bovary*, translated with an introduction by Geoffrey Wall (Harmondsworth: Penguin, 1992), p. 31. Subsequent extracts from this text will be referred to by the translator's name.
10 Alison Fairlie, *Flaubert: 'Madame Bovary'* (London: Arnold, 1962). See also the essays on Flaubert in her *Imagination and Language: Collected Essays on Constant, Baudelaire, Nerval and Flaubert* (Cambridge: Cambridge University Press, 1981).
11 Stirling Haig, *Flaubert and the Gift of Speech: Dialogue and Discourse in Four 'Modern' Novels* (Cambridge: Cambridge University Press, 1986), pp. 7–8.
12 Gustave Flaubert, *L'Education sentimentale*, ed. Edouard Maynial (Paris: Garnier, 1964), p. 272 and notes 554–5; my italics. See also OC II 107.

13 Other examples are given by Philippe Dufour in *Flaubert et le pignouf: essai sur la représentation romanesque du langage* (Saint-Denis: Presses Universitaires de Vincennes, 1993), pp. 94–5.

14 See Aimée Israel-Pelletier, *Flaubert's Straight and Suspect Saints: The Unity of 'Trois Contes'* (Amsterdam and Philadelphia: Benjamins, 1991).

15 Dufour draws attention to these 'sociolects' in *Flaubert et le pignouf*, pp. 42, 122, 133.

16 Haig discusses such amendments in *Flaubert and the Gift of Speech*, especially in his chapter 2, 'Learning dialogue'.

IO

TONY WILLIAMS

The writing process: scenarios, sketches and rough drafts

One of the major developments on the critical scene in France in the last twenty years has been the emergence of genetic studies, a new branch of literary studies concerned with the processes involved in the production of literary works. The focus of genetic studies is not so much on the final, published, work but on the preparatory material – scenarios, sketches, rough drafts, fair copy, author's manuscript – known as the *avant-texte* (a term we shall use throughout this chapter). The rise of genetic studies[1] has been associated with a process of renewal and enrichment in Flaubert studies. The works of Flaubert are increasingly viewed in relation to the work the author invested in their production, as reflected in a series of remarkably extensive *avant-textes*. The emphasis upon the *avant-texte* is not, however, without its detractors and, as we shall see in this chapter, there are a number of theoretical issues in genetic studies that have not been fully resolved. In particular, the nature of the relationship between *avant-texte* and the text itself has been the subject of much debate. For some, the value to be attached to material which, viewed from one perspective, was rejected in order to make way for the definitive version, is problematic. *Avant-texte* and text are, however, in a sense each dependent upon the other. The *avant-texte* can be constituted only because, as the term implies, there is a text that it precedes, but that text itself is the result of the process of production undertaken in the *avant-texte*.

Flaubert is a writer for whom the writing process itself becomes a major preoccupation, reflected in the often illuminating commentary to be found in his correspondence on the difficulties involved in producing each of his works. His attitude to his manuscripts reflects this change in outlook, with a new status being accorded to them. On a number of occasions Flaubert expressed the rather fanciful idea that his manuscripts might be buried with him: 'The thought of remaining unknown the whole of my life does not sadden me in the least. Provided that my manuscripts last as long as I do, that is all I ask. It's a pity that it would require too big a tomb, or I would have them buried with me, as a savage does with his horse' ['La pensée de rester toute ma vie complètement inconnu n'a rien qui m'attriste. Pourvu que mes manuscrits durent autant que moi, c'est tout ce que je veux. C'est dommage qu'il me faudrait un trop grand tombeau; je les ferais enterrer avec moi, comme un sauvage fait de son cheval' (Cor. II 66)]. The remarkable strength of Flaubert's attachment to his manuscripts helps to explain their survival. Flaubert defined himself in terms of his work with the pen: 'I am a man of the quill. I feel through it, because of it, in relation to it, and much more with it' ['Je suis un homme-plume. Je sens par elle, à cause d'elle, par rapport à elle et beaucoup plus avec elle' (Cor. II 42)]. He saw his whole future as consisting in ever more folios to be covered with ink: 'I no longer expect anything more of life than a succession of pieces of paper that one has to daub with black. It seems to me that I am passing through an endless solitude, to reach I know not where, and I am at one and the same time the desert, the traveller and the camel' ['Je n'attends plus rien de la vie qu'une suite de feuilles de papier à barbouiller de noir. Il me semble que je traverse une solitude sans fin, pour aller je ne sais où, et c'est moi qui suis à la fois le désert, le voyageur et le chameau' (Cor. IV 917)]. The manuscripts are important to him because they mark and are marked by a life spent searching for the right words.

The manuscripts also provided a kind of living proof of 'the torments of style' ['les affres du style'] and the endlessly complicated writing process: 'When my novel is finished, in a year, I will bring you the entire manuscript, for curiosity's sake. You'll see the complicated machinery I use to make a sentence' ['Quand mon roman sera fini, dans un an, je t'apporterai mon *ms*. complet, par curiosité. Tu verras par quelle mécanique compliquée j'arrive à faire une phrase' (Cor. II 71)]. But why should writing have become such a painful and protracted exercise? One factor was Flaubert's suspicion of 'inspiration': 'Let's not trust that sort of overheating which is called inspiration, and into which there enters more nervous emotion than muscular strength' ['Méfions-nous de cette espèce d'échauffement, qu'on appelle l'inspiration, et où il entre souvent plus d'émotion nerveuse que de force musculaire' (Cor. II 252)]. He also sensed that he was in the process of establishing single-handedly the basis for the modern novel, that he was the potential Homer of his age: 'I believe that the novel has only just been born, it's waiting for its Homer' ['Je crois que le roman ne fait que de naître, il attend son Homère' (Cor. II 209)]. Prose, traditionally regarded as easier than verse, he considered to be an extremely difficult art, particularly given his dream of producing a new kind of style:

As for me, I can conceive of a style: a style that would be beautiful, that someone will create one day, in ten years, or in ten centuries, and which would be as rhythmical as verse, as precise as the language of science, and with the undulations, the humming of a cello, plumes of fire, a style which would enter your mind like a rapier thrust, and on which finally your thoughts would slide as if over a smooth surface, as when one glides along in a boat with a good tailwind. Prose was born only recently, that is what one should tell oneself.

[J'en conçois pourtant un, moi, un style: un style qui serait beau, que quelqu'un fera à quelque jour, dans dix ans, ou dans dix siècles, et qui serait rythmé comme le vers, précis comme le langage des sciences, et avec des ondulations, des ronflements de violoncelle, des aigrettes de feux, un style qui vous entrerait dans l'idée comme un coup de stylet, et où votre pensée enfin voguerait sur des surfaces lisses, comme lorsqu'on file dans un canot avec bon vent arrière. La prose est née d'hier, voilà ce qu'il faut se dire.   (Cor. II 79)]

Flaubert belonged to a generation of writers from 1850 onwards who, no longer as confident that they can communicate easily with the reading public, tend as Roland Barthes has pointed out to substitute 'work-value' for 'use-value'. Flaubert, Barthes argues, founds a new kind of 'writing as craft' ['écriture artisanale'].[2] He may no longer be sure about his audience but, like Binet producing endless napkin rings on his lathe in *Madame Bovary* (OC I 599), he finds solace in the crafting of perfect prose.

A further complicating factor was his sense of recapitulating the whole evolution of humanity in the process of writing:

Not only does the artist carry humanity within himself, he also reproduces its history in the creation of his work. At first, confusion, a general view, aspirations, bedazzlement, everything is mixed up (the barbarian epoch); then analysis, doubt, method, the arrangement of the parts, the scientific era – finally he returns to the initial synthesis executed more broadly.

[L'artiste non seulement porte en soi l'humanité, mais il en reproduit toute l'histoire dans la création de son œuvre. D'abord du trouble, une vue générale, des aspirations, l'éblouissement, tout est mêlé (époque barbare); puis l'analyse, le doute, la méthode, la disposition des parties, l'ère scientifique – enfin il revient à la synthèse première plus élargie dans l'exécution.][3]

In the initial inspirational phase of creation the subject is grasped as a luminous whole, with the various parts all inextricably linked. In the second 'scientific' phase these parts are divided up methodically and analytically, whilst in the final phase they are reassembled but in a more detailed and artistically coherent manner. This rather abstract overview of the creative process goes some way to explaining why it could be so protracted. In Flaubert's own case, the recapitulation entails passing through a series of stages which can be loosely linked to the evolution of the novel, from a prolonged rumination of the subject, through a 'scientific' phase in which the material is rigorously analysed and organised, to a final stage in which the material, stripped of props and explanation, is presented in a more impersonal dramatic form. Critics have been particularly struck by the way in which Flaubert at an early stage drafts his fictional account as if he were his predecessor, Balzac, but then proceeds to dismantle this account by removing superfluous detail and explicit explanation in order to arrive at a final more concentrated and uncertain version. Finally, it has also often been suggested that Flaubert's relationship with language was in some ways problematic. From an early stage Flaubert was aware of the inadequacy of language as a means of expression. But language for Flaubert possessed a kind of materiality which meant that, rather than functioning referentially, it turned into something more akin to sculptor's clay which needed to be shaped and modelled, a process which contributed in no small measure to the labour of literary production.

The mass of manuscripts left by Flaubert provides an invaluable insight into the writing process. The pattern he followed, from *Madame Bovary* onwards, was remarkably consistent, although each work has its own unique *poétique* or aesthetic rationale. The first and in some respects most crucial phase in the creation of his novels was the planning phase. Prior to the actual composition Flaubert produced for each of his novels from *Madame Bovary* onwards a series of plans and scenarios, which in themselves could run to the length of a novel. Few writers can have planned their work with so much care, with so strong a concern to establish in advance what were to be the main contours of the work, exactly how the plot was to develop, what the characters were to be like and what would motivate their behaviour. The prolonged and repeated anticipation of the future work became for Flaubert a necessary form of quality control, allowing the strength of a narrative line to be tried and tested without reference to the detail and complexity of the whole process of formal and stylistic elaboration. In the scenarios Flaubert is primarily concerned with determining 'what happens', paying less attention to wording and expression than he will later do. Events, characters and situations, all in a simplified, even schematic, form, could be allowed to float in a special kind of conceptual space in which there was constant scope for the provision of additional material and the modification of component elements, according to considerations which were both internal (the overall shape and balance of the work) and external (what he perceived to be the general pattern of things). Flaubert had a deep-seated need to be able to envisage the entire novel and subsequently each of its parts and each of its chapters as a totality in order to achieve the range of artistic effects he desired.

When, in connection with *Madame Bovary*, he writes that 'the reader will, I hope, not be aware of all the psychological work hidden beneath the Form, but he will feel its effects' ['le lecteur ne s'apercevra pas (je l'espère) de tout le travail psychologique caché sous la Forme, mais il en ressentira l'effet' (Cor. II 497)], he is probably thinking of the extensive planning that takes place in the scenarios and which, though never visible, underpins the narrative. The scenarios are of particular interest for a number of reasons. They provide an indication of the different kinds of constraint – generic, ideological and cultural – which help to determine the shape of a work. They offer an insight into the various ways the content of the novel is generated, differentiated and refined. They reveal a constant preoccupation with the structure of the novel, in particular how it is to be divided into parts and chapters. They also contain more direct and uninhibited comments on what happens in the novel, which contrast with the studied uncertainties and decorousness of the final version. As the novel develops, it becomes more refined in more senses than one.

Before embarking upon the composition of his novels Flaubert came increasingly to undertake extensive documentation of his subject. He took detailed notes on a prodigious number of books for *Salammbô*, collected in a dossier entitled 'Sources and Method' ['Sources et méthode']; he claimed to have consulted 132 historical works for *L'Education sentimentale* and wrote over a hundred pages of notes; for *Bouvard et Pécuchet*, which reviews the full range of human knowledge, he claimed to have read over fifteen hundred books (CHH XVI 300) and planned a second volume for the novel which would have been made up largely of the notes made by the two ex-clerks. He would also visit the places in which each novel was set and make detailed notes. Lastly, he would seek out information from those better qualified than himself because they had either been witness to events or had specialised knowledge or access to library resources. The extent to which he was prepared to go often borders on the excessive. For the dinner episode at the Café Anglais in *L'Education sentimentale* (OC II 84–5), for instance, he insisted on obtaining details of a typical menu of the year 1847 (Cor. III 651). The reasons for this exceptionally thorough quest for accurate information are complex. On the one hand, he wanted his description of events and places to conform to what the reader might know. On the other hand, documentary material was often used as a way of 'kick-starting' the writing. Although he did expend a considerable amount of time on documentation, Flaubert was not slavishly bound by it. Of *Salammbô*, for instance, he commented: 'I think I have made something that resembles Carthage. But that is not what matters. I don't care about archaeology!' ['Je crois avoir fait quelque chose qui ressemble à Carthage. Mais là n'est pas la question, je me moque de l'archéologie!' (Cor. III 282)] When it suits his purpose he will invent something he knows to be false. He concedes for instance that in *Salammbô*, the aqueduct which Mâtho and Spendius use to enter Carthage (OC I 762–9) is an invention (Cor. III 284). Often he subtly adapts documentary material to the needs of fiction. For instance, the documentation for the 'terrasse du bord de l'eau' scene in *L'Education sentimentale* (OC II 131) indicated that the defenceless prisoner shot by Roque was a middle-aged landowner from the provinces, but in the novel he becomes an adolescent with long fair hair.[4] What is perhaps most striking is the plasticity of documentary material: pieces of historical information are gathered in order to be reworked subsequently in the fictional mill. There is, however, particularly in the modern novels, a residue of documentary detail which grounds the fictional world in historical reality, and runs counter to an opposing impulse to create a 'book about nothing' (Cor. II 31).

The first stage in the actual composition is marked by a process of sketching out in more detail what has been outlined in the scenarios. In the case of 'historical' scenes, it is at this point that Flaubert will insert documentary material collected with a view to fleshing out the fiction. The often rudimentary notes relating to real places and historical figures and events are then freely expanded in subsequent sketches (*esquisses*). For the purely 'fictional' scenes Flaubert visualises and maps out what happens in greater detail. He continues to show concern over the underlying psychological postulates and is more precise and explicit about what motivates behaviour and links characters. The sketches are drafted in the present tense suggesting a provisional quality about the way the action is conceived.

The most protracted and demanding phase of the writing comes when Flaubert sets out to transform the version of events established in the sketches into a fully fledged, polished, novelistic rendering. Each passage, having already been sketched out several times, will be reworked in a series of three or four rough drafts (*brouillons*). Flaubert's method was to begin by copying out the previous version, once this had become overlaid with additions and corrections to the point of being difficult to decipher. This temporary fair copy would then be subjected to the same treatment as the previous one, with numerous deletions and additions, rendering it in turn difficult to decipher and requiring another fair copy. These manuscripts are characterised by the use of past tenses (imperfect and past historic), a careful modulation from one kind of presentation to another, the gradual introduction of 'point of view', a constant search for *le mot juste*, the avoidance of repetition both of sense and sound, and the quest for colourful and later concise expression. Critics have noted a pattern of expansion and contraction: the first rough draft, typically, is still fairly short, but is expanded in the next rough draft, only to be pared down in the third. The removal of superfluous detail and the generally more concise expression contribute to the characteristic ambiguity of the final version.

On the basis of the fair copy (*mise au net*), which would still be subject to revision, Flaubert would produce a neater version to be given to the professional copyist so that the work could be handed over to the printer in a form which left no room for mistakes. He would then check the copyist's version before sending it off to the printer and finally check the proofs themselves. There is a good deal of evidence to suggest that Flaubert did not sustain the same degree of interest and concentration in this last stage. He did not always spot mistakes that crept in and complains about the tedium of proof-checking in his letters. It would be wrong to suggest that the writing process is completely rigid and unchanging. There were, inevitably, variations in the way Flaubert worked from one novel to the next and the various stages identified here[5] were not each completed before the next began. Planning and documentation would carry on throughout the composition of the novel and the division between sketch, rough draft and fair copy is not always clear-cut. Flaubert was, however, methodical in the way he wrote and there is something reassuring about the way the definitive version repeatedly emerges from the mound of proliferating possibilities.

The opening up of the *avant-textes* of Flaubert's works has led to a huge expansion of the amount of writing available for examination. In volume the preparatory manuscripts of each of the major works represent a much bigger word-mass than the published version; for *Madame Bovary* 3,814 folios; for *Salammbô* 1,933 folios; for *L'Education sentimentale* 2,504 folios; for *La Tentation de saint Antoine* 2,533 folios; for the *Trois Contes* 759 folios; for *Bouvard et Pécuchet* 72 folios of plans, 1,203 folios of rough drafts, and 2,215 folios of notes and documents.[6] In order to present this material to the reader, a new kind of edition, the genetic edition, has come into existence. The central objective of the genetic edition is to recover material that has, as it were, been overlaid by the definitive version. The genetic editor, in a move which is not without its paradoxes, attaches significance to what the writer himself has cleared away in favour of a final version deemed to be superior. The presupposition of the genetic editor is that the material that is being reclaimed possesses value, that its retrieval is a kind of enrichment, leading to a fuller understanding of the literary work. Rather than attempting to establish through the collation and analysis of various 'witnesses' a definitive version of the text, conceived as the best or most authentic version, the aim of a genetic edition is to present as fully and faithfully as possible all the different versions through which a text passes before becoming the definitive text. The emphasis shifts from the literary work as finished product to the scene of writing itself, with all its hesitations, uncertainties and dramas. There are, however, a considerable number of problems and difficulties attached to this new kind of edition, and they are particularly acute in the case of Flaubert's manuscripts.

The material that constitutes the *avant-texte* is often dispersed. The order in which the manuscripts are found will often reflect either the last use to which they were put by the writer or the sometimes questionable notions of the curators who undertook the preliminary classification. Genetic editors have sometimes abided by what might be called the institutional order and published material in a way that does not necessarily correspond to the genetic process. This was the solution adopted by Jeanne Goldin for her edition of the 'Comices Agricoles' chapter in *Madame Bovary* (OC 1 618–26) and Fleury for his edition of the plans of *Un cœur simple*.[7] The more recent editions of the scenarios for *Madame Bovary* and *L'Education sentimentale*,[8] in contrast, rearrange the material in order to reflect the various stages of the planning. A further problem relates to the difficulty of representing manuscript material through the medium of the printed page. A manuscript, by virtue of being hand-written, allows much greater freedom and flexibility in the arrangement of material than the printed page. There will always be a degree of what might be called 'transcription loss' resulting from the use of one technology, that of the printed page, for another – handwriting. The most elaborate code of transcription will never be able to capture the graphic dimension of handwriting, with all its aesthetic and emotional connotations. Genetic editors have shown considerable ingenuity in devising methods for indicating deletions and additions as well as the arrangement of the words on the page. A basic choice has to be made between a diplomatic transcription which respects the lay-out of the words on the page – the now generally preferred solution – and a linearised transcription which pieces together manuscript material in as coherent a way as possible. Respect for a folio as a material object does not automatically lead to an understanding of its conceptual dimension. The fundamental duality of the folio is best brought out by multiple rather than single forms of representation: in particular the combination of a facsimile image and a diplomatic transcription allows the folio to be both simulated in its materiality and deciphered as an apparently inextricable array of signs, whilst a linearised transcription plumps for an order in which the material should be read.

The sheer bulk of the *avant-texte* poses problems of various kinds. Despite the commendable efforts of genetic editors there is still not a single novel by Flaubert for which the complete *avant-texte* has been published, although there are ambitious projects under way.[9] It is significant that a major enterprise, the *Corpus Flaubertianum*, which set out to publish all the manuscript material of all Flaubert's works, has in twenty years succeeded in publishing the complete *avant-texte* of only one work, the *Trois Contes*.[10] Genetic editors tend to be consumed by impossible dreams of completeness and are destined to a life of frustration, given the sheer size of the dossiers they are dealing with and the standards of accuracy to which they subscribe. There is a real danger that, in seeking to present material exhaustively, one simply ends up becoming exhausted and exhausting. It is also often difficult to know where the *avant-texte* of a work ends. For instance, should a genetic edition, in the interests of completeness, include material such as documentary notes, which are not, strictly speaking, part of the compositional process? There have been attempts to demonstrate that notes of this kind are already informed by a concern for how they might be used in the work for which they are destined, and the relation between documentary note and fictional account is a good deal more complex than was once supposed. However, notes of this kind might be regarded as extraneous and certainly do not entail the same grappling for *le mot juste* as is seen in the mainstream writing.

The opening up of the *avant-texte* has led to a huge expansion of the amount of writing available for examination. The size of the complete genetic dossiers of Flaubert's novels is so great that they cannot be reproduced in book form. As a result a degree of selectivity has been necessary and has been achieved by focusing on either one stage of production or one section of a work. A dedicated 'horizontal' trawl through a complete genetic 'dossier', gathering all the material relating to a particular stage of production, has often proved highly revealing. The scenarios of *Madame Bovary* are found on a total of forty-six folios (sixty-one pages in all). The recent edition produced by Yvan Leclerc, with its excellent facsimile reproductions and meticulous transcriptions, combined with a lucid introduction and numerous tables, demonstrates clearly what can be achieved by being comprehensive within narrow parameters. It is significant that the actual material had already been transcribed in linearised form at the beginning of the 'new version' of *Madame Bovary* published by Pommier and Leleu, as long ago as 1949.[11] The comparison of these two editions provides a good indication of the way in which standards and expectations have risen as genetic studies have been established as a discipline. A similar comparison might be made between Durry's *Flaubert et ses projets inédits*, which provided at the time remarkable insights into the very earliest stage of the planning of many novels only some of which were completed, with Pierre-Marc de Biasi's monumental edition of the *Carnets de travail*, in which a thousand pages of dense and erudite commentary threaten to engulf the at times slight material transcribed.[12] Such an edition succeeds by virtue of being so systematic in its charting of a major seedbed of ideas and information, much of which is shown to have a bearing upon the published works. It is less easy to make a 'horizontal' selection when focusing on the actual composition of a work. The edition of *Madame Bovary* which aimed to give an early version of each episode of the novel (*Madame Bovary. Nouvelle version*) has an unsatisfactorily composite quality, since it ended up by piecing together versions which had reached different stages of elaboration. 'Vertical' editions, concentrating on one section of the work and reproducing all the material that relates to this one section, have fewer problems in circumscribing their material but there have been varying solutions to the order in which the material is presented. There is something heroic about Jeanne Goldin's lone labours of transcription: 329 rough drafts for one chapter of the novel, but not the plans or fair copy, which would have made the 'plongée verticale' ('vertical descent') into *Madame Bovary* more complete. Bernard Gagnebin, in contrast, in *Flaubert et Salammbô*, reproduces all the different stages of a central episode in the novel, 'Sous la tente' (OC I 756–62), including the plans. However, he chooses to anchor the material to the final version and this means that individual folios are sometimes truncated. The integrity of each folio needs to be respected and, ideally, transcribed on a single page, if the reader is to have an accurate perception of the way the writing evolves.

Some of the problems associated with the presentation of genetic material are less acute if the editor resorts to hypertext technology, which does not impose limits on the amount of material to be included and allows the user to follow different pathways through a genetic dossier. Hypertext opens up a number of attractive possibilities. Facsimile images of the manuscripts can be provided, allowing direct comparison with transcriptions, using a split screen. Links between the various manuscripts allow easy navigation of a genetic dossier. Compared to the linear and sequential logic of the book, the multiple networks of a hypertext package arguably offer a much better match with the multidirectional geometry of a genetic dossier, allowing the user to move more freely along both a horizontal and a vertical axis. A recent example of the possibilities of hypertext technology when applied to a genetic dossier can be found in the package 'History in the Making',[13] which focuses on a key chapter of *L'Education sentimentale* (OC II 112–31).

As a result of the valiant efforts of genetic editors there are, then, significant portions of the *avant-textes* of Flaubert's works now available. How have they altered our view of the works themselves? The first point to be made is that they have enhanced the image of Flaubert as a painstaking artist. The thousands of folios that constitute the *avant-texte* of the works from *Madame Bovary* onwards are the most eloquent testimony to the way, over a period of years, Flaubert grappled with a different set of artistic problems created by the sheer originality of his conception, gradually elaborated fictional worlds of great density and complexity, and laboured incessantly to produce a prose whose cadences continue to resonate with a richness and subtlety few writers can match. The *avant-textes* endow the works with unsuspected textual depths. Beneath the polished surface of the final version lies a whole world of dense and sustained writing. The potential and possibilities latent in the nexus of ideas that form the initial conception gradually unfold, driven by processes which have an interest all of their own, much as, in the biological sphere, the information coded in a genetic blueprint is gradually expressed in the development of an organism. Each part of the work passes through a kaleidoscopic succession of versions which approximate ever more closely to the final version. As the *avant-texte* becomes available, the works begin to shimmer with alternative possibilities, become encrusted with the mesmerising might-have-been meanings which went into their production, gain in impact from all that they shed in superfluous detail and explicit specification, and perhaps lose something of their aura of glorious finality.

For some, the reconstitution of the *avant-texte* poses a threat to the authority of the definitive version, yet there is no reason why the *avant-texte* should undermine or destabilise the final version. The processes at work in the *avant-texte* are designed precisely to achieve the perfection of the final version and seeing how they work can help the reader to appreciate its 'rightness'. There are, of course, times when the text of the definitive version can be corrected as a result of the establishment of the *avant-texte*. Readers might be puzzled by the adverb 'silencieusement' in the famous forest seduction scene in *Madame Bovary*: 'Alors, elle entendit tout au loin, au delà du bois, sur les autres collines, un cri vague et prolongé, une voix qui se traînait, et elle l'écoutait *silencieusement*, se mêlant comme une musique aux dernières vibrations de ses nerfs émus' (OC I 629) ['And she heard in the distance, beyond the woods, on the far hills, a vague and lingering cry; a murmuring voice, and she listened to it in silence, mingling like music with the last tremors of her stirred nerves']. The word used in the *avant-texte* is, however, 'délicieusement' ['deliciously'], which makes better, more interesting, sense, and it was the copyist who made the change, not Flaubert. As Raymonde Debray-Genette has insisted, there are misguided readings which a little genetic research invalidates.[14] Although the main thrust of genetic studies is not to establish a proper reading, this is nonetheless one of its spin-offs.

Part of the appeal of the *avant-texte* lies in the way it makes visible meanings and structures that are concealed in the final version. The extent to which it is appropriate for this material to shape the reader's responses to the printed text is, however, a matter for debate. Is it legitimate, for instance, to plough into our interpretation of the final version the more explicit account of motives and behaviour that is frequently available in the *avant-texte*, particularly in the scenarios and sketches? Can one always be certain that 'all the psychological work hidden beneath the Form' will in fact make its impact? Indeed, in the case of *L'Education sentimentale*, would supplementing the final version, which often fails to indicate clearly the motives for actions, with information provided in the *avant-texte* make for a more satisfyingly complete understanding, or is it precisely the uncertainty and undecidability of the final version that make it so engrossing? One might also ask whether it is desirable to allow one's visualisation of the fictional scene to include the often more detailed and sometimes more specific descriptions to be found in the *avant-texte*. It might be argued, for instance, that only the prevalent censorship of the 1850s prevented Flaubert from following the instruction he gives himself in a scenario about how to present Emma's seduction in the forest: 'show clearly the way Rodolphe takes her by the fanny with one hand, and the waist with the other' ['montrer nettement le geste de Rodolphe qui lui prend le cul d'une main, & la taille de l'autre' (*Plans, notes et scénarios de 'Madame Bovary'*, p. 43)]. On the other hand, such precise visualisation might be felt to coarsen the definitive version, detracting from the complex and subtle effects created by the indirect but highly suggestive description of the forest setting immediately following the act of seduction.

Part of the interest of the *avant-texte* is that it contains traces of something which subsequently becomes blurred – the living voice of the author, and in particular the ideological position he occupies. Flaubert's view of life, his profound scepticism about the likely success of all forms of human endeavour, his social and political attitudes, all clearly articulated in the correspondence, will on occasion be formulated in the *avant-texte*, only to dissolve in the final version. It is as much the gradual evaporation of personal views as those views themselves that is of interest, throwing into relief as it does the powerful forces making for a more 'impersonal' presentation at work in the writing process. The analysis of the *avant-texte* also allows us to situate the text more precisely in a particular social and cultural context. Pierre Bourdieu, on the basis of his insistence that a writer necessarily operates within a specific social and cultural context, has questioned what he sees as a narrowness of focus in genetic criticism: 'the analysis of the successive versions of a text would gain its full explicative power only if it aimed to reconstitute the logic of the labour of writing understood as a quest pursued within the constraints of the [literary] field and the range of possibilities that it offers' ['l'analyse des versions successives d'un texte ne revêtirait sa pleine force explicative que si elle visait à reconstruire la logique du travail d'écriture entendue comme recherche accomplie sous la contrainte structurale du champ et de l'espace des possibles qu'il propose'].[15] However, as has been pointed out by Raymonde Debray-Genette, 'it is on the basis of the study of manuscripts that one should reread a work. It is in their light that the role of the cultural environment becomes clear, and not the reverse' ['l'étude des manuscrits est [. . .] bien ce à partir de quoi il faut relire une œuvre. C'est à leur lumière que s'éclaire le rôle de l'environnement culturel, et non l'inverse'].[16] In this respect the *avant-texte* might be thought to mediate between literary works and the broad literary, social, ideological and biographical contexts from which they spring.

One dimension of the text that is highlighted by the exploration of the *avant-texte* is its intertextuality. Literary works constitute themselves partly by drawing upon other texts in various ways. The extent to which a writer may be referring to, echoing, parodying, or distorting another text is not always immediately apparent. However, in the *avant-texte* the intertextual link is often much more apparent. For the 'Club de l'Intelligence' episode in *L'Education sentimentale* (OC II 118–20), for instance, Flaubert was heavily indebted to a book on the political clubs which mushroomed in March 1848. Having made notes on Lucas's *Les Clubs et les clubistes*, he integrated a large number of examples of the demands that were made at the time in the early sketches. There is nothing hypothetical about intertextuality at this level. As Raymonde Debray-Genette has insisted: 'It's not something up in the air, it's down on paper' ['La chose n'est pas dans l'air, elle est sur le papier' ('Hapax et paradigmes', p. 80)]. What is most interesting, however, is the way the material which has been clearly taken from a particular source is subsequently developed and transformed. Various demands are attributed to fictional characters, made to follow rapidly one after another and contribute to a pattern of rising chaos. The *avant-texte* allows us to observe how intertextual material is appropriated and activated for fictional purposes.

The *avant-texte* also contains material which points more clearly to structures not immediately apparent in the final version. When mapping out Frédéric's development in 1848 Flaubert initially places more emphasis on his reactions to two older men, Arnoux and Dambreuse. The Guard Room episode (OC II 123) represents a moment of Oedipal confrontation, as murderous impulses towards Arnoux surface in the sketches and drafts, only to be toned down in the final version. Similarly, Roque's shooting of a defenceless prisoner (OC II 131) represents another Oedipal moment, with the repressive response of the father being acted out on the political front. The plans and sketches for the novel expose the deeper structure based upon violent confrontation in both the private and the public sphere. Critics who have seen in Emma Bovary an oral fixation which corresponds to an unsatisfied demand for love might scour the earlier versions of *Madame Bovary* in order to see how this drive shapes the writing. In the *avant-texte* of *La Légende de saint Julien l'Hospitalier*, although the Oedipal configuration at the heart of the story is more apparent, it becomes gradually and deliberately obscured.

There is one kind of comment found in the *avant-texte* that is of particular interest. What are called in French *notes de régie* ('working instructions'), to be found particularly in the scenarios, throw light on the strategies employed by Flaubert in the construction of his fictional worlds. In some cases these would not be apparent from a reading of the final version alone, but, when the reader is made aware of them, the sense of Flaubert's artistic adroitness is increased. In the case of *Madame Bovary*, for instance, Flaubert formulates an important compositional choice in relation to the way Emma is to be presented: 'present these antecedents in the course of later developments' ['poser ces antécédents dans le cours des développements postérieurs' (*Plans, notes et scénarios de 'Madame Bovary'*, p. 1)]. In the case of *L'Education sentimentale* Flaubert repeatedly indicates a wish to mislead the reader: 'Make the reader believe that Frédéric is going to marry the Roque girl'; 'The reader should believe that he is going to fuck Madame Arnoux' ['Faire croire au lecteur que Frédéric va épouser la petite Roque'; 'Le lecteur doit croire qu'il va baiser Madame Arnoux' (*L'Education sentimentale. Les scénarios*, p. 263, p. 251)]. Such comments highlight the way the definitive version of the novel deliberately frustrates the reader's expectations.

The *avant-texte* contains riches and revelations of various kinds. It may well fall short of the final version, but this no longer exists in glorious isolation. Flaubert's case is in many ways exemplary, and genetic studies have gained appreciably from their encounter with such a well-preserved body of *avant-textes*. The *Corpus Flaubertianum* may still be far from complete and even with the aid of new technology the *avant-texte* may never be fully available. However, what has already been published has without doubt enhanced and deepened our appreciation of Flaubertian writing, in its essential duality as elaborate and painstaking process of production on the one hand, and completed masterpieces on the other.

NOTES

1 For a recent survey see Pierre-Marc de Biasi, *La Génétique des textes* (Paris: Nathan, 2000).
2 Roland Barthes, *Le Degré zéro de l'écriture* (Paris: Seuil, 1972 [1953]), p. 47.
3 *Carnet de lecture* 2, folio 4 verso, Bibliothèque Historique de la Ville de Paris (simplified version).
4 Tony Williams, 'From Document to Text: the "terrasse du bord de l'eau" episode in *L'Education sentimentale*', *French Studies*, 47 (1993), 156–71.

5 For a more systematic typology of the various stages through which Flaubert's writing progresses see the following accounts by Pierre-Marc de Biasi: 'Qu'est-ce qu'un brouillon? Le cas Flaubert: essai de typologie fonctionnelle des documents de genèse', in M. Contat and D. Ferrer, eds., *Pourquoi la critique génétique?* (Paris: Editions du CNRS, 1998), pp. 31–60; and 'Processus d'écriture et phases génétiques', in *La Génétique des textes*, pp. 29–49.

6 See J. Neefs, 'Gustave Flaubert. Les aventures de "l'homme-plume"', in Marie Odile Germain and Danièle Thibault, eds., *Brouillons d'écrivains* (Paris: Bibliothèque nationale de France, 2001), pp. 68–75, p. 68. The manuscripts of *La Tentation de saint Antoine, Salammbô, L'Education sentimentale* and the *Trois Contes* are held in the Bibliothèque nationale de France. The manuscripts of *Madame Bovary* and *Bouvard et Pécuchet* can be found in the Bibliothèque municipale de Rouen. Access to all these manuscripts is open to scholars and most are available on microfilm. For a complete list of the manuscripts of Flaubert's works see 'Répertoire des manuscrits de Flaubert' in Yvan Leclerc, ed., *Plans, notes et scénarios de 'Madame Bovary'* (Paris: Editions du CNRS et Zulma, 1995), pp. 180–4.

7 *Les Comices agricoles de Flaubert*, 2 vols. Edition diplomatique établie par Jeanne Goldin (Geneva: Droz, 1984); F. Fleury, ed., *Plans, notes et scénarios d'"Un cœur simple'* (Rouen: Lecerf, 1977).

8 Leclerc, ed., *Plans, notes et scénarios de 'Madame Bovary'*; Tony Williams, ed., *L'Education sentimentale. Les scénarios* (Paris: Corti, 1992).

9 For details of the planned hypertext edition of the *avant-texte* of *Madame Bovary* see the University of Rouen Flaubert website: http://www.univ-rouen.fr/flaubert/

10 *Un cœur simple. Corpus Flaubertianum I. Edition diplomatique et génétique des manuscrits*, ed. Giovanni Bonaccorso et al. (Paris: Les Belles Lettres, 1983); *Hérodias. Corpus Flaubertianum II. Edition diplomatique et génétique des manuscrits*, ed. G. Bonaccorso et al. (vol. I, Paris: Nizet, 1991; vol. II, Paris: Sicania, 1995); *La Légende de saint Julien l'Hospitalier. Corpus Flaubertianum III. Edition diplomatique et génétique des manuscrits*, ed. G. Bonaccorso et al. (Paris: Didier Erudition, 1998).

11 *Madame Bovary. Nouvelle version*, ed. J. Pommier and G. Leleu (Paris: Corti, 1949).

12 M.-J. Durry, *Flaubert et ses projets inédits* (Paris: Nizet, 1950); Gustave Flaubert, *Carnets de travail*, édition critique et génétique établie par Pierre-Marc de Biasi (Paris: Balland, 1988).

13 http://www.hull.ac.uk/hitm/

14 Raymonde Debray-Genette, 'Hapax et paradigmes', *Genesis*, 9 (1994), 79–92, p. 83.

15 Pierre Bourdieu, *Les Règles de l'art: genèse et structure du champ littéraire* (Paris: Seuil, 1992), p. 277.

16 Raymonde Debray-Genette, *Métamorphoses du récit* (Paris: Seuil, 1988), p. 26.

AIMÉE ISRAEL-PELLETIER

Flaubert and the visual

The sheer density of visual information and the pressure placed on the reader to be an observer, to behold the real, make Flaubert's work a model for pictorial representation in fiction. Flaubert is not unique in the history of the nineteenth-century novel for his valuation of the visual. But in his work the visual asserts itself as the single most reliable carrier of signification. The work rests on the power of the visual to sway us or to convince us of the accuracy, realism and truth-telling merit of its representations. Whether or not it ultimately delivers on the meaning it promises, the visual in Flaubert offers nonetheless an open invitation to interpretation and discussion. The centrality of the visual is as true in the *realistic* novels like *Madame Bovary* and *L'Education sentimentale* as it is in the *romantic* works like *La Tentation de saint Antoine* and *Salammbô*. Both styles are marked by a high degree of visuality and both exemplify the dominance of the visual in nineteenth-century literature and culture.

It is a well-accepted fact that, in the nineteenth century, realist novelists were less interested in telling stories than they were in describing them. By the time Flaubert, Maupassant and Zola are squarely on the scene, visual description is no longer an option but instead the compulsory discursive site from which meaning and character are conceived.[1] Vision and visual description occupy a large place, for example, in the novels of Balzac, Hugo and Chateaubriand; and the novels of Restif de la Bretonne in the previous century or, further back, the twelfth-century Arthurian romances of Chrétien de Troyes are examples of writing that gives major importance to the visual. But visual description for these writers has no exclusive priority as a mode of apprehending the real world. Images, tableaux, and optical devices are typically conjured up as part of the décor, to sustain the story, to give it local colour and to construct a more believable fiction. Descriptions strive for clarity, cohesion, and a degree of completion in order to convey the distinctiveness of a character or place. In Flaubert, many of the most visually charged descriptions do not typically serve to supplement or to complete a portrait. Rather, they seem gratuitous and tend to promote doubt in the reader's mind as to the role they play in the narrative. Like Charles's cap, Emma's wedding cake, or the altar in *Un cœur simple*, they seem to say too little with too much; somehow the meaning, when meaning is attended to, does not, at first glance, justify the expenditure of effort and of effect. That is why interpretation in Flaubert is deemed a subversive and problematic activity. How is the reader to process excess? And what value can we place on it? Balzac's reader is a monadic observer (i.e., one and the same throughout all space, and in all time); the world is passed in review in front of his eyes in a straightforward manner. Contrary to Flaubert, meaning in Balzac's novels is not organised around visuality but around a dominant and coherent idea or intrigue. That is why Marc Fumaroli in his study of conversation in the novels of Balzac is able to show that characters in Balzac do more listening and talking than they do actual looking. They are told stories and tell stories all the time. This above all else is how they come to know things.[2]

The visual in the mid-nineteenth century stops being an ornament and becomes exclusively the space in which the characters are constructed and take on specificity.[3] Through vision, they come to know the world. Emma Bovary learns about the world not by hearing people talk but by looking at images promoted in literature, paintings, magazines and popular culture. Her knowledge of the world may admittedly be flawed and limited. But it is nonetheless the only world she understands and responds to. In Flaubert, knowledge of the world and of the Other is visually apprehended and constructed. I am thinking in particular of the opening scene of *L'Education sentimentale* when Frédéric, on the *Ville-de-Montereau*, is represented seeing the movement both on the boat and outside the boat. He is both in the world and inside his consciousness. And Félicité in *Un cœur simple* can fully confuse inside and outside on more than one occasion, and most touchingly when she imagines herself as Virginie in the communion scene. Images serve as instruments of knowledge, of discovery, regardless of how inadequately and inexplicably the characters process that knowledge. To see, in Flaubert, is to know. But seeing is not a guarantee of truth or of accuracy. It is through vision that both Frédéric and Félicité explore the world and that we are allowed access to them. They occupy the novel's visual space fully since they are both the subject of fiction and the tool with which reality is explored in the novel.

The visual is indeed the space where their consciousness and their desires take shape and are revealed, not in a straightforward and unambiguous manner as in Balzac or Stendhal, but in bits and pieces. The reader sees the novelistic world through the character's eyes and through the narrator's. But the reader does not, cannot, see the whole picture at once. No reliable and impartial subjectivity imparts that knowledge to him. Are Emma's eyes brown, black, or blue? Is Félicité simple or cunning? Is the root of saint Antoine's temptation psychological or metaphysical? Unable to identify the narrator and character as a privileged consciousness, the reader in Flaubert can be said to exist embedded as a consciousness apart, solitary and circulating in the world of the novel and occupying varied points of view as he sees fit; he is a roaming eye and a *flâneur* (or wanderer), interested, seriously implicated, but, also, detached. His presence may at times be suspected but it is virtually never acknowledged. He watches and gathers information about the characters and the narrator less from what is said about them than from catching them looking. Charles's delicate gaze and Rodolphe's crude stare as they look at Emma suggest how they feel about her and how we might interpret their attention. In *Un cœur simple* the tall grass at the bottom of the stream which, we are told, is like the hair of dead bodies, explains what Félicité sees and thinks. Through her eyes we understand that she mistakenly assumes Victor died drowning (he died on land of a disease). At the Vaubyessard ball in *Madame Bovary*, Emma is all eyes and we follow most of the action through her gaze. At one point, she looks out of the window and sees peasants looking in. How does Emma process these looks? In the same scene, what is the reader to make of the statue of a woman draped to the chin gazing at the room full of people? And what of the scene where Charles stares at Emma's eyes and sees himself reflected in their depths? How are we to understand the meaning of the scene in *Hérodias* where Salomé and Herod look into each other's eyes? And what about the scene where the dead but open eyes of Iaokanann are placed in front of the dim eyes of Aulus? In *La Légende de saint Julien l'Hospitalier*, how does Julien interpret the look the great stag and the dead father give him? Does he deduce that their stares represent a reproach and a judgment, as do both the reader and the narrator? And is blindness an insight, as we must assume from the examples of *Madame Bovary* and *Un cœur simple*? How do we understand the image of a gigantic Loulou hovering in the sky above Félicité? What does the image tell us about Félicité, Flaubert, and, ultimately, about ourselves as readers? How we interpret what the characters see and how they see become our most intimate and most reliable access to the characters, their world, Flaubert's intentions, and ourselves as thinking and feeling human beings. The Flaubertian reader can occupy any number of vantage points, any number of positions, including and especially the positions occupied by the characters, but, wherever he is, he can never claim to view from the only position possible. No matter what the limitation or the flaws implicit in this partial view, the visual in Flaubert is an instrument, a consciousness and a mode for examining and exploring the world.

The nineteenth-century penchant for visual effects in literature, painting, and everyday life follows closely a larger social and epistemological shift brought about, as Walter Benjamin argued in *Paris, Capital of the Nineteenth Century*, by the circulation and proliferation of objects made possible by the increasing mechanisation of the means of production. New objects, colours and materials appeared in the culture at the same time as objects once in the domain of the privileged few were duplicated and mass-produced, making them accessible to a greater number of people and making them available to the imagination as the promise of prosperity and of happiness. The proliferation and availability of these new and reproduced objects made for a fascination with, if not a survaluation of, the visible and material products of modernity. These objects circulated in literature, in art and in the wider culture where they emerged as more than mere signs of the real but as ideologically loaded and idealised. Models of vision and ways of representing visible objects became inseparable from a reorganisation and definition of what constituted objects of value and valuable knowledge. As Baudrillard has argued, the bourgeois political revolution at the end of the eighteenth century laid the groundwork for the widespread belief and expectation that the rights of man and the pursuit of liberty and happiness were accompanied by the right to *possess* and enjoy commodities made possible by new technologies and new opportunities. These objects functioned as signs of material wellbeing that needed to be visible, material and quantifiable. They had to be out there for all to see.[4] In the mid-nineteenth century, representational practices like literature and painting reflected this new interest. But they also exhibited signs of not fully grasping the meaning and implications of these new forms on society and on the individual. It is significant that, as Philippe Hamon suggests, the flood of images that entered everyday life – through newspapers, museum exhibitions, advertising and so on – introduced by the same token an anxiety in the way reality was recognised and processed.[5] Emma's tragedy, caused by her inability or unwillingness to accept her life, can be blamed only partly on what she reads and how she reads. We must not underestimate the fact that her artistic sensibility and her desire for happiness and sensual delight make her especially vulnerable to the proliferation, the vigorous promotion, and inspired promise of happiness that objects of fancy and affluence encourage. Lheureux, the tool of Emma's perdition, cannot be more aptly named.

In Flaubert, whether we are referring to his obsessive disdain for the cliché or to his distress at not finding the right word, language seems to have reached a moment of crisis. And Flaubert's habit of reading his drafts aloud may be regarded as the process and the call by which he breathes life into language, words and sentences. Novels like *L'Education sentimentale* of 1869 and

Salammbô, written at a time of great political and social change, express both a sense of overwhelming bewilderment and a pronounced feeling of excitement. The problem for writers like Flaubert is that, alongside the old, new forms of the real were being fabricated. Therefore, a new truth about the capacities and the desires of the human subject needed to be articulated. A variety of responses developed to deal with this reality, some as radically different as Rimbaud's poetry. This is why we can expect novelistic characters in Flaubert to serve as test cases for staging, not always clearly and unambiguously, the new epistemology and the new consciousness. For Flaubert and writers of his generation, non-visual language had lost its footing and was considered, by both writer and general reader, a feeble vehicle for invoking and appraising reality. For example, when *Salammbô* was published, it was attacked by critics who thought the story incoherent and outrageously visual. Yet, as Flaubert pointed out to defend his reluctance to have the novel illustrated, representations in art are static and too literal; they fix in a single image what the literary imagination sees as mobile and dizzying. He wrote to Jules Duplan in 1862: 'It was hardly worth using so much art to keep things vague, if some oaf was to come and demolish my dream with his inept precision' ['Ce n'était guère la peine d'employer tant d'art à laisser tout dans le vague, pour qu'un pignouf vienne démolir mon rêve par sa précision inepte' (Cor. III 226)]. Illustrations give the illusion of accuracy and of certainty when, in fact, the characters themselves, and Flaubert himself, are not clear about what it is they are seeing. But the novel's emphasis on the picturesque, on plasticity of form and dazzling effects, was precisely what made it a success with the public. Storytelling barely exists in *Salammbô*, *L'Education sentimentale*, and *Hérodias* where visual descriptions and images threaten to drown out old storytelling forms. In *Madame Bovary*, *La Tentation de saint Antoine*, *Un cœur simple*, and *La Légende de saint Julien l'Hospitalier* the visual and the narrative coexist, albeit at moments uneasily and unevenly. This hybrid quality of Flaubert's texts creates an effect of fragile coherence best described by T. J. Clark in his reading of Manet's *Exposition universelle de 1867*:

> The 1860s are notably an epoch of transition. The great categories of collective life – for instance, class, city, neighbourhood, sex, nation, place on the 'occupational ladder' – have not yet been made over into commodity form, though the effort to do so is impressive. And therefore the spectacle is disorganised, almost hybrid: it is too often mixed up with older, more particular forms of sociability and too likely to collapse back into them. It lacks its own machinery; its structures look flimsy alongside the orders and means of representation they are trying to replace.[6]

In Plato's *Republic* Socrates relates that the painter can make a *likeness* of a cobbler without knowing anything about cobbling, and his picture is deemed good enough for those who judge only by colours and forms. Similarly, the poet does the same with words, verbs and nouns. For Plato, both the painter and the poet are makers of images who know nothing of the true existence of the things they represent but their appearance. Later, Horace in the formula 'ut pictura poesis' ['as is painting, so is poetry'] placed the emphasis on the similarities between the two forms of representation. Lessing, in the eighteenth century, undermined their affinities and accentuated their differences, arguing for the spatiality of painting and the temporality of poetry. By the mid- to late nineteenth century, however, painting was believed to be above anything else a surface covered by colour and brush strokes. John Ruskin in a celebrated passage of 1850 defines the new way of seeing by remarking that 'the whole technical power of painting depends on our recovery of what may be called the *innocence of the eye*; that is to say, of a sort of childish perception of these flat stains of colour, merely as such, without consciousness of what they signify, – as a blind man would see them if suddenly gifted with sight'.[7] Monet repeated the same idea in the form of a desire. In the mid-nineteenth century, both in art and in literature, emphasis shifts from, on the one hand, a primary concern with narrative to, on the other, execution and material. In Flaubert's *La Tentation de saint Antoine* and *Salammbô*, as well as in *L'Education sentimentale*, *Madame Bovary*, *Trois contes* and *Bouvard et Pécuchet*, objects proliferate, colour and optical effects abound, suggesting that, quite apart from what they may imply or expose about the characters, these objects are unerringly expressive of a fascination with the act of seeing and with objects of desire proliferating in nineteenth-century French culture.

L'Education sentimentale could serve as a model for the way objects and visuality function more generally in Flaubert's work. The novel is indeed a good example of their importance and the way visuality is used by Flaubert to construct identity and represent desire in the world. In this novel, like many by Flaubert, objects compete with people and events for the attention of characters, and for the attention of the reader. The glut of objects and images is certainly a token of modernity. But it is also a sign of Flaubert's and of his characters' visual appetite. In *L'Education sentimentale*, such an abundance of objects and the delight in their presence risk undermining Frédéric's integrity as a conscious and knowing character. Like Salammbô, Frédéric often seems nothing more than a reflecting eye, indifferent to events and to knowledge and fascinated with surface effects and flatness. Frédéric lives his life in spaces and landscapes strung together like a series of tableaux which, finally, amount to nothing much. Proust understood Flaubert's penchant for visual constructions when he observed that in *L'Education sentimentale* the visual holds primacy over narrative and that objects are as significant as people.[8] Like Emma and saint Antoine, who see their life as a series of tableaux flashing in and out of their consciousness,[9] Frédéric, inspired by Madame Arnoux, sees his future life laid out in the form of images: 'These images shone like beacons on the horizon of his life' ['Ces images fulguraient, comme des phares, à l'horizon de sa vie' (OC II 39)]. On his way home from her house one night, he asks himself 'whether he would be a great painter or a great poet – and he opted for painting' ['s'il serait un grand peintre ou un grand poète; – et il se décida pour la peinture . . .' (OC II 26)]. As he enters his room the same night, 'his own face looked out at him from the mirror. He decided that he was handsome, and remained there looking at himself for a minute' ['son visage s'offrait à lui dans la glace. Il se trouva beau; et resta une minute à se regarder' (OC II 26)]. Images can be sharp and thus invoke decisiveness. But they can also be vague and disorienting. When Frédéric enters Rosanette's house for the first time, he is struck by light, colour and movement. Forms appear to him fragmented: 'Everything seemed to shimmer in a luminous haze; he stood there contemplating the dancing, *half closing his eyes* in order to see better' ['(tout s'agitait dans une sorte de pulvérulence lumineuse), il resta debout à contempler les quadrilles, *clignant les yeux* pour mieux voir' (OC II 50)] (my italics). Cracks, eyes half-shut, half-closed doors, and half-closed curtains and windows, are numerous in *L'Education* and elsewhere in Flaubert's work; they appear at moments of visual intensity when the characters seem to be at the threshold of an understanding. In the scene above, to get the whole picture, Frédéric must squint or blink. Like Madame Dambreuse, who also squints, he may indeed be literally near-sighted. However, squinting offers Frédéric, and others engaged in extreme looking, a way of organising and absorbing visual experience. By narrowing the field of vision, squinting gives the illusion of grasping, of understanding, the totality of the scene in a single gaze. Félicité endows Loulou with the attributes of the Holy Spirit by means of a visual trick; she places a picture of the Holy Spirit in eyeshot of Loulou's stuffed body and deliberately joins them in her mind. And at the end of *Un cœur simple*, vision once again plays a trick. Loulou is covered with roses; only his blue forehead appears. But as Flaubert closes in on the conclusion, the forehead is magnified until it occupies the entire novelistic space thus leaving the reader a grand image, and a wonderful life, to interpret. Optical effects such as narrowing and magnifying the gaze are frequent in Flaubert.

Frédéric, like all the main characters in Flaubert, receives pleasure and gathers what knowledge he can access by looking at the world. At times, the world returns his gaze. As he waits anxiously for Madame Arnoux to consummate their love, 'the tiniest objects became companions for him, or rather, ironic spectators' ['les objets les plus minimes devenaient pour lui des compagnons, ou plutôt des spectateurs ironiques'(OC II 109)]. Frédéric lives, dreams, and feels through his eyes. What he sees is not always what others see. And yet, mostly, he sees better and sees more than they do. He is a visual narrator in the sense that he is the narrative's main focaliser; we see numerous events through his consciousness. In her study of Flaubert's pictorialism, Adrianne Tooke points out that 'in his early drafts, Flaubert had intended to make Frédéric less impressive as a producer of images than he appears in the final text', that he returned 'again and again to the subject of what exactly it was that stopped Frédéric from being an artist', and that the 'drafts are inclined to emphasise his failure in this respect, just as they are inclined to emphasise the artistic connotations of Frédéric's love for Mme Arnoux'.[10]

Madame Arnoux serves as the canvas upon which Frédéric (like Flaubert) expresses his visual or painterly imagination and his desire for stunning imagery. She is endowed with a powerful visual presence. And this presence is as fictional to Frédéric as if she were a character in a novel he is reading or a painting he gazes at. But she is not alone in presenting a strong visual presence. Before Frédéric sees her, and before he makes out the 'rabble' travelling on the same boat, Frédéric is struck by Monsieur Arnoux's white trousers, black jacket, sparkling emerald buttons, his strange red boots with blue designs. He makes out the gold of a cap, the shiny gold cross around a passenger's neck, and notes the shimmer made by the sun as it strikes metal and water. Frédéric feasts his eyes on objects so intensely colourful and brilliant that we are not, perhaps, at risk of misrepresenting Flaubert's intentions if we declared them in poor taste. And yet we cannot be sure. After all, this scene has all the markings of a *plein air* tableau; and it may be read in this context. It reflects the vivid colours and contrasts earnestly celebrated at the time in the paintings of Manet and Renoir, and which emerged in the new colours introduced at the time by new chemical and industrial processes. Frédéric is so receptive to the nuances of colour and to the effects of light that he does not fail to remark them on many occasions. For example, Frédéric follows Monsieur and Madame Arnoux in the cabin below deck where they have lunch and notes the change in colour on her as Monsieur Arnoux draws the window curtain behind her and the light loses its brilliance. She is now illuminated by the harsh white ceiling. Frédéric is not sitting very close to the couple and yet he is able to observe her lashes, her lips, her fingers, the crumbs, and the lapis-lazuli locket on her bracelet. His eyes, like those of Charles staring into Emma's or noting the beads of sweat on her bare shoulders, serve as a magnifying glass that enables him to see so closely that he misses, or more likely chooses to ignore, the larger picture. In fact, Frédéric sees a lot in a literal sense; he is a prodigious eye. But he is indifferent to the meaning of what he sees. In this scene, for example, he does not, and does not care to, understand why he alone finds Madame Arnoux interesting.

The power of the novel, and for some its weakness, is the frequency and steadfastness with which objects, places and characters are presented in tableaux. These tableaux, readers agree, tend to undermine and immobilise the narrative flow. In Flaubert's work, description and narrative coexist, but they do so more or less easily. Descriptions perturb the narrative function in various degrees. This is true also of *La Tentation de saint Antoine* with its strong linear narrative. After *Madame Bovary*, Flaubert's work becomes more insistently visual and descriptive, with narrative appearing more fragile and diminished.

One of the most memorable tableaux in Flaubert is the notorious description of Madame Arnoux on the *Ville-de-Montereau* where, like a figure in a Manet painting, she sits against a clear blue sky, her straw hat with its pink ribbons fluttering in the wind and her ample pleated polka-dotted dress spread out. Behind her, a shawl with purple stripes rests precariously against the copper railing. Her fingers are so delicate that Frédéric notes the light penetrating her dark skin. What is remarkable is that, moments after he has left the boat, Frédéric recalls more visual details about her. Frédéric has the knack of seeing in retrospect as if his eyes cannot take all in at one time. It is also as if he cannot tolerate the lack of images and must continue constructing visions to satisfy his need for more pictures:

> . . . the entire journey came back so clearly into his mind that he could now pick out fresh details, more intimate qualities. Under the last flounce of her dress, there was her foot in a delicate, brown-coloured silk boot; the drill awning formed a wide canopy over her head, and the little red tassels on its edge shimmered constantly in the breeze.

> [. . . tout son voyage lui revint à la mémoire, d'une façon si nette qu'il distinguait maintenant des détails nouveaux, des particularités plus intimes; sous le dernier volant de sa robe, son pied passait dans une mince bottine en soie, de couleur marron, la tente de coutil formait un large dais sur sa tête, et les petits glands rouges de la bordure tremblaient à la brise, perpétuellement.

> (OC II 11)]

Can we trust Frédéric's memory, his too meticulous recall? We might, after all, suspect him of imagining this. And yet, generally, we are not inclined to doubt him. Sooner or later, the narrative makes clear whether what he sees is fanciful or real. So, we trust him to distinguish actual from imagined, though we understand that the value-judgments he makes on what he sees are not necessarily shared by others. His knack for transforming ordinary people and places into visions is perhaps a mark of his superficiality and penchant for tableaux but it is not a sign of his delusion. Like Félicité, Emma, and even saint Antoine, Frédéric knows when he is fabricating images. He frequently, but also consciously, represents Madame Arnoux in different places and in different costumes. At the Louvre, he substitutes her for figures in the paintings he observes; he imagines her in various landscapes. When she is not a picture, a work of art, she is in his mind's eye a fictional character in a romantic novel. At one point, he closes his eyes half-way and, 'rocked by the motion of the carriage, his eyelids becoming heavy, and gazing upwards to the clouds, he abandoned himself to a dreamy, infinite joy' ['bercé par le mouvement de la voiture, les paupières à demi closes, le regard dans les nuages, il s'abandonnait à une joie rêveuse et infinie' (OC II 11)]. In Flaubert's economy, eyes half-closed or half-opened are signs of deep looking. But here, what is especially suggestive is that by having his eyes half-closed he manages to impose on the outside world the very image his mind creates. Thus he is able to make the image inhabit both his inner world and the real world of the novel. This is not a hallucination but a deliberate, and creative, form of day-dreaming.

Poses and still-life scenes are numerous in *L'Education sentimentale* as they are elsewhere in Flaubert. Madame Arnoux is represented in a variety of forms, some painterly and some sculptural. Like many of the female characters in Flaubert's novels, Madame Arnoux is often still as Frédéric gazes at her. At Creil, he surprises her in a pose that reminds the reader of any number of paintings, illustrations and sculptures exhibited at that time and which appealed especially to the bourgeois viewer:

> Madame Arnoux was standing alone in front of a mirrored wardrobe. The cord of her *half-open* dressing gown trailed down her hips. One full side of her hair formed a black wave down to her shoulder. She had both arms raised and was holding her chignon in one hand while placing a hairpin in it with the other. (My italics)

> [Mme Arnoux était seule, devant une armoire à glace. La ceinture de sa robe de chambre entr'ouverte pendait le long de ses hanches. Tout un côté de ses cheveux lui faisait un flot noir sur l'épaule droite; et elle avait les deux bras levés, retenant d'une main son chignon, tandis que l'autre y enfonçait une épingle.   (OC II 78)]

In this doubly visual and erotic pose, Frédéric, and the reader in tow, gaze at her through the half-opened door as she looks at herself in the mirror.

As for Madame Dambreuse, she is invariably framed and set against a rich and luminous interior:

> He almost always arrived before her; and he would see her come in, arms bare, clutching her fan, with pearls in her hair. She would stop at the entrance, where the doorway surrounded her like a frame, and make a slightly indecisive movement, half-closing her eyes to see if he was there.
>
> [Il arrivait presque toujours avant elle; et il la voyait entrer, les bras nus, l'éventail à la main, des perles dans les cheveux. Elle s'arrêtait sur le seuil (le linteau de la porte l'entourait comme un cadre), et elle avait un léger mouvement d'indécision, en clignant les paupières, pour découvrir s'il était là.
>
> (OC II 143)]

Flaubert underlines the painterly character of Frédéric's experience of Madame Dambreuse. Yet, by showing us Madame Dambreuse squinting he signals that, though she might really be near-sighted, she, like Madame Arnoux and Frédéric, participates in acts of intense looking.

Rosanette alone poses frequently in both interior and exterior scenes and in diverse costumes. She is shown as both erotically and exotically dressed. But she is also depicted as a common, cheery, even cute manifestation of the new emerging classes in the streets of Paris. In one of their walks in the city, Rosanette appears to Frédéric like a delightful flower and altogether different from the grand flower evoked in descriptions of Madame Dambreuse:

> Young women with their children stood eating at the marble counter, on which small cakes jostled together under glass domes. Rosanette swallowed two cream tarts. The icing sugar made little moustaches at the corners of her mouth. From time to time, to wipe it, she pulled out her handkerchief from her sleeve; her face, surrounded by a green silk hood, was like a rose blossoming between its leaves.
>
> [Des jeunes femmes, avec leurs enfants, mangeaient debout contre le buffet de marbre, où se pressaient sous les cloches de verre, les assiettes de petits gâteaux. Rosanette avala deux tartes à la crème. Le sucre en poudre faisait des moustaches aux coins de sa bouche. De temps à autre, pour l'essuyer, elle tirait son mouchoir de son manchon; et sa figure ressemblait, sous sa capote de soie verte, à une rose épanouie entre ses feuilles. (OC II 63)]

For Frédéric objects, like people, are potentially works of art. Madame Arnoux's possessions, 'her comb, her gloves, her rings, were special objects for him, as important as works of art' ['son peigne, ses gants, ses bagues étaient pour lui des choses particulières, importantes comme des œuvres d'art' (OC II 28)]. In her absence, 'Frédéric, standing in front of the stove, contemplated the walls, the shelves, the floor: and charming images crowded into his memory, *or rather, before his eyes*' ['Frédéric, debout contre le poêle, contemplait les murs, les étagères, le parquet: et des images charmantes défilaient dans sa mémoire, *devant ses yeux plutôt*' (OC II 31)] (my italics). The narrator's emphasis on the eyes invests Frédéric's hallucination of charming images with physical presence. It is as if the narrator wanted to be sure we did not miss the keenly visual quality of Frédéric's mind. Of course we are inclined to believe that the mundane objects he sees in Madame Arnoux's dining room attract his attention *because* they belong to Madame Arnoux. However, the objects described are so intensely material, present, and fascinating to Frédéric that we cannot help but suspect that what seduces him is less people, less Madame Arnoux, less ideas and sentiment, than the objects themselves. This focus on objects to the detriment of meaning and sentiment is portrayed most dramatically in *Salammbô*. But the tendency to privilege objects and the act of seeing is in all Flaubert. In the following passage Frédéric is reminded of Madame Arnoux by every type of woman in the street. But, more tempting than the thought of her as a person is his fixation on the objects he imagines her wearing. He gazes at objects in streets and shops with a pleasure that betrays not only knowledge of their value but, also, a giddy delight at the chance encounter of seeing them:

> He looked at all the cashmeres, laces and jewelled pendants in the shop windows, and imagined them draped around her waist, sewn into her bodice, or glittering in her black hair. In the flower-girls' stalls, blossoms opened out to make her choose them as she passed by; in the shoemaker's displays, little satin slippers edged with swan's down seemed to await her feet.

> [Il regardait, le long des boutiques, les cachemires, les dentelles et les pendeloques de pierreries, en les imaginant drapés autour de ses reins, cousues à son corsage, faisant des feux dans sa chevelure noire. A l'éventaire des marchandes, les fleurs s'épanouissaient pour qu'elle les choisît en passant; dans la montre des cordonniers, les petites pantoufles de satin à bordure de cygne semblaient attendre son pied.   (OC II 33)]

Frédéric's desire does not move him to undress Madame Arnoux in his mind, rather, it moves him to dress her up. Objects are a source of pleasure *not* because they are part of her sphere. The opposite is actually more exact. Objects add to her desirability. As in the Louvre, Madame Arnoux is an object of desire because she is, like a mannequin, available to Frédéric's fancy. Curiously, more than Rosanette, Madame Dambreuse or Louise, she offers Frédéric what seems to him a *tabula rasa* on which a promiscuous range of pictorial effects could be produced. Is this because of something in Madame Arnoux herself, attributable to her social class or her type of beauty, for example? Or can it be explained, more simply, and, perhaps, less convincingly, by the love Frédéric feels for her?

There is a deciding moment in the novel when Frédéric is unable to transform Madame Arnoux into visual delight but, instead, must deal with the unpleasantness of what he sees. Returning to Paris to see him for the last time, she asks to go out for a walk. The pleasures of Paris are not available to her in Brittany where she now lives. Like Frédéric, an inveterate *flâneur*, Madame Arnoux enjoys wandering in the city, and vision is a source of pleasure to her as it is to him. When they return to his apartment, she steps into the light of a lamp and he sees her grey hair. Immediately, words, clichés of love, take over like a fury as he tries to conceal his feeling of disappointment: 'To hide his disappointment from her he went down on his knees, and taking her hands, started uttering tender words to her' ['Pour lui cacher cette déception, il se posa par terre à ses genoux, et, prenant ses mains, se mit à lui dire des tendresses' (OC II 161)]. In the past, he used to be able to sit silently, not uttering a word, and contemplate her hair, her eyes, her costume. 'He would scarcely talk during those dinners; he watched her. On her right temple she had a small beauty spot. The swept back sides of her hair were darker than the rest' ['Il ne parlait guère pendant ces dîners; il la contemplait. Elle avait à droite, contre la tempe, un petit grain de beauté; ses bandeaux étaient plus noirs que le reste de sa chevelure' (OC II 28)]. He would note the smallest detail: 'He knew the shape of each of her fingernails' ['Il connaissait la forme de chacun de ses ongles' (OC II 28)]. Is the unabashed barrage of words he churns out to conceal his disappointment made up of lies like Emma's famous declarations to Rodolphe? Does Frédéric not mean what he says? And is language the lie that saves him from betraying what would be otherwise apparent to her by looking at his face, his body, and his gestures? Is Flaubert suggesting that words distort or mask the truth that can be plainly seen? Not really, because we are told that this excessive language affects Frédéric as powerfully as it affects her. He ends up believing what he says and is ready to act on his words and make love to her. Besides, nothing can assure us that Madame Arnoux would correctly see the discomfiture on Frédéric's face. Yet, if we insist that these words represent lies, we must concede they are lies that reconfigure reality until it is effectively acceptable, convincing and, ultimately, even sincere. Frédéric takes his words seriously, as Emma does hers. For Flaubert, language and words are not lies; they are tools for amending fictions, for remapping desire. In the same way, eyes don't lie and distort – but neither do they privilege the truth; rather, like words, they reframe, recontextualise and revise fictions. In the same episode, Madame Arnoux spots in Frédéric's apartment, slightly hidden behind a curtain, Pellerin's painting of Rosanette: 'The portrait of the Marshal was *half-hidden* behind a curtain. But the gold and white hues, which stood out in the midst of the darkness, drew his attention' ['Le portrait de la Maréchale était *à demi caché* par un rideau. Mais les ors et les blancs, qui se détachaient au milieu des ténèbres, l'attirèrent' (OC II 160)] (my italics). The fact that the painting is half-hidden intensifies Madame Arnoux's gaze. As with the dilapidated figure of Loulou, in *Un cœur simple*, camouflaged in the altar until only the beautiful blue spot of lapis-lazuli shows and expands imaginatively into the skies above, here, Pellerin's work behind the half-open curtain reveals only the bright and visually striking fragments of the portrait. By imagining Madame Arnoux, and others, as he would a work of art, Frédéric, like Félicité and Emma, falsifies nothing that is not already fictionalised. Images and words do not fictionalise reality. They reframe, represent and evoke an already fictionalised world. Throughout his work, Flaubert suggests that eyes like words, by managing detail, restate fictions thus preserving them from debasement and disillusionment. Frédéric, Félicité, Emma, Salammbô, saint Antoine, and others see with a vengeance. And, with the exception of Iaokanann, his characters do more looking than speaking or listening. But they do not understand more clearly or feel more fully through their eyes than they do through words. Both systems are controlled to offer them no more knowledge than they are willing or capable of receiving.

We would expect that Flaubert's keen sense of the visual and the significant presence of pictorial effects in his work would betray a strong interest in painting and in contemporary issues on art. It does not. Discussions of major figures of the times like Courbet and Manet, as well as passionate debates on movements like Impressionism, sparked superficial comments or no interest on his part. How are we to understand a writer so visual and yet who seems to have very little to say about the big questions circulating at that time about art? Flaubert shows no indication that he knew how to *read* Manet or Courbet or that he was aware that they used colour, brush stroke, subject position, and subject matter in new ways to solve the same types of problems that he was wrestling with in writing. He understood that literature offered the writer positions from which to interpret what he saw. However, he did not extend this understanding to painting and considered it, as Pellerin's failure at representation demonstrates, a form typically preoccupied with copying the real without concern for its interpretation and, at best, as a conjurer of visual fantasies not a conjurer of universal truths, like literature. True, he discussed

Courbet, disagreeing with his views on Realism; and he admired Gustave Moreau for his capacity to *make one dream*. The Romantic idea that works of art should make one dream is not a concept unique to Flaubert. Baudelaire, Delacroix, Fromentin and others refer to it. But whereas Baudelaire gives due consideration to aesthetic features such as strokes, colour and treatment of the subject, in Flaubert the idea of *faire rêver* stands on its own undeveloped. However, it suggests an interesting conceptual position. Norman Bryson argues that the very idea of a painting making us dream means, at heart, that we are thinking about it linguistically. Speaking of Watteau, Bryson writes, 'by reverie one should understand not simply a mental state but a linguistic activity with distinct and analysable features'.[11] It is well known that Flaubert did not like to include illustrations in his work, believing that the visual could not attain language's subtlety and complexity. But less well known, perhaps, and as important, is that he also believed that language could not comment on art.

Reading Flaubert's novels, we have the sense that visual figuration is the manifestation of Flaubert's fascination with the visual as a way of representing and apprehending a world he found exhilarating but that he did not fully grasp and could not assess. Flaubert cannot explain the world in which his characters live any more than he can put into words how all the parts of their lives add up. All that he can do, and it is significant, is relate his fascination and his incomprehension at the fragmentary, discontinuous, chaotic and visually stimulating world he shares with his characters. We can say that in his work, especially after *Madame Bovary*, Flaubert acts on a realisation, a partial knowledge, that what cannot be understood can nonetheless be described.

NOTES

1 See Isabelle Daunais, *Frontière du roman. Le personnage réaliste et ses fictions* (Montreal: Presses de l'Université de Montréal, 2002).

2 Marc Fumaroli, *Le Genre des genres littéraires français: la conversation* (Oxford: Clarendon, 1992), p. 32.

3 See Daunais, *Frontière du roman*, p. 92.

4 Jean Baudrillard, *La Société de consommation* (Paris: Gallimard, 1970).

5 Philippe Hamon, *Imageries. Littérature et image au XIXe siècle* (Paris: Corti, 2001).

6 T. J. Clark, *The Painting of Modern Life. Paris in the Art of Manet and His Followers* (Princeton: Princeton University Press, 1984), p. 64.

7 See Jonathan Crary, *Techniques of the Observer. On Vision and Modernity in the Nineteenth Century* (Cambridge, MA, and London: MIT Press, 1991), p. 95.

8 Marcel Proust, 'A propos du "style" de Flaubert' (1920), reprinted in *Contre Sainte-Beuve, précédé de Pastiches et mélanges et suivi de Essais et articles*, ed. Pierre Clarac and Yves Sandre (Paris: Gallimard, 1971), pp. 586–600.
9 See Jean-Pierre Richard, *Littérature et sensation* (Paris: Seuil, 1954), p. 157.
10 Adrianne Tooke, *Flaubert and the Pictorial Arts. From Image to Text* (Oxford: Oxford University Press, 2000), p. 219.
11 Norman Bryson, *Word and Image. French Painting of the Ancien Régime* (Cambridge: Cambridge University Press, 1981), p. 73.

12

ALAN RAITT

The theatre in the work of Flaubert

Anyone who decides to look at the question of Flaubert's attitude to the theatre is likely to have at least two surprises. The first is to do with his childhood. Every reader of a biography of Flaubert is aware that, with his sister and some school friends, he had used his father's billiard-room to put on plays, but it is less well known that this was close to being an obsession. Flaubert wrote plays, he acted in them, he organised performances with costumes, playbills and tickets. Here is how at the age of seventeen he remembered this period of his young life:

> Oh God, God, why did you make me be born with so much ambition? For what I have really is ambition. When I was ten years old, I was already dreaming of glory, and I started composing as soon as I knew how to hold a pen. I imagined for myself delightful pictures: I dreamt of a theatre full of light and gold, hands clapping, cries of acclamation, bouquets of flowers. People are calling 'the author! the author!': the author really is me, it is my name, me, me! People are looking for me in the corridors, in the dressing rooms; they crane their necks to catch a glimpse of me, the curtain rises, I step forward: what bliss! They look at you, they admire you, they envy you, they are proud to love you, to have seen you.

> [Ô mon Dieu, mon Dieu, pourquoi donc m'avez-vous fait naître avec tant d'ambition? Car c'est bien de l'ambition ce que j'ai. Quand j'avais dix ans, je rêvais déjà la gloire et j'ai composé dès que j'ai su écrire. Je me suis peint tout exprès pour moi de ravissants tableaux: je songeais à une salle pleine de lumière et d'or, à des mains qui battent, à des cris, à des couronnes. On appelle 'l'auteur! l'auteur!': l'auteur c'est bien moi, c'est mon nom, moi, moi – ! On me cherche dans les corridors, dans les loges; on se penche pour me voir, la toile se lève, je m'avance: quel enivrement! On te regarde, on t'admire, on t'envie, on est fier de t'aimer, de t'avoir vu! (OJ 732)]

What inspired this obsession was an impulse fundamental to his whole career as an artist, the impulse to create and embody imaginary roles, which he did, not just on the billiard-table stage, but also in front of his family and friends, and even when he was completely alone. One of the characters he loved acting has remained famous, the celebrated and monstrous 'Garçon' who represented a spirit of universal, anarchic and obscene denigration. But there were others whom he acted out with such intensity that his father took fright, as he later confided to Louise Colet:

> In the end, my father forbade me to imitate certain people, convinced that it must make me suffer greatly, which was true though I denied it, among others an epileptic beggar whom I had met one day at the seaside. He had told me the story of his life, he had been a journalist, and it was marvellous. It is certain that when I was pretending to be this chap, I really was in his skin. One could not see anything more hideous than me at such a time. Do you understand the satisfaction I felt? I'm sure you don't.

> [Mon père à la fin m'avait interdit d'imiter certaines gens persuadé que j'en devais beaucoup souffrir, ce qui était vrai, quoique je le niasse, entre autres un mendiant épileptique que j'avais un jour rencontré au bord de la mer. Il m'avait conté son affaire, il avait été journaliste, et c'était superbe. Il est certain que quand je rendais ce drôle j'étais dans sa peau. On ne pouvait rien voir de plus hideux que moi à ce moment-là. Comprends-tu la satisfaction que j'éprouvais? Je suis sûr que non.   (Cor. I 380)]

When he was twenty, he wrote: 'I'm always acting comedy or tragedy, it is so difficult to get to know me that I don't even know myself' ['Je joue toujours la comédie ou la tragédie, je suis si difficile à connaître que je ne me connais pas moi-même' (OJ 756)]. Elsewhere he declared: 'If I had been properly trained, I could have been an excellent actor, I felt I had the inner strength for it' ['J'aurais pu faire, si j'avais été bien dirigé, un excellent acteur, j'en sentais la force intime' (Cor. I 49)]. In 1846 he admitted: 'Whatever people say, the essence of my nature is the clown' ['Le fond de ma nature est, quoi qu'on dise, le saltimbanque' (Cor. I 278)], and later his best friend told him: 'You were born a ham-actor!' ['Tu es né cabotin!' (Cor. III 910)]

The second surprise would be the persistence of this obsession. The billiard-table theatre survived for some five years, roughly 1829–34, but all his life Flaubert loved acting. Maxime Du Camp tells us that for several weeks in the 1840s he would only speak with the accent and intonations of the actress Marie Dorval; the Goncourt brothers noted that he practised imitating Henry Monnier in the role of Joseph Prudhomme or that he mimicked the gestures and hesitant diction of Napoleon III; Emile Bergerat remembers seeing him perform the 'Creditor's Dance' with Gautier; and one day in 1852, in the Goncourts' salon, 'someone asks Flaubert to dance *The Salon Idiot*: he borrows Gautier's tail-coat, he turns up his collar, I don't know what he does to his hair, to his face, to his expression, but suddenly he is transformed into a formidable caricature of stupidity' ['l'on demande à Flaubert de danser *L'Idiot des salons*: il demande l'habit de Gautier, il relève son faux-col; je ne sais ce qu'il fait de ses cheveux, de sa figure, de sa physionomie, mais le voilà transformé en une formidable caricature de l'hébètement'].[1] Moreover, rather than lending the manuscript of works he was writing, he preferred to read them aloud. The reading of the first version of *La Tentation de saint Antoine* for Du Camp and Bouilhet has remained famous, but there is evidence of many more readings for friends, including *Salammbô*, *L'Education sentimentale*, *La Légende de saint Julien l'Hospitalier* and *Hérodias*.

To come back to his youthful dramatic experiments, it is apparent that if he also wrote stories he was principally concerned with the theatre and that he was bold enough to compose five-act historical dramas before he ever thought of undertaking a real full-length novel. Thus, in 1838, he wrote a vast cloak-and-dagger tragedy entitled *Loys XI*, which still exists. But if *Loys XI* shows that the sixteen-year-old had strong dispositions for the theatre, it also reveals an emotional development which was going to take him away from the theatre as normally understood. The first three acts are full of colourful action, but the last two are largely devoid of events, being mainly concerned with the terrors of the ailing king at the thought of death and nothingness, ideas which were preoccupying the adolescent author. At about the same time, he discovered two works which suggested to him a way of reconciling his love of the theatre with his desire to pursue philosophical meditations difficult to adapt to the demands of the stage. These were Edgar Quinet's *Ahasvérus* and Goethe's *Faust*, two 'total dramas' which used a quasi-dramatic form, without thought for scenic practicalities, in order to present, in grandiose visions, the loftiest metaphysical speculations. Inspired by these two works, in 1838 and 1839, he composed two 'mysteries' (in the Romantic sense of the word), *La Danse des Morts* and *Smar*.

These two 'mysteries', episodic and ill constructed, differ from their models in that they include, in the 'stage directions', passages of narration and description, whereas *Ahasvérus* and *Faust* consist almost exclusively of dialogue. So they are already somewhat closer to the novel form. Shortly afterwards, in late 1841, Flaubert began his first real novel, *Novembre* (in 1838, the *Mémoires d'un fou* had been more of a collection of literary and personal meditations). If, at this stage, he turned towards the novel, it was partly to continue his philosophical speculations and partly because his experience of life had become richer, notably by his liaison with Eulalie Foucaud de Langlade at Marseille in 1840, which encouraged him to use the personal or autobiographical novel to explore the secrets of his emotional life. Thus in *Novembre* he visibly imitates two novels he particularly admired,

Chateaubriand's *René* and Goethe's *Werther*. But the theatre is by no means absent from this work, especially in one violently lyrical passage, where the narrator combines his passion for the theatre and his erotic daydreams: 'There was nothing I loved so much as the theatre, even the hum of conversation in the intervals, even the corridors that I tramped with a trembling heart to find a seat' ['Je n'aimais rien tant que le théâtre, j'en aimais jusqu'au bourdonnement des entractes, jusqu'aux couloirs, que je parcourais le cœur ému pour trouver une place' (OJ 763)]. The theatre also occupies a prominent position in the next novel, the 1845 *Education sentimentale* (which has only the title in common with the great novel of 1869). There, Jules, one of the two heroes, a budding playwright, is seduced by the false promises of the manager of a travelling company and by the charms of the leading lady into believing that they are going to produce a great historical drama he has composed, until the company decamps in the middle of the night. One has the impression that Flaubert is becoming more sceptical about his own dreams of fame and riches in the theatre. However, Jules does not abandon literature, and by the end of the novel we learn that after long reflections on aesthetic matters, he has become a 'grave and great artist' ['grave et grand artiste' (OJ 1075)], though Flaubert gives us few hints as to what this artistic vocation consists of, except that the theatre clearly forms part of it.

But between the composition of *Novembre* and the completion of the 1845 *Education sentimentale*, there occurred an unexpected event which completely changed Flaubert's life. This was of course the nervous or epileptic crisis which struck him down in January 1844 on the road to Pont-L'Evêque. The illness compelled him to abandon the law studies which he detested and to return to Croisset to pursue his convalescence, and in mid-1845 he noted with satisfaction that he was being allowed to devote himself exclusively to literature. Then, on his return from a trip to Italy with his family, something extremely strange happened. For about six months, Flaubert spent his time on a detailed study of Voltaire's theatre, taking hundreds of pages of notes, summarising and commenting on thirty-three of Voltaire's tragedies and comedies. For a long time, it was supposed that he had undertaken this task because he was so fond of Voltaire and admired the structure of his plays. But when his notes were finally published in 1967, it transpired that this was far from the truth and that, on the contrary, he felt only scorn for Voltaire's theatre, which he later summed up in a single word: 'Pitiful' ['Pitoyable' (Cor. II 417)]. He pretended to his friend Le Poittevin that this study could be useful to him later, implying that he wanted to train himself seriously to be a playwright. There seems to be only one possible explanation for such paradoxical behaviour. There could be no question of Flaubert becoming something as disreputable as an actor, but it was perfectly respectable to be a dramatist, and of course he wanted nothing more desperately than to be allowed to go on writing. But his father, while by no means the philistine depicted by Du Camp, had very conservative views on literature, with a marked preference for eighteenth-century authors, and his library contained seventy-two bound volumes of Voltaire. It is entirely plausible that, in order to please his father, whom he loved but of whom he was in awe, Flaubert pretended to want to revive the neo-classical theatre of the previous century. Indeed, at that time, the idea was not totally absurd. Romantic theatre seemed to be running out of steam, with the failure of Hugo's *Les Burgraves* in 1843 at the same time as the great success of Ponsard's *Lucrèce*. But however insincere Flaubert may have been in applying himself to the analysis of Voltaire's theatre, it does at least indicate that at this stage he saw his future as a dramatist rather than a novelist.

However that may be, in January 1846 Achille-Cléophas Flaubert died, and his son at once dropped his work on Voltaire's theatre, never to speak of it again, except that a few years later he took his revenge for so much wasted time by persuading his friends Du Camp and Bouilhet to join him in composing a parodic verse tragedy in conformity with the strictest rules of neo-classicism. *Jenner ou la découverte de la vaccine* was never finished, but important fragments survive in which the characters use pompous circumlocutions to utter hair-raising obscenities in perfectly regular alexandrines.

But, naturally eager to profit from his new-found creative freedom, Flaubert resolved to write *La Tentation de saint Antoine*, a subject inspired by a Brueghel painting he had seen in Genoa in 1845. The composition of this work, in some ways not unlike an extension of the 'mystery' genre he had experimented with in *La Danse des morts* and *Smar*, occupied him for fifteen months in 1848 and 1849, during which time he refused to tell his closest friends anything about the project. Then, in September 1849, he invited Bouilhet and Du Camp for a solemn reading of the finished work he believed to be a masterpiece. For eight hours a day, during four days, he declaimed *La Tentation*, after which his friends delivered this implacably severe verdict: 'You must throw that into the fire and never speak of it again' ['Il faut jeter cela au feu et n'en jamais reparler'].[2] Their criticisms were that it was confused and diffuse, that the language was prolix and disorganised, that the action was a torrent of uncontrolled lyricism, and that the saint was a dull and static character. To counteract these defects, they suggested to Flaubert that he should write a novel on a more comprehensible, down-to-earth subject like Balzac's *Cousine Bette* or *Cousin Pons*. Though devastated by this rejection, Flaubert gradually came to recognise that some of their reproaches were not unjustified, with the result that, two years later, on returning from a journey to the Middle East, he set to work on *Madame Bovary*.

But despite having embarked on a crushing task which was to last almost five years, Flaubert was far from having given up his concern with the theatre, especially because of his friendship with Louis Bouilhet. After abandoning the medical studies he had started under Flaubert's father, Bouilhet devoted himself to lyric poetry, eking out a living by giving private lessons. But Flaubert knew that lyric poetry alone would never bring in enough money for Bouilhet's own needs, let alone those of his mistress and his adopted son, and did all he could to convince his friend that he had the ability to succeed in the theatre. As far back as 1847 and 1848 he had joined Bouilhet in producing a series of scenarios for plays. These rarely went beyond bare plot summary, and one supposes that their object was to provide training in the elaboration of dramatic structures. Eventually, Bouilhet, whose disposition was gentle, depressive and pessimistic, allowed himself to be persuaded that he did perhaps have the qualities needed to write for the stage. His first experiment, written in collaboration with Flaubert, was, of all things, a pantomime entitled *Pierrot au sérail*. But simultaneously, in 1855, he had, on his own, completed a five-act historical verse drama, *Madame de Montarcy*, which, with Flaubert's help, he induced the Odéon to accept. The first performance took place in September 1856 and, to Bouilhet's astonishment, was a triumphant success, leading to over eighty performances. This success was in no small measure due to Flaubert, who took over the rehearsals from his friend. Maxime Du Camp witnessed Flaubert's exaltation on this occasion:

> He wouldn't leave the theatre; he had taken it over. He was in a new milieu which interested him and brought out in him unaccustomed activity, and had him wholly in its grip. He strode about the stage, making actors repeat their speeches, showing them the gestures they should make, demonstrating the style he wanted, shifting the characters round, talking familiarly to everyone, the stagehands, the actors, the prompt and the scene-shifters; if it had been his own work, he could not have gone to greater lengths to make it a success.

> [Il ne quittait pas le théâtre. Il en avait pris possession; il était dans un milieu nouveau qui l'intéressait, développait en lui une activité inaccoutumée et l'avait saisi tout entier. Il arpentait la scène, faisait reprendre les tirades, indiquant les gestes, donnant le ton, deplaçant les personnages, tutoyant tout le monde, les garçons d'accessoires, les acteurs, le souffleur et les machinistes; l'œuvre de Bouilhet eût eté la sienne qu'il ne se serait pas tant démené pour la faire réussir.
> (Du Camp, *Souvenirs littéraires*, II, p. 135)]

In fact, his literary closeness to Bouilhet was such that he could legitimately consider himself the godfather, if not the father, of the play.

Having been convinced by the success of *Madame de Montarcy* that after all he did have some talent for the theatre, Bouilhet went on until his death writing for the stage. Not all his plays had the same success, but they followed one another very regularly: *Hélène Peyron* in 1858, *L'Oncle Million* in 1861, *Dolorès* in 1862, *Faustine* in 1864 and *La Conjuration d'Amboise* in 1866. Each time Flaubert flung himself into action with the same enthusiasm, negotiating with theatre managers, choosing theatres and hiring actors. So for ten years Flaubert was able to satisfy that obsession with the theatre which had never left him since his childhood. Admittedly, at the same time he was becoming disillusioned with the theatrical milieu in general, its commercialism, its meanness, its jealousies, its lack of respect for true art. Even so, from time to time he had thoughts of returning to his own theatrical experiments once *Madame Bovary* was out of the way. In the end, having spent five years reflecting on the art of the novel, he preferred to give priority to a second novel, *Salammbô*, which he began in 1857 after revising and abridging *La Tentation de saint Antoine*. But it may be that in writing *Salammbô* Flaubert was thinking obliquely of the theatre. At all events, before it was even published he contacted the composer Ernest Reyer, who was an acquaintance of his, to see if it could be converted into an opera. When Reyer approved, Flaubert asked Théophile Gautier to write the libretto and sent him a detailed scenario. However, Gautier was so dilatory that he produced nothing before his death in 1872. In the meantime Flaubert turned down approaches from several other composers eager to turn it into an opera. Reyer did not give up, and after many more delays the opera had its première in Brussels in 1892, and remained in the repertoire for a good half-century. It is significant that in 1884 Maupassant, well placed to assess his master's intentions, should have asked in relation to *Salammbô*: 'Is that a novel? is it not rather an opera in prose?' ['Est-ce là un roman? n'est-ce pas plutôt un opéra en prose?']³

But after the publication of *Salammbô*, Flaubert had the idea of a totally unexpected dramatic experiment: he decided he wanted to regenerate the 'fairy play' (*féerie*), a genre which had originated in the early years of the century. By the 1860s, the *féerie*, which had never had any literary pretensions, had become a mere pretext for spectacular effects loosely attached to some fairy story (in other words, it was very like an English Christmas pantomime). It is hard to guess why Flaubert believed that the *féerie* could become a poetic and literary genre, but he stubbornly pursued his idea, recruiting Bouilhet and another friend, Comte d'Osmoy, to assist him. Bouilhet was a great help, but d'Osmoy, who was reputed to have had some modest stage success in Paris, proved very recalcitrant. Flaubert composed a first version of *Le Château des cœurs* very rapidly in 1863 and at once set about offering it to a succession of theatre managers, who all turned it down. Their decision is understandable: it is very long and disconnected, with cardboard characters and a glaring discrepancy between the fantastic side, which sets the good fairies against the wicked gnomes, and the social satire which underlies most of the scenes. Maurice Bardèche's severity is by no means misplaced: 'All these great projects had led only to the insertion, in a vast assembly of stage machinery and wild inventions, of a summary and caricatural social satire' ['Tous ces grands projets n'avaient abouti qu'à insérer, dans un grand déploiement de machineries et d'extravagances, une satire sociale caricaturale et sommaire' (CHH VII 21)]. Incomprehensibly, Flaubert attached much importance to his *féerie* and could never fathom why theatre managers persisted in rejecting it. Towards the end of his life, he resigned himself to having it serialised in *La Vie moderne*, a luxury review belonging to his publisher Charpentier. Then, when Flaubert died suddenly, Charpentier dropped the idea of publication in book form and it only appeared in 1885 in the sixth volume of Flaubert's complete works. Right to the end, Flaubert regretted not having seen certain scenes on the stage, but Zola, who had much affection for him, wrote: 'He never saw them, and his friends think it is better that way' ['Il ne les a pas vues, et ses amis pensent que cela vaut mieux ainsi'].[4] *Le Château des cœurs* remains a mystery, since no one has been able to prove why Flaubert wrote it and was so attached to it, though Marshall Olds has recently put forward the plausible argument that Flaubert's original intention had been to use the *féerie* to create a 'modern fantastic' based on contemporary science, but was deflected from this idea by his two collaborators, who induced him to produce something much more traditional.[5] If he thought he could provide a viable work by grafting onto a discredited popular genre some of the fantastic and spectacular aspects of *La Tentation de saint Antoine*, he was certainly wrong.

In July 1869, Louis Bouilhet died after a short illness. This bereavement was a terrible blow to Flaubert who, during all the rest of his life, devoted himself indefatigably to securing and extending his friend's reputation. Just before he died, Bouilhet had finished a new historical verse drama, *Mademoiselle Aïssé*. Flaubert immediately took it upon himself to find a theatre and a publisher for the play, but the upheavals of the war and the Commune prevented it from being produced until 1872. To Flaubert's despair, it was a total failure. But he had found among his friend's posthumous papers another play, a prose comedy entitled *Le Sexe faible*. Whether what Flaubert discovered was a scenario or a full text is open to doubt, but he certainly put in a lot of work adapting it, which is why it figures in editions of his complete works. However that may be, *Le Sexe faible* is a light comedy, solidly constructed and containing some extremely amusing scenes. The message of the play is simple and as politically incorrect as possible, and in 1864 Bouilhet had defined his intentions in these words: 'I shall show there all the cowardly acts which women make us commit, and the terrible power which, day by day, they are usurping in the most important business in the world' ['Je montrerais, là-dedans, toutes les lâchetés que nous font commettre les femmes, et la puissance terrible qu'elles usurpent, de jour en jour, dans les affaires les plus importantes du monde' (Cor. III 973)]. The comedy relates the misfortunes of Paul, a young man about town, victim successively of his mother, his wife and his mistress until he admits total defeat at the hands of feminine domination. Despite its sexist theme, *Le Sexe faible* is a reasonably good comedy, with a lively action, unexpected reversals of fortune, some truly comic lines and an effective structure (no doubt due to Bouilhet's experience of the theatre).

Flaubert had no difficulty in getting the play accepted by Carvalho, manager of the Vaudeville, who wanted to produce it early in 1873. But this production did not take place because Flaubert, having acquired a taste for dialogue as a result of the work he had done in adapting the play, had the idea of himself writing a play, a satirical comedy entitled *Le Candidat*. This play was finished in November 1873, but Flaubert had indiscreetly told Carvalho that he was preparing it. The manager realised that a play written by the great novelist would be much more profitable than one by Bouilhet and only adapted by Flaubert, and so began making difficulties over *Le Sexe faible* while promising to produce *Le Candidat*. Seduced by the flattery and the cunning of the enterprising Carvalho, Flaubert accepted his offer, and *Le Candidat* had its première at the Vaudeville on 11 March 1874. The public and the critics, however, reacted with such coolness that, after four performances, Flaubert himself withdrew it. *Le Candidat*, as its title implies, is a political satire principally directed against universal suffrage, which Flaubert detested. Rousselin, the eponymous candidate, is obsessed with becoming a deputy, whether for the left or the right is a matter of indifference for him, and promises his daughter's hand to the leaders of the rival parties in turn, in order to secure their votes. But he does not realise that the journalist Julien is courting his wife, so that at the very moment when he manages to get elected, he becomes a cuckold. In many ways, the failure of the play was foreseeable: Flaubert drags all the parties through the mire, there is not a single sympathetic character, and the action moves far too fast to be credible. There are a few amusing scenes, and overall the play is worth more than its poor reputation. A revival at the Cité Universitaire in 1988 was reasonably well received, and a German adaptation by the dramatist Carl Sternheim was successfully produced in 1915 and has been regularly revived ever since; likewise an Italian version was well received in 1979. That is to say that, if one corrects some clumsy devices and abridges some rather prolix dialogue, *Le Candidat* is not a bad play at all. After the failure of *Le Candidat*,

Carvalho dropped the idea of producing *Le Sexe faible*, which was accepted the following year at the Théâtre de Cluny. Yet, shortly before it was due to be put on, Flaubert cancelled the production because he was afraid it would be unworthy of the play. So it is that the only play associated with Flaubert's name which might have been a success has never been produced in France.

The failure of *Le Candidat* finally disillusioned Flaubert with the theatre, and from 1874 to the end of his life there is no trace of any theatrical project, except for his continuing efforts to find a theatre for *Le Château des cœurs* and the hope that some day *Salammbô* would be made into an opera. If one tries to assess why this novelist of genius was unable to adapt his remarkable gifts to the stage, one reason is immediately apparent: namely that he believed that a play should be written at breakneck speed. Whereas a novel on average took him five years to plan and write, a version of *Le Château des cœurs* took him no more than three months, and *Le Candidat* was ready in only two months of part-time work. This speed was a matter of principle: 'Anyway, I believe that a play (once the plan is clearly established) should be written in a sort of fever. That speeds up the movement: one can correct afterwards' ['Je crois, du reste, qu'une pièce de théâtre (une fois que le plan est bien arrêté) doit s'écrire avec une sorte de fièvre. Ça presse davantage le mouvement: on corrige ensuite' (Cor. IV 666–7)]. But this conviction in itself betrays a certain disdain for what, after *Madame Bovary*, he considered to be an inferior genre. He was convinced that theatre audiences had no appreciation of art and that, in order to please them, one had to aim at people with no sensitivity to nuances, to subtle intentions, to the beauty of style. More than once he averred that lack of distinction was indispensable in the theatre, and he once declared, about the theatre: 'It's all very well for people who don't love style for its own sake' ['C'est bon pour les gens qui n'aiment pas le style en soi' (Cor. IV 732)], and as what he prized above all was style for its own sake, one can understand that he was unable to give of his best in the theatre. In his novels, direct speech could be reduced to a minimum and, especially with free indirect speech, he could make the narratorial discourse highly literary, but in the theatre he was largely confined to dialogue, which could not be too highly wrought if it was to be convincing. Equally, stage usage deprived him of description, so vital in the economy of his novels. Striving in his plays for the tone of natural conversation, he was always on the brink of banality and inexpressiveness.

In terms of technique, his novels thus owe little or nothing to his long preoccupation with the theatre – it has been pointed out that the original plan for *Madame Bovary* was more descriptive than narrative, and he himself admitted that drama did not play a large part in it, and wrote to someone who wanted to adapt the novel for the stage: '*Madame Bovary* is not a theatrical subject' ['*Madame Bovary* n'est pas un sujet théâtral' (Cor. II 806)]. As for *L'Education sentimentale*, dramatic crises are continually postponed or eluded: it has been well said that what interests him in this novel is what happens between the crises, or rather what happens instead of the crises, and *Bouvard et Pécuchet* contains so little conflict that it hardly has a plot and the stuff of drama is almost completely absent from it. Even *Salammbô* is more spectacular than properly dramatic. It is true that the theatre as an institution figures prominently in all the 'modern' novels. It is at a performance of *Lucie de Lammermoor* that Emma meets up again with Léon and that some of the romantic aura of the opera rubs off onto the prosaic lawyer's clerk. In *L'Education sentimentale* the actor Delmar makes frequent appearances, and his empty-headed vanity and concern with outward show is emblematic of a soulless society preoccupied only with how things look and indifferent to inner values. Bouvard and Pécuchet, in the novel that bears their names, have long discussions about drama which do no more credit to the theatre than to their intelligence. But if the published text of the novels seems to owe little to Flaubert's interest in the theatre, the same is not true of the way in which they came to be written. It is well known that, before setting pen to paper, Flaubert had the habit of declaiming his novels at the top of his voice, to such an extent that in his letters he often complains of being absolutely hoarse after a long session of work. In other words, he acted the parts of all the characters and the narrator, identifying totally if momentarily with them, as the Goncourt brothers noted one day:

> Tells us of his mania for acting and furiously declaiming his novel as he writes it, straining his throat so much that he empties jugfuls of water, getting drunk on the noise he makes, to the extent of making a metal dish vibrate, of the sort he has here, so that one day, at Croisset, he felt something coming up from his stomach, and was afraid that he was about to start spitting blood.

> [Nous parle de sa manie de jouer et de déclamer avec fureur son roman à mesure qu'il écrit, s'égosillant tant qu'il épuise de pleines cruches d'eau, s'enivrant de son bruit, jusqu'à faire vibrer un plat de métal pareil à celui qu'il a ici, si bien qu'un jour, à Croisset, il sentit quelque chose lui monter de l'estomac et qu'il eut peur d'être pris de crachements de sang.   (Goncourt, *Journal*, I, p. 899)]

This custom derived at least partly from his theatrical experiments, from the pleasure he took in reading aloud for his friends his works or those of other authors, from his joy in acting out parts and imitating people. His disciple Guy de Maupassant has given an excellent account of this aspect of his personality:

This man saw everything, understood everything, suffered everything, in an exaggerated, agonising and delightful way. He was the biblical dreamer, the Greek poet, the Barbarian soldier, the Renaissance artist, the peasant and the prince, the mercenary Mâtho and the doctor Bovary. He was even also the coquettish middle-class woman of our own times, as he was Hamilcar's daughter. He was all that, not in imagination but in reality, for the writer who thinks like him becomes all he feels.

[Il a tout vu, cet homme, il a tout compris, il a tout souffert, d'une façon exagérée, déchirante et délicieuse. Il a été le rêveur de la Bible, le poète grec, le soldat barbare, l'artiste de la Renaissance, le manant et le prince, le mercenaire Mâtho et le médecin Bovary. Il a été même aussi la petite bourgeoise coquette des temps modernes, comme il fut la fille d'Hamilcar. Il a été tout cela non pas en songe, mais en réalité, car l'écrivain qui pense comme lui devient tout ce qu'il sent. (Maupassant, *Pour Gustave Flaubert*, p. 127)]

This means that it is misleading to claim, as some critics have done, that for him the theatre was only a temptation and a distraction. The impulse which drove him towards the theatre was of crucial importance in all he wrote: if he had not had that irresistible desire to put himself in the place of the creatures of his imagination, he would not have been the great novelist he was.

NOTES

1 Edmond et Jules de Goncourt, *Journal*, ed. Robert Ricatte (Paris: Fasquelle/ Flammarion, 1956), vol. I, p. 1048.
2 Maxime Du Camp, *Souvenirs littéraires* (third edition) (Paris: Hachette, 1906), vol. I, p. 314.
3 Guy de Maupassant, *Pour Gustave Flaubert* (Brussels: Complexe, 1986), p. 53.
4 Emile Zola, *Les Romanciers naturalistes* (Paris: Charpentier, 1895), p. 296.
5 Marshall C. Olds, *Au pays des perroquets: féerie théâtrale et narration chez Flaubert* (Amsterdam: Rodopi, 2001).

13

LAWRENCE R. SCHEHR

Flaubert's failure

Each of the canonical realist novelists – Stendhal, Balzac, Flaubert and Zola – takes a pessimistic view of human happiness. Flaubert stands out as the one who shows no belief in a progress narrative. His characters fail repeatedly and decline. Each of his works is a construct of insufficiencies on the level of the plot and in the formation of character; the depicted world, while arguably realist, often seems a slightly lesser version of the real world. His characters' foibles are seldom explored with sympathy: there will be no tragedy here, just a kind of de-dramatised apathy marking time.

A glance at the correspondence might provide us with a way to think about failure *in* Flaubert's work and the failure *of* Flaubert's work, which are by and large the same thing (and with the caveat that an author is certainly no guarantor of the meaning of his own texts). Flaubert struggles while trying to produce what will become his first masterpiece, *Madame Bovary*. In a letter to Louise Colet, dated 24 April 1852, he complains about his slow pace, and indicates that he has written only twenty-five pages in the six weeks since he last saw her (Cor. II 75). His general plan is in place for the novel and he indicates that he will start to write the ball scene on Monday. The process is problematic, for the slowness of the progress is producing a kind of lassitude in him, a sort of self-defeat, as he says that he is 'annoyed/disappointed at not advancing' ['ennuyé de ne pas avancer']. So it is more than just disappointment, but *ennui*, a boredom and a *Weltschmerz* (or world-weariness) that weigh heavily on him. Failure then is always imminent, if even progress can produce this feeling.

Part of the reason for the slowness is the constant rewriting and reorganisation of these pages: 'As for me, I have worked, copied, changed, and manipulated them so much that, for the moment, I see only fire' ['Quant à moi, je les ai tellement travaillées, recopiées, changées, maniées, que pour le moment je n'y vois que du feu']. Progress is illusory, because the work done is constantly undone, almost as if Flaubert were Penelope undoing her sewing every night so that her canvas would never be finished, or as if he were Sisyphus condemned to repeat his task *ad infinitum*. Whether he has an inner demon or an external one, Flaubert is possessed. Moreover, the undoing of his work negates what he has previously written: the series of rewrites is a constant condemnation of his writing. Whatever progress there is comes at the expense of seeing value in his writing. Whatever word he writes is only minimally better than yesterday's failure.

Failure as an artist is also ambiguously interwoven with failure as an individual: 'Sometimes, when I find myself empty, when the expression refuses to come, when, after having scrawled long pages, I discover that I have not written one sentence, I fall on my couch and remain stupefied in an internal swamp of *ennuis*' ['Quelquefois, quand je me trouve vide, quand l'expression se refuse, quand après [avoir] griffonné de longues pages, je découvre n'avoir pas fait une phrase, je tombe sur mon divan et j'y reste hébété dans un marais intérieur d'ennuis' (Cor. II 75)]. If he does not make progress, despite intensive work, there is a dissipation after the recognition that the work was all for nought. From the impotence as an artist he automatically discerns an impotence as an individual, a lack of success, and a disorder in his very being. So the scrawlings, which are a kind of disordered writing, lead naturally and inevitably to disorder within. Scrawlings become *hébétude* (stupor) and a swamp of problems, in that curious French combination of boredom and trouble. Failure is infectious. What will happen, one wonders, if the subject itself is failure? Will there be an overflow of that failure into all corners of being? Before turning to that, let us consider a strategy around it.

In his magisterial and massive study of Flaubert before *Madame Bovary*, entitled appropriately enough *L'Idiot de la famille*, Jean-Paul Sartre has created a somewhat materialist, existentialist psychoanalysis of the individual Gustave Flaubert.[1] Sartre's explanation goes on for well over two and a half thousand pages and he suggests at length that Flaubert's coming to language would inevitably be a losing battle. Sartre underlines an insoluble set of problems for Flaubert. Coming to language late means that he can never write the famous 'book about nothing' (Cor. II 31), for there will always have been something there before him. If that something is a living thing, bringing his language to it means killing what is there in order to have that nothing. As Sartre puts it very early in *L'Idiot*, 'to analyse – and language for Flaubert is analysis – is to kill' ['analyser – et le langage, pour Flaubert, est analyse – c'est tuer' (Sartre, *L'Idiot*, I, p. 37)].[2]

If writing is tantamount to an act of murder, it is not the worst thing, for there is something that cannot be killed: *bêtise*, or stupidity.[3] Sartre puts it pithily in his chapter title 'Stupidity as substance' ['De la bêtise comme substance' (*L'Idiot*, I, p. 613)]. Flaubert will always face the undead of language, vampires of stupid opinion, and the intransigence and inevitability of generalised public opinion that can never be killed with a swift stab of the stiletto. Whatever the path taken, he will fail to conquer the inevitable demons: the material world that demands some scant recognition, however feeble, and the juggernaut of stupidity.

Flaubert does not start with stupidity, but with fragmentation. In the early work, *Novembre*, rather than presenting a movement towards a solidification of knowledge, Flaubert chooses to emphasise the partial and subjective nature of his narrator's knowledge, as he proposes a present attached to a lived, non-literary past: 'For a long time, I cherished my lost life; I told myself with joy that my youth was over, for it is a joy to feel cold enter your heart and to be able to say, touching it with your hand like a hearth that is still smoking: it is no longer burning' ['J'ai savouré longuement ma vie perdue; je me suis dit avec joie que ma jeunesse était passée, car c'est une joie de sentir le froid vous venir au cœur, et de pouvoir dire, le tâtant de la main comme un foyer qui fume encore: il ne brûle plus' (OJ 760)].[4] By his choice of words and by the ambiguous nostalgia in this implicit movement towards death, the narrator inscribes his protagonist in a Romantic tradition marked by loss. Thus the stage is set for one of the major articulations of failure: the persistence of romantic longing doomed to fail in a realist world. Whether it is the failed relationships or unrequited loves in the various versions of *L'Education sentimentale* or the pathetic love affairs of Emma Bovary, romantic and Romantic loves are doomed to fail. Flaubert bundles that failure early on by joining linguistic inadequacy to the failure of desire. He will eventually let that situation mutate, as he moves towards a solidification of the narrator's position in an omniscient third-person narrative, while shifting the linguistic and emotional failure entirely onto his characters and marking them as the victims of the *doxa*, or generalised public opinion.

Love is illusory and it must be surpassed to achieve the recognition of disillusion (not dissolution). For the young Flaubert, life itself is already marked as incapable of being a success by 'the eternal monotony of its hours that flow and its days that return' ['l'éternelle monotonie de ses heures qui coulent et de ses jours qui reviennent' (OJ 774)]. Life is repetition, much as the act of writing, for Flaubert struggling with the redaction of *Madame Bovary*, will also be a Sisyphean repetition. In *Novembre*, the individual feels the weight of that repetition and, in that he cannot create, progress, or develop, he feels condemned. This failure is cast as isolation, in that he is different from others, those who have the illusion (a false one already in Flaubert's mind) that they can progress: 'What to do on earth? What to dream there? What to build there? Tell me then, you whom life amuses, who walk towards a goal and torment yourselves for something' ['Que faire ici-bas? qu'y rêver? qu'y bâtir? dites-le-moi donc, vous que la vie amuse, qui marchez vers un but et vous tourmentez pour quelque chose!' (OJ 774)].

Flaubert begins to solidify the narrative discourse in the first version of *L'Education sentimentale*, even as he alternates between a more objective third-person narrative and epistolary interludes between the novel's two main characters, Jules and Henry. Significantly, Flaubert takes a different strategy from the very first, as if he were separating the narrative function from the characters: 'The hero of this book, one October morning, arrived in Paris with the heart of an eighteen-year-old and a school leaver's certificate in the arts' ['Le héros de ce livre, un matin d'octobre, arriva à Paris avec un cœur de dix-huit ans et un diplôme de bachelier ès lettres' (OJ 835)]. By separating the two functions, Flaubert moves towards a lack of failure in style, in order to talk magisterially about what remains a failure in the verisimilar world of his characters. If we already have an inkling that a 'sentimental education' will be a lesson in disillusion for Henry and an ultimate failure, Flaubert can still keep his own illusion of success through writing. One way of marking that distinction – and we see this in this very first line – is in the development of what will come to be Flaubert's signature style of phrases separated by commas. Yet the first seed of the failure of that style to present (or the first success of the eventual 'book about nothing', which amounts to the same thing) is contained in the zeugma of that phrase: yoking a young man's heart and a diploma grammatically, but not semantically, is the first step towards the follies of description, the failures of description that will mark all subsequent work.

Flaubert sets up his characters by insisting on their isolation, and in so doing, he manages to predict that they will not form successful relations, social bonds, happy marriages, or enduring partnerships. Already he does so early on in this first version of *L'Education sentimentale*: 'He thought as well of those three young men, his oldest friends, those with whom he used to play cops and robbers: one had become a sailor, the second had died in Africa, the third had already married; all three were dead for him' ['Il pensait aussi à ces trois jeunes gens, ses plus vieux camarades, ceux avec qui autrefois il avait joué au gendarme et au voleur: l'un s'était fait marin, le second était mort en Afrique, le troisième s'était déjà marié; tous trois étaient morts pour lui' (OJ 839)]. The developing rhetoric increases the ways in which the social structures are broken down by language. Thus, in this quick description a parallel is made between loss to what might be called a homosocial order (the navy), loss from death, and loss to marriage. It is a gesture he will repeat in *Madame Bovary*, in a passing comment on Madame Rouault's first pregnancy: the Rouaults' son, had he lived, would now be thirty (OC 1 584). In the early version of *L'Education sentimentale*, no attempt is made to provide a means by which a social bond can be constructed. And even the basic plot mechanism reinforces that message. There is no valid social bond: marriage, friendship, association by interest, and concubinage are all mere accidents of association. No human bond can form and it is only the retrospectively viewed one, understood through the false consciousness of nostalgia, that is perceived as being solid. And what bond there is cannot last: 'Their passion, which had fermented for a long while, began to sour like old wines' ['Leur passion, longtemps fermentée, commençait à s'aigrir comme les vieux vins' (OJ 950)].

Flaubert also does something here that he will do intermittently in the works that follow, which is to reflect directly on what writing might mean, and how it might succeed or fail. In *Madame Bovary* and in *Bouvard et Pécuchet*, there will be scattered references to the way in which writing does fail: being or becoming part of the *doxa*, misrepresenting (or even just representing), and setting up false knowledge, romantic clichés, or false hopes. And such a situation is also present in this early novel: 'Henry lent books to Mme Emilie – poems, some novels. She read them secretly at night in bed, and she returned them to him with a thousand nail marks in the delicate spots' ['Henry prêtait des livres à Mme Emilie – des poésies, quelques romans. – Elle les lisait en cachette, le soir dans son lit, et elle les lui rendait avec mille marques d'ongle aux endroits délicats' (OJ 873)]. Literature fails through its success: it fails to be pure literature, in the sense that Flaubert envisions it, to the extent that it succeeds in inspiring romantic notions, a romanticism to which Flaubert is completely antipathetic. Elsewhere in the novel, Flaubert already predicts the nihilism and pessimism of *Bouvard et Pécuchet*: 'The ladies said nothing, or chatted about literature, which is the same thing' ['Les dames ne disaient rien; ou causaient littérature, ce qui est la même chose' (OJ 857)].

The mature works are rife with illustrations of failure, as the author spends much time inscribing failure for his characters and constantly paring his writing so that more and more it too, in moving away from the object, inscribes both its own self-sufficiency and its total incapacity. With the exception of *Bouvard et Pécuchet* and the *Dictionnaire des idées reçues*, functioning as meta-texts, *Madame Bovary* is the work most consistently dedicated to failure, in part because it is a verisimilar text when compared to the others. (Of the other narratives of Flaubert's maturity, all but two are marked by a wilful movement away from the reality of the nineteenth-century. *L'Education sentimentale* and *Un cœur simple* occur in a world in which verisimilitude must be operative. As a *Bildungsroman* set in Paris, and therefore, as a revision of Balzac's *Illusions perdues*, *L'Education sentimentale* can set up failure without any justification necessary. And *Un cœur simple* will be the streamlined, compact, and ironic version of *Madame Bovary*.) *Madame Bovary* is unmarked by any Parisianism, the defeat or success of the protagonist not being part of the initial set of expectations in a novel set in the provinces, whereas it is always there in a Paris novel. So *Madame Bovary* is all the more radical in its *mise en scène* precisely because it sets failure against a neutral background. The early pages of the novel show the first examples of Flaubert's mature inscription of a movement towards decline and chaos, even as Flaubert is only initially presenting his character of Charles Bovary. Meaning and sense only *seem* to happen. Charles's initial entrance and subsequent dysphasia are an interruption in the order of things; if the first word of the novel is 'We' ['Nous'], that unity and community is broken by Charles, never to be re-established. After that initial word, plenitude will exist only nostalgically in the past. Thus, it is only after the death of his first wife, following a rather pathetic and melodramatic bad marriage, that Charles can reflect that she had loved him after all (OC 1 581).

Flaubert raises the stakes by bringing disorder to his text through the imposition of the arbitrary and through an imposed, false logic. Jean Ricardou has analysed the famous description of Charles's cap and has shown how Flaubert's organisation of physical space depends on the imposition of a temporal order through the use of adverbs and related semantic fields.[5] He demonstrates that Flaubert fakes the construction of the cap through the artifice of language, and therefore he fails to present the object by virtue of his success in not presenting anything or in presenting nothing. Moreover, the different parts of the cap are both arbitrary and interchangeable; there is no consequence at all to any specific detail about it. This is the first major example of the ways in which the arbitrary will begin to take over in Flaubert's writing. As Jonathan Culler also stresses, there is no coherence, no order, and no 'orchestration' to Flaubert's descriptions: one detail can substitute for another without any problem, and all of them, taken as some fictional whole, illustrate nothing.[6] Beyond that, as Leslie Hill states, 'stupidity, for Flaubert, is less a given content of discourse than a particular *order* of that discourse itself'.[7] While streamlining his text, Flaubert is also making it more *bête*.

Flaubert augments the breadth of the failure of his characters by preventing them from developing, regardless of what they undergo. (This was already in the process of development in the previous works at which we have looked, and will reach its apogee in the consistent turgidity of the minds of Frédéric and Deslauriers in the final version of *L'Education sentimentale* and the total *bêtise* of the protagonists of *Bouvard et Pécuchet*.) Haplessness, inadequacy, incapacity describe most of his characters, their ethos, and their views of the world. As Jonathan Culler remarks, 'Flaubert's characters are poor reflectors in that they do not compose the world for us, do not organise it in ways that reveal new possibilities of feeling and perception' (Culler, *Flaubert*, p. 129). Milad Doueihi calls Frédéric Moreau a failed lover and a failed author.[8] Stathis Gourgouris points to Bouvard and Pécuchet's 'dauntlessness in the face of ignorance, confusion, and failure'.[9] The list goes on and on. But the matter is more radical, revolutionary, and dire. Consider the consequences of the incapacity to learn of the doltish Charles:

> Returning that evening, Charles went one by one over the sentences she had spoken, trying to recall them, to complete their meaning, in order to figure out the portion of her existence that she had lived before he knew her. But he could never see her differently in his thoughts from the way he had seen her the first time, or as he had just left her.

> [Le soir, en s'en retournant, Charles reprit une à une les phrases qu'elle avait dites, tâchant de se les rappeler, d'en compléter le sens, afin de se faire la portion d'existence qu'elle avait vécue, dans le temps qu'il ne la connaissait pas encore. Mais jamais il ne put la voir en sa pensée différemment qu'il ne l'avait vue la première fois, ou telle qu'il venait de la quitter tout à l'heure.   (OC 1 582)]

Charles cannot learn. Not only can he not serve as a reflector for us; he cannot even reflect for himself. He does not remember a perfect moment, and what he remembers is constructed by a very weak, imperfect consciousness of a limited mind. The same can be said for the eventual ball scene that Emma remembers retrospectively as she waxes nostalgic about its brilliance (OC 1 593). In both cases, readers can see to what extent Flaubert successfully weakens his characters' position by reducing their memory not merely to some memory different from what we have witnessed filtered through the narrator's periodising writing, but also to accepted public opinion: 'Sometimes she thought that those were the most beautiful days of her life, her honeymoon, as they said' ['Elle songeait quelquefois que c'étaient là pourtant les plus beaux jours de sa vie, la lune de miel, comme on disait' (OC 1 588)]. Emma and Charles may have had a tacky wedding cake, but her life is no better than a *bêtise* or an *idée reçue*, even if she does not even go to Italy to make the *bêtise* of her honeymoon complete.

In most of Flaubert's nostalgically remembered events, we have only the characters' perception to go on: this includes the final scene of *L'Education sentimentale* in which Frédéric and Deslauriers remember a youthful adventure (yet we have as little confidence in their opinions as we do in *Madame Bovary*, so it does not matter). In *Madame Bovary*, we were there with the narrator, and we saw not perfection, but Flaubert's construction of a narrative description for the sake of that narrative description. Emma is no more a retrospectively remembered bit of perfection than Charles's cap would be were it mentioned again. The fancy ball is no greater than the descriptions that do not work coherently to illustrate a world.

Flaubert creates a *mise en abyme*, a reflected image within the narrative, of the predicament of the reader. He enacts the futility of individual acts of writing coupled with the inscription of received opinions, most often of romantic love. Thus in the 1845 *Education sentimentale*, Henry writes a five-page love letter (OJ 882) and in *Madame Bovary*, Léon doesn't know how to write love letters (OC 1 608). And in *Bouvard et Pécuchet*, the failed pedagogy is itself a kind of writing, generalised to the sense of communication in an active sense, as opposed to the passive reception associated with reading.

In *Madame Bovary*, Flaubert also enacts the inconsequence of reading. All readers remember the famous chapter (1, 6) that Flaubert devotes to Emma's education in the convent. Rather than learn the meaning of history or appreciate the literary value of a novel, Emma retains clichéd images from which she creates her own personal museum of details that combine in no real constellation of meanings. Her images are screens onto which she can graft her desires, wishes and emotions; she can create received meaning out of her reading, by turning, for example, a heroine into a 'heroine', the perfect image of an idealised and melodramatically rewritten figure. Emma therefore fails to learn any lesson from her reading. Beyond that, however, is what the reader learns about reading: reading does not matter. For the learned Charles, country doctor, not reading is the same as reading, as he does not even bother to cut the pages of his medical dictionary (OC 1 585). If Flaubert is telling the reader that the author's writing will have no consequence, that the act of reading or not reading will have no effect, he has succeeded in communicating his failure, our failure, the failure of language, and paradoxically even the failure of the author himself to communicate. After this, we shall be endlessly in that paradox, in which the only success is failure.[10]

Flaubert does not hesitate to weaken his characters psychologically even further by having them fall into a trap of reading, the trap of believing that there can be consequences: 'She wanted to learn Italian: she bought dictionaries, a grammar book, and a provision of white paper. She tried serious reading, history, and philosophy' ['Elle voulut apprendre l'italien: elle acheta des dictionnaires, une grammaire, une provision de papier blanc. Elle essaya des lectures sérieuses, de l'histoire et de la philosophie' (OC 1 616)]. It is a danger to be avoided: 'Thus it was resolved to prevent Emma from reading novels. [. . .] Wouldn't one be able to warn the police if the bookseller nevertheless persisted in his profession of poisoner?' ['Donc, il fut résolu que l'on empêcherait Emma de lire des romans. [. . .] N'aurait-on pas le droit d'avertir la police, si le libraire persistait quand même dans son métier d'empoisonneur?' (OC 1 617)] Flaubert's characters fail even further because they are not allowed to read the writing on the wall, the message that says there is no message, or the writing that says nothing has ever been learned from reading. And they fail to recognise what we know now, which is that there is no truth nor any essence to language:

> From that moment on, her existence was nothing more than a set of lies in which she wrapped her love, as if in veils, to hide it.
>
> It was a need, a mania, a pleasure, to the extent that if she said that she had taken the right side of a street yesterday, it was necessary to believe that she had taken the left side.

> [A partir de ce moment, son existence ne fut plus qu'un assemblage de mensonges, où elle enveloppait son amour comme dans des voiles, pour le cacher.
>
> C'était un besoin, une manie, un plaisir, au point que, si elle disait avoir passé, hier, par le côté droit d'une rue, il fallait croire qu'elle avait pris par le côté gauche.   (OC I 666)]

From the very beginning of the Flaubertian enterprise, descriptions are undermined by the impossibility of presenting objects and individuals all at once, as if in a photograph or a hologram. There is also an act of destruction and decline, generally kept in check until the last part of *Madame Bovary*, and then given free rein both in *Salammbô* and *L'Education sentimentale*. There is a hint of it in the early version of *L'Education sentimentale*, in the reference to 'his desk completely marred by knife gouges and black from ink' ['son pupître tout abîmé de coups de canif et noirci d'encre' (OJ 839)]. This image of damage and abrasion resurfaces in the final version of the novel, where clothes are 'shredded by rubbing against the desk' ['râpés par le frottement du bureau' (OC II 9)]. It is as if, in being devoted to creating perfectly rhythmic, balanced descriptions and in having eschewed the object itself, Flaubert feels compelled to introduce that damage in his descriptions. He knows full well that he will never succeed, for destruction, damage and decline always have a measure of chance. Where will the crack, hole or break be? How will things fall away exactly? Flaubert can never write this; we can never know.

Flaubert introduces destruction as a way of marring his own text, and as Jean-Pierre Richard has shown, the more layers one strips away from Flaubertian description the more liquid the text becomes.[11] It desolidifies to become aqueous and unpredictable. Thus does Flaubert introduce rot, for example with the pharmacist's foetuses rotting in bottles (OC I 599). The examples of destruction are legion: Hippolyte's botched operation followed by an infection that forces an amputation; Emma's death from arsenic, liquefying her, defying the reader to maintain her as an object; the *catoblépas*, the mythological creature at the end of the final version of the *Tentation* that once ate its own paws (OC I 570); the various explosions in agriculture and anatomy in *Bouvard et Pécuchet*. *Salammbô* is rife with such scenes, of which the torture and death of Mâtho (OC I 796) is only the best known. But one could mention in the same breath any of the crowd scenes or the singularity of the decrepitude of Hannon's rotting, festering body (OC I 731).

From Emma's death onwards, Flaubert's characters fail to exist. In her cogent analysis of *L'Education sentimentale*, Michal Ginsburg points out the interchangeability of the characters in that novel, like the interchangeability of details already mentioned.[12] It little matters who is in what scene, who says what to whom, or what happens. Flaubert does not fail at his workmanship; his vision of the world, getting ever darker as he goes on, insists that human relations are a failure: they do not matter. By the time he writes *Bouvard et Pécuchet*, the last turn of the gyre has occurred. The success and the failure of words themselves have no consequence.

Decline and destruction mark every aspect of the structures of *Bouvard et Pécuchet*. In that novel, which, as Marina van Zuylen indicates, is marked by the 'absence of a centre', Flaubert moves beyond the uncertainty of *Bovary* and *Salammbô*.[13] He goes beyond the obstinate irony of *Un cœur simple* and *L'Education sentimentale* and reaches a level of decline and insufficiency theretofore unheard of. Language and knowledge, while once in support of received ideas in the earlier works, translated into nostalgia in *L'Education sentimentale*, are, in Flaubert's last work, marks of a monstrous epistemology and a rhetoric of failure.

On every page of *Bouvard et Pécuchet*, there is an implicit or explicit battle of words: a logomachy. On one side, one set of opinions; opposed to it, seemingly an equally valid set of opinions. There is no way to reconcile the opposing interpretations; no adequation or dialectic can move the hapless receivers of opinion to a felicitous conclusion. These logomachies are Pyrrhic victories in which both sides lose. Consider the pithy summary of the French Revolution: 'For some, the Revolution is a diabolical event. Others claim it is a sublime exception. The conquered on either side, naturally, are martyrs' ['La Révolution est, pour les uns, un événement satanique. D'autres la proclament une exception sublime. Les vaincus de chaque côté, naturellement, sont des martyrs' (OC II 239)]. There is no reconciliation of opinions and there is thus total failure to understand. Nothing can tip the balance because there is no objective position from which to assert, nor any from which to hypothesise and test. And if we think that having a total assessment of the situation will help determine the truth, we would be wrong, for the whole truth can never be had – the marks of absence and decomposition are endlessly present now, and error is the condition of all enquiry: 'To judge that era impartially, one must have read all the histories, all the memoirs, all the newspapers and all the hand-written works, for an error can depend on the slightest omission, an error that could bring on others in turn *ad infinitum*. They gave up' ['Pour la [cette époque] juger impartialement, il faudrait avoir lu toutes les histoires, tous les mémoires, tous les journaux et toutes les pièces manuscrites, car de la moindre omission une erreur peut dépendre qui en amènera d'autres à l'infini. Ils y renoncèrent' (OC II 239)].

Beyond the renunciation, which is after all an acceptance, submissive or not, of failure, there is a radical change from works like *Madame Bovary* and *L'Education sentimentale*. For in those novels, there is the hope offered by nostalgia to recuperate the plenitude of the past. Even if the characters' perspective on that past is different from the one offered the readers by the narrator, who thus puts an ironic distance between us and them, the characters have the possibility of turning away from their failure and towards the illusion of success and happiness. No such escape mechanism exists in *Bouvard et Pécuchet*:

> They remembered when they had been happy.
> Nothing now could cause such sweet hours as those filled by distillery or literature. An abyss separated them from those hours. Something irrevocable had occurred.
>
> [Et ils se rappelèrent le temps où ils étaient heureux.
> [. . .] Rien, maintenant, n'occasionnerait ces heures si douces que remplissait la distillerie ou la littérature. Un abîme les en séparait. Quelque chose d'irrévocable était venu. (OC II 275)]

No return is possible. The protagonists are condemned to exist in a failure they recognise from time to time. What is left, in spinning out these lives, but to pass along their lack of knowledge and become teachers?

An assessment of Flaubert's figures of failure shows an ever-widening gyre, which, starting from characters marked by a kind of romantic longing, eventually invades the entire corpus. Where Flaubert moves away from the irony and cynicism of someone like Balzac or where Flaubert's total pessimism outstrips the darkness of later writers like Dostoevsky, Kafka, and even Beckett, is the way in which that failure creeps into the very writing itself. The success of Flaubert's writing is in the fact that it attains total failure: there can be no hermeneutic code, there can be no interpretation, nor can there be any successful evocation of an object in time and space. The more precise the descriptions seem to become, the more they are accidental and contingent. Values and meaning collapse at the level of the writing, as it begins to reproduce the collapse of meaning and values for the characters. In the end, there is no solution but to go on, endlessly, working at doing nothing: 'Literature. Occupation for the idle' ['Littérature. Occupation des oisifs' (OC II 311)]. No author in recorded history will have worked harder than Gustave Flaubert to fail at his task.

NOTES

1 Jean-Paul Sartre, *L'Idiot de la famille: Gustave Flaubert de 1821 à 1857*, 3 vols. (Paris: Gallimard, 1988 [1971–2]), translated by Carol Cosman as *The Family Idiot, Gustave Flaubert 1821–1857*, 5 vols. (Chicago and London: University of Chicago Press, 1981–93).

2 Christopher Prendergast relates Flaubert's insistence on form to radical loss or absence, one figure of which is precisely that figure of death: 'Flaubert's insistence on the autonomy and the purity of literary "form" rests, in part at least, on an experience of radical loss or separation' (Christopher Prendergast, 'Flaubert: Writing and Negativity', *Novel*, 8 (1975), 197–213, p. 199). On figures of death in Flaubert, see also Yvonne Bargues-Rollins, *Le Pas de Flaubert. Une danse macabre* (Paris: Champion, 1998).

3 On the consequences of stupidity for the Flaubertian text, see Françoise Gaillard, 'A little story about the *bras de fer*, or, how history is made', in Naomi Schor and Henry F. Majewski, eds., *Flaubert and Postmodernism* (Lincoln, NE: University of Nebraska Press, 1984), pp. 84–99.

4 For a reading of the problematics of *Novembre*, including matters relating to duality, incompletion, and paradox, see Timothy Unwin, '*Novembre* and the Paradox of the New in Flaubert's Early Work', in Tony Williams and Mary Orr, eds., *New Approaches in Flaubert Studies* (Lewiston, NY: Edwin Mellen, 1999), pp. 32–48.

5 Jean Ricardou, *Nouveaux problèmes du roman* (Paris: Seuil, 1978), pp. 24–33.

6 Jonathan Culler, *Flaubert: The Uses of Uncertainty* (London: Elek, and Ithaca: Cornell University Press, 1974), pp. 91–109.

7 Leslie Hill, 'Flaubert and the Rhetoric of Stupidity', *Critical Inquiry*, 3 (1976), 333–44, p. 336.

8 Milad Doueihi, 'Flaubert's Costumes', *Modern Language Notes*, 101 (1986), 1086–109, p. 1086.

9 Stathis Gourgouris, 'Research, Essay, Failure (Flaubert's Itinerary)', *New Literary History*, 26 (1995), 343–57, p. 349.

10 See Christopher Prendergast, 'Flaubert: Quotation, Stupidity and the Cretan Liar Paradox', *French Studies*, 35 (1981), 261–77.

11 Jean-Pierre Richard, *Littérature et sensation* (Paris: Seuil, 1954), pp. 126–7.

12 Michal Peled Ginsburg, *Flaubert Writing: A Study in Narrative Strategies* (Stanford: Stanford University Press, 1986), pp. 144–7. As Ginsburg later points out, 'we know that Bouvard and Pécuchet do not fail all the time, and that the success they enjoy every now and then has precisely the same function in the narrative as their failure; success and failure have the same effect of prompting them to change their subject of study' (p. 159).

13 Marina van Zuylen, 'From *Horror Vacui* to the Reader's Boredom: *Bouvard et Pécuchet* and the Art of Difficulty', *Nineteenth-Century French Studies*, 22 (1993–4), 112–22, p. 113. On ambiguity in Flaubert more generally, see Culler, *Flaubert: The Uses of Uncertainty*.

14

MARIO VARGAS LLOSA

Flaubert, our contemporary

What can a novelist today learn from *Madame Bovary*? Everything that is essential to the modern novel: that it is art, created beauty, a construct that produces pleasure. As in poetry, painting, dance or music, this is brought about through formal success, which is the determining factor in the novel's content.

Before Flaubert, novelists sensed intuitively that form played a key role in the success or failure of their stories. Instinct and imagination led them to give stylistic coherence to their themes, to organise point of view and time in such a way that their novels could give an appearance of autonomy. But only after Flaubert does this spontaneous, diffuse and intuitive idea become rational knowledge, theory, artistic consciousness.

Flaubert was the first modern novelist, because he was the first to understand that the main problem to be resolved when writing a novel is that of the narrator, the person who tells the tale – the most important character in any story – who is never the author, even when the narrator uses the first person to take on the name of the author. Flaubert understood before anyone else that the narrator is always an invention. The author is a being of flesh and blood, the narrator is a creature made up of words, a voice. While an author's existence precedes, succeeds and exceeds his tales, a narrator lives only when telling them, and only lives to tell them. A narrator lives and dies with the tale, and the two are interdependent. One cannot exist without the other.

With Flaubert, novelists lost the innocence that had once allowed them, when they transformed themselves into narrators – or believed that they had done so – to tell their stories from the perspective of an intrusive first person who was never a part of the reality being described. Such narrators constantly revealed their arbitrary presence, because they knew everything – always much more than one character could possibly know about another character – and because they gave their own opinions quite shamelessly as they were telling the story. They interfered in the action and limited their characters' freedom through their meddling, stripping these men and women of free will, and turning them into puppets by their persistent intrusion. It is true that, in the great classical novels, the characters manage to release themselves from this yoke and achieve freedom, like Don Quixote. But even in these exceptional cases, the freedom of the character was guarded and provisional, always under threat of being cut back by the sudden and abusive appearance of the narrator-God, that egotist and exhibitionist who is capable at times, as in Victor Hugo's *Les Misérables*, of interrupting the plot of the novel and introducing long parentheses – true *collages* – on the Battle of Waterloo or the importance of human excrement as a fertiliser.

Flaubert introduced into narrative the 'suspicion' which Nathalie Sarraute describes in *L'Ere du soupçon*. In order to be 'believable', it was not enough for a narrator to have a wonderful turn of phrase and a fertile imagination. On the contrary, anything that accentuated this arbitrary presence – a presence not justified by the needs of the plot – conspired against the persuasive power of the story and weakened the verisimilitude of the narrative. The narrator could no longer, as before, become a spectacle without destroying the credibility of the story – the only permissible spectacle within a novel – because the essential prerequisite of the novel's success was the way that the characters managed to convey to the reader the illusion that they had freedom of action. Since a novel must always have a creator, or be formed in the brain, or shaped by the hand, of someone outside itself, then in order for the spectacle to appear as spontaneous and as free 'as life itself', Flaubert perfected a series of narrative techniques designed to make this irredeemable intruder invisible. He turned his narrators into the ghostly figures that they remain today in modern novels – unless they play the part of being just one of the characters in the story, enjoying no special privileges of omniscience or ubiquity, as limited as any other character in what they can know, do and see.

Flaubert was the first novelist fully to realise that, if he was to convince his readers that his fiction had a life of its own – something that all good stories achieve – then his novel had to be seen by them as a sovereign, self-sufficient reality, not in any way parasitic on life outside itself, real life. And he realised that this illusion of sovereignty, of total autonomy, could only be achieved through the success of the novel's form, that is, through the style and structure governing that representation of life to which all fiction aspires.

To achieve this fictional autonomy, Flaubert made use of two techniques that he employed with genius in the first of his great works, *Madame Bovary*: the impersonality or invisibility of the narrator, and *le mot juste*, the precision and economy of a language which gave the sense that it was absolutely necessary, that there was nothing lacking or superfluous, that it was the perfect expression of what was to be narrated.

After Flaubert, good novelists were good not merely because of the scope of their imagination, the attractiveness of their stories, the prominence and well-rounded nature of their characters, but rather – and above all – because of their choice of words, their technical virtuosity, their shrewd use of time, and the originality of design in their stories. After Flaubert, novelists continued to be dreamers and fantasists, overwhelmed by their own memories; but, in addition to that, they were stylists, craftsmen of words, architects of chronology, detailed planners of the human adventure. Hallucinations and clairvoyance were still permissible, so long as they were expressed in an appropriate language and a functional structure. The genius of Proust, of Joyce, of Virginia Woolf, of Kafka and of Faulkner would have not been possible without the lesson of Flaubert.

Instead of ushering in 'realism' as the deep-rooted critical commonplace would have us believe, with *Madame Bovary* Flaubert revolutionised the traditional notion of 'realism' in literature as an imitation or a faithful reproduction of reality. All of Flaubert's ideas on the novel, developed throughout his life and expressed through his correspondence – the most lucid and profound treatise on narrative art ever to have been written – lead us to dismiss that idea of realism as mere fantasy. Rather, they confirm the opposite view, that between real reality and fictional reality there is no possible identification, but rather an unbridgeable distance. It is the distance between a ghost and a person of flesh and blood, or a mirage in the desert in which fresh springs and welcoming oases appear. The novel is not a mirror of reality: it is *another* reality, made up entirely of a combination of imagination, style and craft. It is always 'realist' (and not realistic at all), irrespective of whether it tells a story as verifiable in reality as that of Emma Bovary or Frédéric Moreau, or as fabulous and mythical as the temptations that Saint Anthony resisted in the desert, or the operatic battles of the mercenaries in *Salammbô* in the exotic land of Carthage.

After Flaubert, 'realism' is also a fiction, and any novel that has sufficient power of persuasion to captivate the reader is realist – because it communicates an illusion of reality – and every novel that lacks this power is unreal.

That briefest of expressions, *le mot juste*, encompasses a whole world. What is it? How can one measure the accuracy and precision of literary discourse? Flaubert believed that it could be measured by submitting each phrase – each word – to the test of the *gueuloir*, or the ear. If, when it was read out loud, a sentence sounded harmonious, and nothing grated or was off key, then it offered the perfect expression of the thought, there was a total fusion between words and ideas, and the style achieved its maximum potential.

'The more beautiful an idea, the more sonorous the sentence. Believe me: precision of thought determines (and is itself) that of the word.' ['Plus une idée est belle, plus la phrase est sonore; soyez-en sûre. La précision de la pensée fait (et est elle-même) celle du mot' (letter to Mlle Leroyer de Chantepie, 12 December 1857, Cor. II 785)]. By contrast, if, when subjected to this aural test, something – a syllable, a silence, a cacophony, a gap – broke the musical fluidity of the expression, then it was not the words but rather the ideas themselves that were stumbling and in need of revision. This formula was valid for Flaubert, but the principle of the *mot juste* does not imply that there is just one way of telling all stories. Rather, it suggests that each story has a privileged way of being told, through which it appears at its most persuasive.

Le mot juste must be appropriate to what the words seek to express. The economy of language in Borges's short stories is as indispensable to his tightly argued parables as are the fluid meanderings of Proust's language to his reminiscences. What is important is that the words and what they say, suggest or imply should form an indestructible identity, an unbroken whole. There should be no suggestion of what occurs in bad novels – which is why they are bad – when the story and the voice that narrates that story suddenly become distanced because, as in failed marriages, they no longer get on and have become incompatible. This divorce takes place whenever readers of a novel realise that what they are reading is not unfolding naturally before their eyes as if by magic, but that it is being told to them, and that there is a certain incompatibility between the teller and the tale. This realisation that the form and the content are different and incompatible kills the illusion and discredits the story.

Le mot juste is also a functional notion, in the sense that it is a style that fits the story like a glove and becomes fused with it, like those boots that become feet in the famous surrealist painting by Magritte, *Le Modèle rouge* (1935). There is not, therefore, one style, but as many styles as there are successful stories, and the styles can change in the same author, as happened in Flaubert. The precise, succinct, cold and 'realist' prose of *Madame Bovary* and *L'Education sentimentale* becomes lyrical, romantic and at times visionary and mythical in *La Tentation de saint Antoine* and *Salammbô*, then erudite, scientific and full of irony or sarcasm, with flashes of humour, in his unfinished *Bouvard et Pécuchet*. The 'awareness of style' that characterises the modern novelist owes much to the desperation with which Flaubert fought all his life to write the impossible 'book about nothing' which would consist 'solely of words', as he wrote to Louise Colet. All books are this, of course, just words. But the great paradox is that masterpieces, like the ones he wrote, seem to be precisely the opposite. They seem to be history, reality, life. They seem to exist and to develop by themselves, by their own truth and force, without the need of the words that have melded into them, so that the events, characters and landscapes they describe appear more truthful and clear.

When *Madame Bovary* appeared, some critics accused it of being cold and almost inhuman because of the objectivity with which the story was told. They were judging it through the filter of Romantic novels, in which an intrusive narrator lamented and sympathised with the misfortunes of the heroes. In Flaubert's novel, the emotional reactions to the events of the story are felt by the reader. The function of the narrator is to present these events to readers in as objective a way as possible, leaving them complete freedom to decide for themselves whether to be saddened by, rejoice in, or simply yawn at, the developments in the story. This means, in other words, that when Flaubert developed a mode of narration that turned the characters of a novel into free beings, he at the same time liberated the reader from the servitude imposed by classical novels, which forced upon their stories a single way of reading and living them. That is why, if we wish to sum up Flaubert's contribution to the novel in a single phrase, we can say that he was the *liberator* both of his characters and of his reader.

Lima, March 2004

SELECT BIBLIOGRAPHY

Gustave Flaubert: reference texts used throughout this volume

Œuvres complètes, 2 vols. (Paris: Seuil, 1964)
Œuvres complètes, 16 vols. (Paris: Club de l'Honnête Homme, 1971–6)
Œuvres complètes, vol. I: *Œuvres de jeunesse* (Paris: Gallimard, 2001)
Correspondance, 4 vols. (Paris: Gallimard, 1973–98)

Gustave Flaubert: other works cited in this volume

Carnet de voyage à Carthage, ed. C.-M. Delavoye (Rouen: Université de Rouen, 1999)
Carnets de travail, édition critique et génétique établie par Pierre-Marc de Biasi (Paris: Balland, 1988)
Correspondances. Gustave Flaubert – Alfred Le Poittevin, Gustave Flaubert – Maxime Du Camp, texte établi, préfacé et annoté par Yvan Leclerc (Paris: Flammarion, 2000)
Par les champs et par les grèves, ed. Adrianne Tooke (Geneva: Droz, 1987)
Voyage en Egypte, ed. Pierre-Marc de Biasi (Paris: Grasset, 1991)

Translations

Early Works

Early Writings, translated with an introduction by Robert Griffin (Lincoln, NE and London: University of Nebraska Press, 1991)
Intimate Notebook 1840–1841, introduction, translation and notes by Francis Steegmuller (London: W. H. Allen, 1967)
Mémoires d'un fou/Memoirs of a Madman, parallel translation and critical edition by Timothy Unwin (Liverpool: Liverpool Online Series, 2001). Also available online at: http://www.liv.ac.uk/sml/LOS/Madman.pdf
November, edited with an introduction by Francis Steegmuller (London: Michael Joseph, 1966)

Mature Works

Madame Bovary, translated with an introduction by Geoffrey Wall (Harmondsworth: Penguin, 1992)

Madame Bovary. Life in a Country Town, translated by Gerard Hopkins, with an introduction by Terence Cave, and notes by Mark Overstall (Oxford: Oxford University Press, 'Oxford World's Classics', 1998)

Salammbô, translated by Robert Goodyear and P. J. R. Wright (London: New English Library, 1969 [1962])

Sentimental Education, translated with an introduction by Robert Baldick (Harmondsworth: Penguin, 1964)

A Sentimental Education, edited and translated by Douglas Parmée (Oxford: Oxford University Press, 'Oxford World's Classics', 2000)

Sentimental Education, translated with an introduction by Adrianne Tooke (Ware: Wordsworth, 'Classics of World Literature', 2003)

The Temptation of Saint Anthony, translated with an introduction and notes by Kitty Mrosovsky (Harmondsworth: Penguin, 1983)

Three Tales, translated with introduction and notes by A. J. Krailsheimer (Oxford: Oxford University Press, 'Oxford World's Classics', 1999)

Bouvard and Pécuchet. Dictionary of Received Ideas, translated with an introduction by A. J. Krailsheimer (Harmondsworth: Penguin, 1978)

Correspondence

The George Sand – Gustave Flaubert Letters, translated by Aimée L. MacKenzie (Chicago: Academy Chicago, 1979)

The Letters of Gustave Flaubert, 1830–1857, selected, edited and translated by Francis Steegmuller (London: Faber, 1981 [1980])

The Letters of Gustave Flaubert, 1857–1880, selected, edited and translated by Francis Steegmuller (London: Faber, 1984 [1982])

Biographical and other

Barnes, Julian, *Flaubert's Parrot* (London: Cape, 1984)

Bart, Benjamin F., *Flaubert* (Syracuse: Syracuse University Press, 1967)

Douchin, Jacques-Louis, *La Vie érotique de Flaubert* (Paris: Carrère, 1984)

Lottman, Herbert J., *Flaubert: A Biography* (London: Methuen, 1989)

Oliver, Hermia, *Flaubert and an English Governess: The Quest for Juliet Herbert* (Oxford: Clarendon, 1980)

Spencer, Philip, *Flaubert: A Biography* (London: Faber, 1952)

Starkie, Enid, *Flaubert: The Making of the Master* (London: Weidenfeld, 1967)
  Flaubert the Master (London: Weidenfeld, 1971)

Wall, Geoffrey, *Flaubert: A Life* (London: Faber, 2001)

Critical and general

Abrams, M. H., *The Mirror and the Lamp: Romantic Theory and the Critical Tradition* (Oxford: Oxford University Press, 1953)

Addison, Claire, *Where Flaubert Lies: Chronology, Mythology, History* (Cambridge: Cambridge University Press, 1996)

Auerbach, Erich, *Mimesis. The Representation of Reality in Western Literature*, translated by Willard R. Trask (Princeton: Princeton University Press, 1953 [1946])

Barnes, Julian, *Something to Declare* (London: Picador, 2002)

Barthes, Roland, *Le Degré zéro de l'écriture* (Paris: Seuil, 1972 [1953])

'L'Effet de réel' (1968), reprinted in Roland Barthes et al., *Littérature et réalité* (Paris: Seuil, 1982), pp. 81–90

Beizer, Janet L., *Ventriloquized Bodies. Narratives of Hysteria in Nineteenth-Century France* (Ithaca and London: Cornell University Press, 1994)

Bem, Jeanne, *Le Texte traversé* (Paris: Champion, 1991)

Bloom, Harold, ed., *Gustave Flaubert* (New York and Philadelphia: Chelsea House, 1988)

Emma Bovary (New York and Philadelphia: Chelsea House, 1994)

Bourdieu, Pierre, *Les Règles de l'art: genèse et structure du champ littéraire* (Paris: Seuil, 1992)

Brombert, Victor, *The Novels of Flaubert* (Princeton: Princeton University Press, 1966)

Bruneau, Jean, *Les Débuts littéraires de Gustave Flaubert, 1831–1845* (Paris: Armand Colin, 1962)

Burton, Richard D. E., 'The Death of Politics: The Significance of Dambreuse's Funeral in *L'Education sentimentale*, *French Studies*, 50 (1996), 157–69

Carlut, Charles, *La Correspondance de Flaubert: étude et répertoire critique* (Columbus: Ohio State University Press, 1968)

Culler, Jonathan, *Flaubert: The Uses of Uncertainty* (London: Elek, and Ithaca: Cornell University Press, 1974)

De Biasi, Pierre-Marc, *Flaubert: les secrets de 'l'homme-plume'* (Paris: Hachette, 1995)

Debray-Genette, Raymonde and Jacques Neefs, eds., *L'Œuvre de l'œuvre: études sur la correspondance de Flaubert* (Saint-Denis: Presses Universitaires de Vincennes, 1993)

Diamond, Marie J., *Flaubert: The Problem of Aesthetic Discontinuity* (London and New York: National University Publications, 1975)

Donatio, Eugenio, *The Script of Decadence: Essays on the Fictions of Flaubert and the Poetics of Romanticism* (Oxford and New York: Oxford University Press, 1993)

Dufour, Philippe, *Flaubert et le pignouf: essai sur la représentation romanesque du langage* (Saint-Denis: Presses Universitaires de Vincennes, 1993)

Durr, Volker, *Flaubert's 'Salammbô'. The Ancient Orient as a Political Allegory of Nineteenth-Century France* (New York: Peter Lang, 2002)

Fairlie, Alison, *Flaubert: 'Madame Bovary'* (London: Arnold, 1962)

Imagination and Language: Collected Essays on Constant, Baudelaire, Nerval and Flaubert (Cambridge: Cambridge University Press, 1981)

Falconer, Graham, 'Le travail de "debalzaciénisation" dans la rédaction de *Madame Bovary*', *Revue des Lettres Modernes*, 865–72 (1988), 123–56

Gans, Eric, *The Discovery of Illusion: Flaubert's Early Works, 1835–1837* (Berkeley: University of California Press, 1971)

'Madame Bovary': The End of Romance (Boston: G. K. Hall, 1989)

Genette, Gérard, 'Silences de Flaubert', in *Figures I* (Paris: Seuil, 1966), pp. 223–43

Ginsburg, Michal Peled, *Flaubert Writing: A Study in Narrative Strategies* (Stanford: Stanford University Press, 1986)

Green, Anne, *Flaubert and the Historical Novel: 'Salammbô' Reassessed* (Cambridge: Cambridge University Press, 1982)

Haig, Stirling, *Flaubert and the Gift of Speech: Dialogue and Discourse in Four Modern Novels* (Cambridge: Cambridge University Press, 1986)

  The Madame Bovary Blues: The Pursuit of Illusion in Nineteenth-Century French Fiction (Baton Rouge, LA: Louisiana State University Press, 1987)

Heath, Stephen, *Flaubert: 'Madame Bovary'* (Cambridge: Cambridge University Press, 1992)

Hill, Leslie, 'Flaubert and the Rhetoric of Stupidity', *Critical Inquiry*, 3 (1976), 333–44

Huss, Roger, 'Some Anomalous Uses of the Imperfect and the Status of Action in Flaubert', *French Studies*, 31 (1977), 139–48

  'Nature, Final Causality and Anthropocentrism in Flaubert', *French Studies*, 33 (1979), 288–304

Israel-Pelletier, Aimée, *Flaubert's Straight and Suspect Saints: The Unity of 'Trois Contes'* (Amsterdam and Philadelphia: Benjamins, 1991)

James, Henry, 'Gustave Flaubert' (1914), in *Literary Criticism. French Writers, Other European Writers* (Cambridge: Cambridge University Press, 1984), pp. 314–46

Kaplan, Louise J., *Female Perversions: The Temptations of Emma Bovary* (New York: Doubleday, 1991)

Kenner, Hugh, *Flaubert, Joyce and Beckett. The Stoic Comedians* (London: W. H. Allen, 1964)

Knight, Diana, *Flaubert's Characters: The Language of Illusion* (Cambridge: Cambridge University Press, 1985)

LaCapra, Dominick, *'Madame Bovary' on Trial* (Ithaca, New York and London: Cornell University Press, 1982)

Lloyd, Rosemary, *Flaubert: 'Madame Bovary'* (London: Unwin Hyman, 1989)

Lowe, Margaret, *Towards the Real Flaubert. A Study of 'Madame Bovary'* (Oxford: Clarendon, 1984)

Neiland, Mary, *'Les Tentations de saint Antoine' and Flaubert's Fiction. A Creative Dynamic* (Amsterdam: Rodopi, 2001)

Olds, Marshall C., *Au pays des perroquets: féerie théâtrale et narration chez Flaubert* (Amsterdam: Rodopi, 2001)

Orr, Mary, *'Madame Bovary': Representations of the Masculine* (Bern: Peter Lang, 1999)

  Flaubert: Writing the Masculine (Oxford: Oxford University Press, 2000)

Paulson, William, *Sentimental Education: The Complexity of Disenchantment* (New York: Twayne, 1992)

Porter, Laurence M., ed., *Critical Essays on Gustave Flaubert* (Boston: G. K. Hall, 1986)

  A Gustave Flaubert Encyclopedia (Westport, CT: Greenwood, 2001)

Porter, Laurence M. and Eugene F. Gray, eds., *Approaches to Teaching Flaubert's 'Madame Bovary'* (New York: MLA, 1995)

Gustave Flaubert's 'Madame Bovary': A Reference Guide (Westport, CT: Greenwood, 2002)

Poulet, Georges, *Etudes sur le temps humain* (Edinburgh: Edinburgh University Press, 1948), translated by Elliott Coleman as *Studies in Human Time* (Baltimore and London: Johns Hopkins University Press, 1956)

Poyet, Thierry, *Pour une esthétique de Flaubert d'après sa correspondance* (Saint-Pierre-du-Mont: Eurédit, 2000)

Praz, Mario, *The Romantic Agony* (London: Oxford University Press, 1933)

Prendergast, Christopher, 'Flaubert: Writing and Negativity', *Novel*, 8 (1975), 197–213

'Flaubert: Quotation, Stupidity and the Cretan Liar Paradox', *French Studies*, 35 (1981), 261–77

The Order of Mimesis: Balzac, Stendhal, Nerval, Flaubert (Cambridge: Cambridge University Press, 1986)

Proust, Marcel, 'A propos du "style" de Flaubert' (1920), reprinted in *Contre Sainte-Beuve, précédé de Pastiches et mélanges et suivi de Essais et articles*, ed. Pierre Clarac and Yves Sandre (Paris: Gallimard, 1971), pp. 586–600

Raitt, Alan, *Flaubert: 'Trois Contes'* (London: Grant and Cutler, 1991)

Flaubert et le théâtre (Bern: Peter Lang, 1998)

The Originality of 'Madame Bovary' (Bern: Peter Lang, 2002)

Ramazani, Vaheed K., *The Free Indirect Mode: Flaubert and the Poetics of Irony* (Charlottesville: University Press of Virginia, 1988)

Reed, Arden, *Manet, Flaubert and the Emergence of Modernism. Blurring Genre Boundaries* (Cambridge: Cambridge University Press, 2003)

Richard, Jean-Pierre, *Littérature et sensation* (Paris: Seuil, 1954)

Robert, Marthe, *En haine du roman. Etude sur Flaubert* (Paris: Balland, 1982)

Roe, David, *Gustave Flaubert* (Basingstoke: Macmillan, 1989)

Rousset, Jean, *Forme et signification* (Paris: Corti, 1962)

Sarraute, Nathalie, *Paul Valéry et l'enfant de l'éléphant; Flaubert le précurseur* (Paris: Gallimard, 1986)

Sartre, Jean-Paul, *L'Idiot de la famille: Gustave Flaubert de 1821 à 1857*, 3 vols. (Paris: Gallimard, 1988 [1971–2]), translated by Carol Cosman as *The Family Idiot, Gustave Flaubert 1821–1857*, 5 vols. (Chicago and London: University of Chicago Press, 1981–93)

Schehr, Lawrence R., *Flaubert and Sons. Readings of Flaubert, Zola and Proust* (New York: Peter Lang, 1986)

Rendering French Realism (Stanford: Stanford University Press, 1997)

Schmid, Marion, *Processes of Literary Creation: Flaubert and Proust* (Oxford: Legenda, 1998)

Schor, Naomi and Henry F. Majewski, eds., *Flaubert and Postmodernism* (Lincoln, NE: University of Nebraska Press, 1984)

Sherrington, R. J., *Three Novels by Flaubert* (Oxford: Clarendon, 1970)

Tanner, Tony, *Adultery in the Novel. Contract and Transgression* (Baltimore and London: Johns Hopkins University Press, 1979)

Thibaudet, Albert, *Gustave Flaubert* (Paris: Gallimard, 1935)

Tillett, Margaret G., *On Reading Flaubert* (London: Oxford University Press, 1961)

Tooke, Adrianne, *Flaubert and the Pictorial Arts. From Image to Text* (Oxford: Oxford University Press, 2000)

Toulet, Suzanne, *Le Sentiment religieux chez Flaubert d'après sa correspondance* (Montreal: Editions Cosmos, 1970)

Traire, Sylvie, *Une esthétique de la déliaison: Flaubert (1870–1880)* (Paris: Champion, 2002)

Unwin, Timothy, 'Flaubert and Pantheism', *French Studies*, 35 (1981), 394–406
    Art et infini: l'œuvre de jeunesse de Gustave Flaubert (Amsterdam: Rodopi, 1992)

VanderWolk, William, *Flaubert Remembers: Memory and the Creative Experience* (New York: Peter Lang, 1990)

Vargas Llosa, Mario, *The Perpetual Orgy* (London and Boston: Faber and Faber, 1987)

Williams, D. A. *Psychological Determinism in 'Madame Bovary'* (Hull: University of Hull Publications, 1973)
    'The Hidden Life at its Source': A Study of Flaubert's 'L'Education sentimentale' (Hull: Hull University Press, 1987)

Williams, D. A. and Mary Orr, eds., *New Approaches in Flaubert Studies* (Lewiston, NY: Edwin Mellen, 1999)

Bibliographical

Colwell, David J., *Bibliographie des études sur Gustave Flaubert*, 4 vols. (Egham: Runnymede, 1988–90)

Online and electronic resources

Gustave Flaubert, *Madame Bovary*, CD-ROM (Paris: Ubi Soft, 1997)
    L'Œuvre romanesque, texte intégral, CD-ROM (Paris: Egide, 1997)
Site Flaubert (University of Rouen): http://www.univ-rouen.fr/flaubert/
Gustave Flaubert (site maintained by Jean-Benoît Guinot): http://perso.wanadoo.fr/jb.guinot/pages/accueil.html

INDEX

Allen, Woody 1
antiquity 34, 45, 86, 89, 90, 95
aporia 16
asceticism: *see* mysticism
Austen, Jane 137, 147
avant-texte 5, 165, 172, 174–8

Balzac, Honoré de 2, 7, 19, 22–6, 34, 48,
    49, 148, 158, 168, 180, 181, 208,
    218
  Cousine Bette, La 7, 23, 200
  Cousin Pons, Le 200
  Illusions perdues 23, 24, 26, 146, 212
  Louis Lambert 23
  Lys dans la vallée, Le 23, 26
  Père Goriot, Le 22, 23
Barnes, Julian 1, 67
Barthes, Roland 23, 26, 30
  Le Degré zéro de l'écriture 2, 20, 167
Baudelaire, Charles 4, 19, 36, 51, 67, 145,
    146, 157, 194
Beckett, Samuel 1, 4, 23, 27, 163, 218
Bergerat, Emile 197
Bergson, Henri 132
bêtise 8, 12, 14, 15, 39–40, 107, 213, 214
Beyle, Henri: *see* Stendhal
Blanchot, Maurice 163
Borel, Petrus 21
Borges, Jorge Luis 1, 223
Bouilhet, Louis 1, 11, 18, 57, 63, 78, 80–1,
    89, 90, 198, 200, 201–2, 203–4
  Conjuration d'Amboise, La 202
  Dolorès 202
  Faustine 202
  Hélène Peyron 202
  Madame de Montarcy 201–2
  Mademoiselle Aïssé 203
  Oncle Million, L' 202

  Pierrot au sérail 201
  Sexe faible, Le 203–5
Bourdieu, Pierre 1, 176
Brainne, Léonie 82
Brueghel, Pieter 72, 200
Byron, Lord 2, 21, 36, 45

Caillebotte, Gustave 18
Calvino, Italo 1
Carvalho, Léon 204, 205
Céard, Henri 29
Cervantes, Miguel de 2, 18, 45, 71, 221
Césaire, Aimé 124
Chabrol, Claude 1
Champfleury (pseudonym of Jules Husson)
    17
Charpentier, Georges 203
Chateaubriand, François-René de 36, 45, 94,
    104, 140, 145–6, 158, 180, 199
Chéruel, Adolphe 34, 86
Chevalier, Ernest 21, 50, 71, 85
Chrétien de Troyes 180
Colet, Louise 1, 2, 5, 7, 10, 18, 23, 35, 48,
    68, 69, 71, 73, 74, 76, 77, 146, 153, 197
comedy 160–2
Commanville, Caroline (Flaubert's niece) 68,
    71
Constant, Benjamin 145, 156
Cormenin, Louis de 67, 71
Courbet, Gustave 17, 193–4
Cousin, Victor 93

Damas, Léon-Gontran 124
Darwin, Charles 22
Daudet, Alphonse 82
Degas, Edgar 18
Delacroix, Eugène 194
Delavigne, Casimir 85

CAMBRIDGE COMPANIONS TO LITERATURE

CAMBRIDGE COMPANIONS TO CULTURE